THE GLASS FACTORY

Braxton McCoy

To those wandering through chaos.

Contents

Caveats and Admissions

In its current form this book is, like its author, deeply imperfect on multiple levels. I wrote much of the story ten years after the fact. The mind is not a supercomputer. Information sitting untouched is not stored perfectly; it erodes with time. Despite that admission I did my very best to ensure accuracy. Anywhere it was possible I consulted other people, often asking what they remembered of an event before showing them what I had written.. If the information that I was attempting to verify was from military or combat experience I asked several people before I proceeded. Where there were discrepancies in recollection, I changed the text to accommodate. A side note that may be of interest to some of you: almost never was there a fact in need of change if it was combat related. We all shared the same details in our collective memories. I think that says something about the profundity of the razor's edge.

Like all others, any wisdom gained throughout this process came not just from analyzing my own life experience, but from reading the thoughts of titans such as, Nietzsche, Shakespeare, Tolstoy, Hitchens, and many more. Most influentially perhaps, was a psychology professor from the University of Toronto. I did not discover him until I had written the first draft of this memoire, but Dr. Jordan Peterson's lectures helped form and clarify my thoughts in such a profound way that I am not sure I could point out each idea that has his mark of influence upon it. Suffice it to say, I feel very blessed to have found his work and I owe him a great deal.

Lastly, my concept of "ownership," which is sort of a higher form of accountability and responsibility, was shaped by Navy SEALs Jocko Willink and Leif Babin. Their book *Extreme Ownership* is a treatise on leadership and personal development that has not been matched in contemporary literature. I see it as the go-to for any who are trying to gain a deeper understanding of what it means to take "extreme ownership" of one's own mistakes and decisions. It is a true must read for all who wish to grow.

Acknowledgments

I was blessed to have edits and suggestions from many smart and talented people like, David H. Madsen, Lexi Stuivenvolt-Allen, April Wilder, James Morgan, Cody Hasson and Adam Larson. I could never have completed this project without their help, professional or otherwise.

The magnificent cover and interior design was done by Matthew Madsen, a former Army medic who heroically worked on the wounded in the aftermath of the suicide bombing at the Glass Factory. It would be impossible to overstate my gratitude for his lending his powerful talents to this project.

The first edition of this book was funded by a crowdsourcing campaign. My family and I are deeply grateful for the support this manuscript project received. Four of my good friends, all of them military men—not one a wealthy man—contributed mightily to our project. Dusty Winkle, Chad Ray Williams, Mike Hales, and Rob Smith all backed the book with hundreds of their own dollars. To have men who have served our country themselves show that kind of belief in this story and my ability to tell it gave me a confidence without which I feel I never could have finished.

Everyone is overloaded these days, just stop someone on the street and ask them how they're doing. They won't be able to get through two sentences without using the word *busy*. I think that is something we all ought to give a bit of consideration to; nevertheless, I was busy as hell throughout the writing of this book. My wife was pregnant; she, our son, and I had a few health problems, we are remodeling our home in order to get it ready to sell, the list goes on—but I always kept in my mind that I owed this book to many people who had bet their own money on me:

Chris Beckstrand; Chris Radcliff, Cody Hasson, Travis Hale, Tammy Graham, Marty and Sherry Mecham, Jerod Button, Val Niehaus, Debra Peterson, Jace Torgerson, Connie Bess, Asher Rindlesbach, Denise Caristi, Catherine Shepherd, Riley Rogers, Lauri Mathews, Jackie Perron, Jamie Stone,Shane Johnson, Charles Triplett, Jessica Stone, all paid five times what this book is worth. Just to help us out. I never lost sight of it. That fact kept me focused on producing the best product possible, and I think we succeeded there. This book is as good as I can make it. I hope it lives up to all of your expectations.

When I launched the project I naïvely hoped that people would view it as a chance to buy the book at a reduced rate, sort of like pre-buying a novel from an author that you love. As you can see, that isn't what happened at all. The folks backing us were not just buying the book, but *giving* to it. The charitable aspect was deeply moving, so we decided that the only way to truly show our appreciation for those gifts was to give back to others. To pay it forward.

We looked around for a few months until we found a 501c3 charity that fit our desires most perfectly. I then reached out to Jacob Nold and told him that we wanted to donate a percentage of the profits that will come from future book sales to his organization, Labs for Liberty. Rather than try to explain LFL to those who are unaware of the organization and its mission, I asked him to provide us with a blurb:

"Labs for Liberty's mission is to provide custom-trained service dogs for military veterans with PTSD and physical limitations. Additionally, we seek to offer a non-clinical, naturally therapeutic respite for military families for the purpose of empowering them to reconnect and rejuvenate. All of this is accomplished with a 100% volunteer staff and is provided at no cost to the veteran or their family.

Labs for Liberty's goal is to empower our veterans and their families to find a "new normal" and to assist our veterans with their transition into civilian life. By doing so we will build stronger families and better communities.

Background (as of June 2017): Labs for Liberty was born out of a passion for American Veterans who have sacrificed so that we may remain free. That passion has resulted in the growth of a nationwide family. A family of Veterans and those who appreciate them and their service. Since the inception of Labs for Liberty in December 2014, Labs for Liberty has trained and placed over 50 service dogs with veterans in 28 states. Additionally, Labs for Liberty has hosted 20 veterans and their families at the Liberty Outpost for respite retreats. This has been accomplished with a combined effort of over 50,000 volunteer hours and generous donations from family foundations, corporations, and private entities. What perceivably started as a mom & pop 501c3 organization has blossomed into a full-fledged operation with 3 full-time volunteer staff and over 50 part-time volunteers."

Lastly, and most importantly—like nearly all things worthwhile in this life—it could not have been done without the support of a strong and generous woman: Lauri Mathews. Love you a million suns, Mom. Thank you, it is always for you.

Introduction

In 2004 the US, British, and Iraqi militaries launched Operation Phantom Fury, a joint-force mission to crush the insurgency in Fallujah. The US Marine Corps spearheaded the attack. Some called it the fiercest urban fighting the Marines had seen since Hue City in Vietnam. Our coalition forces fought bravely and many men died in the fight. Though the battle destroyed many insurgents within the stronghold, it also forced some underground and others to flee for the nearby town of Ramadi. This left Ramadi a war-torn and volatile place.

Sunni extremists controlled the majority of the city. Gunfights and IED explosions were a daily occurrence for the men and women who took over the Area of Operation in 2006.

On Camp Ramadi, incoming mortar and rocket fire was so common that any soldier who had been there for more than a week, hardly batted an eye at shelling if it didn't strike virtually at their feet. Sometimes though, an incident would remind you that those incoming projectiles were very real.

One morning, a young Marine was walking with his best friend to the dining facility to fetch some breakfast. While en route he was struck directly in the chest by an enemy rocket, killing him instantly and spreading his unlucky remains across a few meters worth of sand.

We all called the Forward Operating Base's softball grounds "Rocket Field," because it had been hit so many times. However, aside from the ominous presence of impact craters, those of us lucky enough to hit a weak line drive up the middle every now and again benefited greatly from the small cavities. We weren't able to play very often, due to the fact that everyone from infantrymen to logistical support was constantly busy handling their own parts of the fight, but when we were able to gear up for sport, the games were a welcomed alleviation from the austere environment.

The streets of the city were covered in trash making spotting IEDs nearly impossible. I recall one Marine bomb technician (EOD) responding to the question: "How do you tell the difference between the garbage on the streets and an IED?" with, "If it doesn't blow up when you step on it, it's just trash."

Most of the resistance we met came from Iraqi-born Sunni Muslims, but it was not uncommon to encounter foreign-born Islamists who came to Iraq for the sole purpose of taking pot shots at the American military.

The different tribes and sects within Islam clashed—and are still clashing—in Anbar Province, particularly in Ramadi, in a way that they had not since the rise of the Ottoman Empire. Shiites killed Sunnis because they felt like they had been politically oppressed and murdered by Sunnis for years. Meanwhile, Sunnis hated and killed the Shiites, ostensibly over political grievances spurred by the Commander in Chief's decision to remove and bar from future service all members of Saddam Hussein's Ba'ath Party.

This decision was widely and highly criticized by military historians, anthropologists, sociologists, Islamic scholars, and others such as journalists, politicians, and lawyers long before the writing of this book. Frankly, a decision like that is made too far above my pay grade to comment on without bias, so I will do them the courtesy of avoiding said disparagement.

I find the urge to use the clarity of hindsight to criticize someone else's foreign policy decisions a bit reprehensible. It is like social media users criticizing the actions of troops on the ground in Iraq and Afghanistan based on combat footage alone. It may look like the warfighter is doing something egregious, but sometimes the viewer forgets that they are only seeing about 40 degrees worth of a 360 degree environment. Oftentimes, the stuff that is going on outside of focal range is the important bit.

That said, the fact that the administration chose to bar Ba'athists plays an important role in the first chapter, so I think it worth noting.

Despite all this turmoil and the angst it caused the people of Ramadi, things were going to change while my unit was there. US forces took control of the city during 2006 in an extremely costly fight, generally called The Battle of Ramadi. It is widely considered to be the bloodiest era of the war in Iraq, but at its end, I am told, the city was a different place.

In fact, in 2007, Americans and Iraqis together ran a 5K down route Michigan, a road that was once so dangerous that US logistical convoys took a four hour detour around Lake Habbaniyah just to avoid driving down it for about fifteen minutes.

All the lives lost and blood shed in Ramadi did have a positive impact for the Iraqis who lived there—I am proud to say—short-lived as it may have been. It took a helluva fight to clear the place out, but in the end, locals and soldiers were running 5Ks together. That is a happy ending if ever I have heard of one. I only wish I had been able to see it.

CHAPTER ONE

Soaked in Blood

I am young, I am twenty years old; yet I know nothing of life but despair, death, fear, and fatuous superficiality cast over an abyss of sorrow. I see how peoples are set against one another, and in silence, unknowingly, foolishly, obediently, innocently slay one another.

— Erich Maria Remarque, *All Quiet on the Western Front*

It was roughly 0400hrs in local time. We were in Ramadi, the capital of Anbar Province, which sits about 70 miles west of Baghdad. Ramadi, aside from being in the news so often in recent years because of the rise of ISIS, is most famously known by Americans as the city that US Navy SEALs such as Chris Kyle and Marcus Luttrell portrayed in their books and movies.[1] However, to those of us who fought there, it is an enigma. A place in our own histories that somehow holds memories of both the best and the *worst* days of our lives.

Though it was early, I was busy inspecting my kit to ensure I had the proper load-out for the mission ahead. This mission was going to demand as much crowd control as it would perimeter security. I elected to take only a single frag grenade and flash bang, several canisters of

1 Chief Chris Kyle's book centered on his life and his many engagements on multiple tours in Iraq, but some of its more significant happenings took place in Ramadi during his time with Task Force Bruiser. A unit lead by Navy SEAL Jocko Wilink, a warrior whose name is becoming more renowned in its own right—deservedly so. Marcus Luttrel is widely known for his first book *Lone Survivor,* but his second book *Service: A Navy SEAL's Time at War,* details his return to combat in Ramadi during the 2006 Battle of Ramadi.

smoke, eleven magazines for my M-4 (to prevent jamming I loaded each with only 27 rounds rather than the full thirty that they are capable of holding), and a shotgun with both "less-than-lethal" and "lethal" rounds of buckshot.

My pre-mission routine was always the same. First, I'd go through my gear to guarantee it was structurally sound and fit for duty. Next, I went over a multitude of potential future situations in my mind: How would we react if we took fire from the buildings to the south, or from the village to the west? What would our team do if the enemy was able to breach the security checkpoint to the east? What if we were attacked by indirect fire (i.e., mortars, rockets, and artillery shells)? Where would our Casualty Collection Point (CCP) be? What were our evacuation routes?

Whenever it was possible, I liked to spend a half an hour doing this kind of hybrid meditation before I headed out on a mission. It gave me a firm sense of confidence, the kind that can only be attained through thorough preparation. I mapped out many possible scenarios and outcomes that morning, but I *never* imagined—though perhaps I should have—what actually lay in store for us that day. During my personal mission prep my mind often wandered home.

It was January. Only three months earlier I had taken my standard two weeks of leave to marry my girlfriend. Everyone on my team advised me against it, but I was young, stupid, and "in love." She was a short, pretty blonde girl from Minnesota. I met her during a fishing trip her brother, an old platoon mate of mine, had planned. Before I flew out there to fish with him and his family he said, "I only have one rule: no talking to my sister!" The best way to ensure a human being will do something is to tell him never, ever, do it. If you've any doubt of that just consult Adam and Eve.

But, at this time she and I were in a fight. I was even considering getting an annulment. My good friend and one of our machine gunners was going through a divorce of his own, so he acted as the typical barracks lawyer: "Bro, you were only married to her for a week before you came back overseas. I guarantee you can get the marriage annulled!" I wondered what that process would be like—or if it was even the right thing to do.

Alright, forget that shit. It's time to focus.

During my morning soldiering ritual I noticed that something in the world was different. I had this bizarre feeling that I was going to get hit, a feeling I have since learned to listen to, but I could not quite figure out why. I did my best to ignore the premonition and prepare for my duty day. The thought lingered in my subconscious. *Something is wrong.*

Generally, when soldiers are severely wounded in their legs, medics are forced to cut the injured warrior's boots off. This makes the removal of footwear much faster and circumvents the need to forcefully pull the boots off their body, which may cause additional trauma to a patient whose legs are broken or badly burned. I, for whatever reason, was so sure that I was going to get hit that day that I opted not to wear my favorite boots. I had grown so attached to them that I just could not handle the idea of having to watch them being cut up and ruined.[2]

Luckily, we had all been issued cold weather boots that I found terribly uncomfortable and extremely hot in the Iraq sun. *I'll wear those pieces of shit,* I thought to myself. I hated those awful things and would not miss them for a second after they were sliced up and thrown onto the scrap heap.

Later on, we rallied up at our Intelligence Officer's (S2) building for our pre-mission intel briefing. He told us that they had strong reasons to believe we would be attacked by a Vehicular Borne Improvised Explosive Device (VBIED). As I listened to our S2 tell us what to expect from the day ahead, I realized that internally it was all starting to make sense to me, when that VBIED detonated—and it was going to— I would be within its blast radius.

There had been missions where I was nervous before they began, and others where I didn't feel those butterflies until they were in full-swing, but there had never been anything like what I felt that morning. I was sure of it: *this is going to be my last day on earth.*

---

2 Those boots, my favorite pair, now sit on a display at my house next to my shot-up piece of body armor. I keep them there as a reminder that the cost of war is both blood *and* sweat; miles walked, and miles that will never be walked again.

When the briefing ended, we gathered up our teams and discussed the security plan, revealing our new intelligence to everyone else as we went along. All eyes and ears seemed a little more attentive than usual. It was almost as if everyone around me was just as sure that we were making a stupid move as I was.

Our mission was to protect the Iraqi civilians, as well as a group of Marines who had been assigned the job of recruiting the men of Ramadi and its surrounding villages to become local police officers. We were to guard the Glass Factory where they would be processing candidates.

The whole recruitment push had gone smashingly thus far, but we were on the fourth day of this same drive and we had already hugely surpassed our initial goal of 200 new recruits. The men of Ramadi had lined up in droves for the opportunity to become one of the guys chosen to fly to Jordan for the high-speed training the US government had funded for them, and later return to their hometown to clean it up. In fact, we had processed hundreds of candidates already. The catch was, this was going to be day four of this particular mission and we had only been promised three peaceful days.

The problem was all the spots that we had for these future IPs (Iraqi Police) had been filled days ago; this was all just for show. No one on our team felt like it was a good idea to put ourselves at risk for almost nothing, but we were soldiers and that is just part of the job, or so we are told. Look, I don't want to be too cavalier about this situation. It could have been that command was right, we did need to keep the doors of recruitment open even though there were no slots left for these men to fill. Sometimes, especially in a so-called Hearts and Minds campaign, showing the local populous that you will go the extra mile is the *important* part. But, as the guys on the ground about to stick their faces near the meat grinder for what feels like a charade, it can be difficult to see the big picture and even harder to care about it if you do.

When we got into our Humvee I cracked a joke: "Well, let's go get blown up boys!" I was just trying to cut the tension—probably mine more than any others, but I'm not sure it had the desired effect.

In five short minutes we had arrived at the Glass Factory on the western edge of town. We had previously secured this facility because it sat too close to our Forward Operating Base (FOB) not to have annexed it. It had become a sort of quasi part of Camp Ramadi, so it only made sense to use this otherwise wasted space to conduct this mission. But, when we arrived there it was clear that something was very wrong.

We pulled into the rear of the facility and then walked straight to the main entrance to figure out what was happening. There were nearly a thousand fighting-age Iraqi men lined up in three single-file lines already there waiting for us. Something like this happening in America may not seem too far out the ordinary because we see it all the time at sporting events, concerts, and movies; but in Ramadi, this kind of self-organization never happened.

Johnny, my first line leader and the leader of our Alpha Team, quickly decided that we needed to report this to the TOC (Tactical Operations Center). He took out his radio and asked Major Shark, who was with us, whether we should call up a situational report. The Major decided that we had better. We waited for a response before proceeding. The reply came quicker than we expected, "Roger. Continue mission."

Roger? *That's it? Are you kidding me?*

We grabbed our interpreter whom we lovingly called Carlos, because he looked more like he was from Juarez, Mexico, than Southern Iraq, and headed to the entrance to start asking some questions. When we reached the steel, man-sized gate, we let a few Iraqis in, patted them down, ran a metal detecting wand over their bodies, and inspected them for potential contraband such as weapons, explosives, etc. After we had determined them clean, we began asking questions, namely, "What the hell are you doing here early?" The average answer ranged between 'Someone told us to be here at this time,' and 'We just wanted the greatest opportunity to get the job, so we did our best to be here first.' Not fully satisfied and slightly reluctantly, we then sent them to the Marine element who had been charged with the screening and recruitment process. Under normal circumstances neither of these answers would be cause for concern, but war is nothing if it is not consistent abnormality.

Soldiers for generations have described battle in the same way as an unnamed British Cavalryman did during WWI: "War is months of boredom punctuated by moments of sheer terror." I guess I might even take it a step further and say something like, war is spending the best days of your youth, bored out of your mind, hoping for something to happen, occasionally interrupted by sporadic states of extreme confusion and dangerous levels of adrenaline. That is exactly where we had found ourselves: caught somewhere between boredom, fear, and confusion.

Johnny decided that we had better get out into that crowd and get a firmer handle on what was going on, but neither of us was interested in sending members of our teams out there; so we did what had to be done. We put our team members in their places inside the Glass Factory's walls and went out ourselves.

I was oddly calm as we walked out the gate; not that I generally feared being among Iraqi people, it's just that in a situation like this, where you are surrounded by roughly a thousand men whom you have no ability to directly communicate with, things can spiral out of control very quickly. The otherwise peaceful crowd could be overtaken by the chaos of a mob in an instant, and that should be frightening to anybody. We were outnumbered something like a hundred to one; and the tools we generally used to even the odds were completely useless. Despite what some in the global media would have you believe, American soldiers have no intention of using their automatic weapons as a form of crowd control.[3]

Up and down the line of Iraqis we walked, checking the crowd for threats as we went. We stopped frequently to interrogate Iraqis who looked eager, agitated, or uncomfortable. Honestly, most of them looked nervous and unsettled—which was perhaps the most reasonable way to

---

3 I have heard numbers like 14 million civilian casualties in Iraq bandied about on different media outlets. I do not wish to get into any sort of political discussion, but I feel honor-bound to point out how grossly misrepresented American conduct in Iraq has been by many in the media.

It is true that if you would have quizzed our security team that day you would not have found a majority of them holding high opinions of the Iraqi people, but that doesn't mean we would shoot civilians indiscriminately as it seems some on the far left seem to believe. Dislike, contempt, even flat out disdain for the people does not then equal murderous conduct. Particularly in a military as professional as the one we are blessed to employ.

feel in that moment. These guys knew they were in danger just as well as we did; after all, they *lived* in the city that we fought in. The danger of terrorist attacks had become just another part of daily life to the citizen of western Anbar Province.

At one point a man approached us uneasily, instantly causing my blood pressure to rise. He stood close to me as he began to talk, too close:

"Back up!" I said.

"He has something important to tell you," Carlos leaned in and told me defensively. "Grenade? You found a grenade?" our interpreter continued the conversation.

"Yes!" the man responded.

"A grenade and wire," Carlos relayed to us in English.

"You have got to be shitting me," I said. "There's a *fucking* tripwire out here somewhere? Ask him where the hell it's at, Carlos!"

Carlos turned to the man and asked, but they were having a hard time communicating because the guy was so scared. It was like watching a kindergartner tattletale on his classmates on the playground.

"Goddammit! We are out here in a crowd of a thousand unpredictable Iraqis and there is a fucking booby-trap somewhere," I said aloud, but to no one in particular.

We had dealt with plenty of IEDs (Improvised Explosive Devices) by this time in our deployment, but a booby-trap amongst a crowd of civilians was the last thing we had expected to find ourselves encountering on this tour. We were supposed to be attacked by a VBIED—what the hell happened to that? What happened to the bad guy driving a vehicle where we could use our rifles and our skill-sets to mitigate the threat? I felt like we were in grave danger with no foreseeable way to defend ourselves. No chance at good guys versus bad guys. No hope for the white-hat-wearing cowboys to vanquish the black-hatted foe. This was just helpless chaos, and that is the reality of war. However strategic and organized combat may appear from a bird's eye view, or from the safety of a command position, or with the clarity of hindsight, to the guy on the ground experiencing it in real time, it is random, terrifying, often almost totally helpless chaos. And that is why we miss it so deeply when it is gone.

We continued to interview Iraqis, our eyes more thoroughly examining the ground and the crowd than ever before. In the back of my mind I thought, What the hell am I going to say to these people if I do spot the tripwire before it goes off? If I call out to them to stop moving they will just get agitated and move around more. At each interaction I found myself waiting for an explosion to be triggered by some unknowing Iraqi. I was both worried and distracted, but doing my best not to show it to my friends, or more importantly, to our enemies who were surely in the crowd.[4]

Then I heard a strange sound to my left, followed by the report of rifles and bursts from the machine guns set atop an Abrams tank that had been positioned to block a street. I dropped to a knee and began to scan for targets.

BANG! BANG! BANG! CR–ACK! CRACK! CRACK! The rounds sounded off as they struck their target.

Men began shouting in two different languages. The confusion of combat sets in rapidly. Iraqis were running around frantically screaming in high-pitched tones and flailing about in the streets. Others stood frozen as if fear and curiosity had stiffened them as they had once done to Lot's wife. Pillars of salt seemed a fitting end for any decent person caught living in that modern day Sodom anyway.

Still scanning for a target that I could positively identify and engage, but coming up with none, I was getting worried that I was missing some obvious ambush coming from the buildings to our south. Then I saw it.

A semi-truck had crashed through our outer perimeter a few hundred

---

4 I need to clear something up here because I am not sure that the average person understands why most soldiers had a tendency to treat *all* Iraqis in Anbar Province as if they were potential threats. We didn't treat them as if they were all homicidal terrorists, or subhuman beings, or anything like that, we simply treated them as if they were all *potential* threats—similar to the way a police officer behaves as he or she walks up to a vehicle they've just pulled over.

It's a basic matter of arithmetic: if it is thought that 1 in 5 civilians may be hostile, then in a crowd of roughly a thousand men, there are 200 insurgents. When one is outnumbered that heavily, it is wise to be aware of that *fact*, and to acknowledge it before one finds oneself wishing they had.

meters away. Our fellow soldiers and marines had immediately recognized the threat and eliminated it before it could do any more damage to our position. *That's one helluva VBIED,* I thought to myself. The acute problem had been solved, I hoped, for all I knew that thing might be filled with explosives. But an even larger threat now loomed: a terrified mob.

Civilians were running around horrified; shoving each other, climbing over jersey barriers (the concrete barriers that separate Interstates in most developed countries), screaming, lost in the confusion of the moment. As frustrated as I was at their behavior, I understood its roots. They thought themselves stuck between a proverbial rock and a hard place. In this case they were sandwiched between a gunfight and a brick wall, but in truth it was all a lie, the exchange was happening only in their own minds. There was no active gunfight. Our side had stopped shooting and there had never been any returned fire. But, as is common in mobs, fear ruled the day. Critical faculties had long since lost sway and group think devolved in to a turbid self-preservation-at-all-costs mindset.

It did not take long to decide that we could not allow them to get any more riotous; it was time to start wrangling non-combatants. We were, I think justifiably, irritated at their behavior, but we all knew that this situation needed our more professional sides to take control before the frantic crowd continued to devolve into an angry mob.

Johnny was well within earshot, so I asked him what the new plan of action was. He radioed the TOC again and briefed them on the current situation. Our commanding officers verified that reinforcement troops were now en route. All we could do in the time being is keep the Iraqis contained until we had enough help to reorganize them. *With all of these guys running around in circles, how had no one stepped on that grenade yet?* I wondered. *Maybe the guy who told us about the grenade was lying, or maybe he was just confused about what he saw.* Perhaps, as hindsight teaches us, I should have been open to the possibility that there was something *I* wasn't seeing.

We started yelling at the civilians to get back into line as Carlos translated for us. A few listened, but most pretended not to hear what he was saying, or were just plain too afraid to move. We ratcheted up our anger a little and looked them dead in the eye to let them know we were still in command of this circus, but it was of little use. Whether we wanted to be or not it soon became apparent that we were going to have to be more forceful. Some men had to be physically dragged off the tops of barriers, some had to be shoved, others conformed when they saw that we were no longer messing around; still others ran away and escaped the scene altogether. I knew we needed help getting this situation back in order before someone stepped on that booby-trap, but it seemed it was not going to arrive in time. Just then, the radio on my right hip rang out. It was our battalion command center letting us know that reinforcements should have arrived at the gate by now.

The soldiers they had promised had not actually arrived yet, but when we reached the main gate that we had first walked through earlier that morning, we were met with some good news. Two of our new Marine friends were there asking us whether we wanted them to go get their dogs. "Roger!" We said emphatically. "Please do." These two Marines were canine handlers, and by reputation, damn good ones, too. One of them, SGT Cann, had already deployed to Iraq before. This round for him had started at a small base out in western Iraq near the Syrian border, but that area lacked the action he longed for so he had requested transfer to the hottest area of the fight: Ramadi. He was a true badass warfighter and, in my experience, the US Military has no better tool for safely changing the minds of stubborn Iraqi men than a canine warrior at one end of a leash and a cocksure Marine at the other. We were glad to have them on our side and as the events played out, lucky, too.

Most Iraqi civilians were petrified of dogs. We had heard all kinds of different theories about where that fear stemmed from—none were likely to be fully true. One such barracks myth was that if a devout Muslim man were to contact a dirty animal like a dog just before he died, he would not be allowed into heaven. Maybe it was contact with a dog at all that voided said ticket. I can't remember exactly. Either way, I have since been informed that neither of those theories is doctrinal. The reality is, those four-legged Marines are incredibly intimidating. No social or religious pressure is going to top that primal fear, and I had no problem capitalizing on that. We needed all the help we could get, and at least one of these dogs was trained to detect explosives. *Maybe we'll even find that tripwire before it goes off*, I thought hopefully.

Since we were at the gate and there were some soldiers there to help too, I decided that this would be a good time to offload some of the less useful parts of my kit. I was carrying a couple of smoke grenades on the upper left portion of my body armor. I took them off first, fearing that if one were punctured by shrapnel and its smoke deployed, the subsequent rising heat might sear my face. Next, I removed all but one of my fragmentation grenades. I remembered reading about how when cavalrymen fought Indians on the American frontier they were commonly ordered to save the last bullet for themselves. Iraq was not a whole lot different in that regard. We had heard all the horror stories about coalition forces who had been captured by enemy Iraqis. Rape, torture, and mutilation were thought of as a fate that was certain to befall anyone captured by Al-Qaeda in Iraq (AQI). I was not about to willingly give up *all* of my last resort weaponry. Lastly, I made possibly the strangest choice I ever made in my military career; in fact, I still slightly shudder at the thought: I handed over my rifle.

I felt that in the turmoil of this crowd carrying two long weapons was a liability, so I chose to keep my shotgun over my rifle. I thought that my scattergun was the more practical weapon for this application, because it could fire both less-than-lethal and lethal rounds. On top of that, any likely attack visited on us in which I was going to be of any use to my team would take place well within 50 meters. Perfect range for a 12-gauge. For more distant targets, we had above us, placed in both buildings and towers, dozens of American rifles. They could cover any threat that manifested itself beyond the crowd, and it is likely that I would not be able to engage those targets anyway. Should that happen, there would be dozens—if not hundreds—of civilians between me and the potential threat, making it impossible for me to safely fire. One of the secondary jobs for a young NCO in modern urban combat is to limit collateral damage and we took that directive very seriously, from both a humanistic point of view and a professional one. Still, in all honesty—even after all these years—I question my logic. I never should have taken off my rifle, but I did.

As I walked back out to the fragmented crowd I noticed one of our Iraqi Police officers, and brother-in-arms, was surrounded by civilian men who were screaming at him in Arabic. They had him completely encircled and were slowly closing in as we started over to help. Anxiety twisted his face. He trembled as he brandished his AK-47 and spun around in a full circle to make sure each screaming civilian got a good look at its business end. Undeterred, they continued shouting and slowly approaching him. He stiffened his back with courage and wrapped his hand around the charging handle of his weapon. The unmistakable metallic *clink* reverberated over the voices of the mob as he violently jacked a fresh round into the chamber. I'll never know exactly what he screamed back at them, but I think we can safely assume that it was something impolite.

"HEY!!!" I heard yelled in an authoritative and powerful new American voice. "WE DON'T FUCKING ACT LIKE THAT AROUND HERE! That's Saddam tactics! We don't pull that shit!"

Lieutenant Colonel Mac had arrived, and he was not pleased with the behavior of our Iraqi comrade.[5] Apparently, Colonel Mac had heard that things were getting out of hand and had decided to gather up his Personal Security Detail (PSD team) and come see the mission through. With the help of Mac's team, and the dog handlers, we began to regain control of the crowd. We separated the civilians into three lines heading east and west along the large concrete wall that formed the outer border of the Glass Factory.

The first line, closest to the wall, was designated for men who had

---

5 The issue here is that Iraqi civilians simply do not respect other Iraqis who are in positions of authority. Perhaps this is because they endured decades of maltreatment by their corrupt government before we arrived in Iraq, or maybe it was a symptom of our being there. One can't be sure; but what we do know is that the attitude was real and prevalent. If it were an American in the same position as this young man, he could have simply showed them his rifle, shouted "Back up!" with as much vigor as he could muster and it is highly likely that he'd get his desired response. This was not the case for IPs, and our commander knew it just as well as we did. However, in his mind this was no excuse to threaten a group of disarmed civilians.

no form of Iraqi identification documents. The second, for men who had an ID issued by the Iraqi government, but who had never worked for the government before. The last, for men who had formerly been employed by the state, whether as a police officer; firefighter, elected official, or otherwise. This line was the most important because US Central Command had issued a ban on the hiring of civilians who had once been a member of the Ba'ath Party, or the former Iraqi state department under Saddam.

In a move that has been highly criticized by the global press, the politicians back home decided that removing the dictatorship of Iraq simply did not go far enough to foil potential conspirators, so they elected to banish the entire government, and *all* Ba'ath party members. Whether they had ever been involved in a crime didn't matter to the American administration, they felt as if there was no real way to separate the uncorrupted men of the Ba'ath party from the criminals, so for our part, we needed to be sure that none of these men had been removed from office during that time, nor could they have ever been involved with Saddam's party. Additionally, there was a large group of former Iraqi Police officers who had been fired and forever banned from civil service by the US military when they refused to support US efforts in "Operation Phantom Fury," otherwise known as "The Battle of Fallujah." Luckily for me, I did not have to do any of the background checking on these folks; my job was just to get them into their appropriate lines and keep them, and us, safe. Simple enough. Drive on.

The entire morning my good friend, and medic, whom we affectionately called "Z," had been hounding me to have him relieved of his post. He was manning our .50 caliber machine gun within the walls of the Glass Factory, which we had set up to defend us and the crowd from potential attacks. The weapon system was mounted on our Humvee so that it could provide support by fire from a few different angles, while simultaneously presenting our military might to the Iraqis within the complex. As Sun Tzu said, "The supreme art of war is to subdue the enemy without fighting."[6] We, and the rest of the Coalition Forces on

---

6 I understand there is some debate as to whether Sun Tzu ever actually existed at

the ground in Iraq during the occupation, heeded and applied that advice whenever possible.

For me, though, the problem at hand was a personal one: Z was not just our medic, he was also a former Airborne Infantryman. The last place he wanted to be stuck was in a vehicle somewhere away from the action. Over and over he buzzed my radio, practically begging to get out there with us, and each time he did I told him I would get him relieved as soon as possible—never once actually intending to do so. I knew our situation was risky, and the last thing I wanted was to have one of my dearest brothers walk out those gates and be put in harm's way for a mission that I fully believed to be foolhardy.

About that time, I received another transmission alerting me to the fact that there were more augment troops waiting for us at the gate, so I headed over to check it out. Of the soldiers they had sent our way, two of them were carrying a light machine gun called a M249, or more commonly, a SAW (Squad Automatic Weapon). Like I said before, the last thing we want to do is introduce a machine gun to a crowd control situation. As an NCO, one of the most important jobs one has is to reduce collateral damage whenever possible, and following the same logical progression that had made me drop off my rifle, I could not use a machine gunner in a crowd. I told the only soldier there who was armed with a rifle that he would be coming along with me when I went back out. It was not enough help, but, *Ours is not to reason why, ours is but to do and die.* Drive on.[7]

---

all. Either way, someone wrote that line in *The Art of War* and attributed it to him, and its wisdom has proved itself numerous times throughout history in battles that you've never heard of—because they never happened. Perhaps the best example of this maxim, though, which you have heard of, is the Cold War.

7 There is a complex bit of logic at play here that I feel worth mentioning. I knew that we needed more help out there, but as I said earlier, I did not want to use my teammates to provide that help. However; when presented with the option of using soldiers from other companies and battalions, I *was* willing to ask them to come out. It's not that I had no feeling of brotherhood with other troops, because I did—and I still do. It is simply that these other soldiers had not been through the hardships of war *with* us, and some of them had hardly left the base at all, so we almost felt like it was their turn. Whatever that meant. Additionally, our guys were

The soldier with the rifle was a Specialist called "Rick." He was visibly younger than me and justifiably nervous at the idea of leaving those protective walls. I talked to him directly as we walked out, but with a supportive smile. We were all nervous the first time we put ourselves blatantly into harm's way. Anyone who says he was not is either lying, or just too immature to understand the gravity of the situation he was in. He was obviously, and justifiably so, nervous. But he was still willing, my kind of guy.

When we got back to my position between the lines of civilians I began to explain what had happened beforehand, what we were doing about it, and what he should look out for, including tripwires.

"Hey Corporal McCoy, get over here!" LTC Mac yelled to me.

"I will be right back. You know what to do," I told Rick before I jogged over to the Colonel.

"Hey McCoy, you got any dip?"

"Yes, Sir."

Mac was a commanding, but warm leader. You could not help but feel a little stronger when you talked to him. He was straight to the point, and I would not use the word "friendly," per se, but he certainly was not the typical overbearing, massively insecure curmudgeon that some officers, or even NCOs, for that matter, can be. He was a warrior, a man you respected and admired.

He went on to give me some new set of instructions that I cannot quite recall, and then sent me off. Each of us heading back to our positions about 50 meters apart.

When I got back to Rick I stood in front of him, but with my back turned to his direction and picked up instruction right where I had left

---

already in overwatch positions. I was not going to move them and heighten their risk to keep a new guy safe. Especially, since this would require that at the same time I place a troop that I inherently trusted less than my own teammates in a place to watch our backs while we were in the crowd. Putting new troops in place of my teammates would weaken us in our strongest and most important positions, the overwatch. Anyone could stand out there and handle the crowd with us, but our safety depended not so much on our own skills, but those of the rifles and machine guns above our heads. Really, it was in a way *better* for both the new guys and for us if the less experienced troops were brought out to the front.

off. Then Z called me on my radio again to say he was on his way out because he had found relief (maybe Johnny relieved him, I'm not sure). I reached up with my left hand to key the microphone on my left shoulder and bent my neck to respond:

"Rog. See you out here."

Suddenly, there was a loud bark followed with a violent growl coming from somewhere just in front of me. I peered under the brim of my helmet, to figure out what was going on, neck still bent to the radio mic.

SGT Cann's dog, Bruno, had grabbed an Iraqi man in the midst of the first line, dressed in a blue thawb[8] by the arm and began to shake violently. SGT Cann threw himself at the guy. BOOM! BOOM! deafening blasts rumbled out back-to-back, accompanied by two rapid white flashes.

A burning, stinging sensation shot through my entire body. It was as if I had been struck by lightning. I felt my muscles and bones contort fiercely; almost like they had all flexed in succession so swiftly that their mere compression had been enough to shatter my skeleton. Then followed an unimaginable pain. It felt like every nerve in my body had been set ablaze in the same instant. Then blackness.

---

8 Thawb or thobe is the garment most commonly worn by Arab men.

CHAPTER TWO

The Evacuation

The only thing that makes battle psychologically tolerable is the brotherhood among soldiers. You need each other to get by.

— Sebastian Junger

... the body fell beside him, badly broken and disfigured, but not yet dead. After a while consciousness returned to the shattered man, and he saw Zarathustra kneeling beside him. 'What are you doing there?' he said at last, 'I knew long ago that the devil would trip me up. Now he will drag me down to hell: will you prevent him?'

— Friedrich Nietzsche, *Thus Spoke Zarathustra*

I awoke face down in blood soaked sand. The world spun around me. What little sounds I could make out were muffled and indistinct. It was like I had been twirled around on an old tire swing, then flung into a swimming pool. I couldn't gather my wits any more than I could get my bearings. The harder I tried to get a handle on the world around me the more slippery my grip became. My eyes strained to adjust to the scene. Pain sunk its fangs permanently. We have just been hit by rockets, I assumed. *This must be a coordinated attack.* My confusion turned to panic.

"Oh, God!"

"Oh, God!"

"Please, God!!!"

"Ohhhh…"

The sounds that surrounded me became clearer. I could decipher some individual words, but they seemed to only add uncertainty. *Who is groaning?* I heard gurgling as someone tried to force air through a blood filled throat. The wounded and dying were bellowing in both English and Arabic. Screams of death filled the air. Rage filled our hearts.

"Ahhhhhh!"

"Medic!" "Medic!"

"Allahu akbar!" "Allahu akbar!"

I propped myself up as much as I could. The inch or two that I was able to manage was not enough to make a significant difference in my field of view. I thought I heard the reports of rifles. *Is that AK fire? I need to start helping my guys*, I thought to myself, *We're being ambushed!* Shock was setting in. I tried desperately to locate my weapon and return fire, but I was totally unable to move. I wanted to figure out why, but I couldn't get my body positioned in a way that would allow me to look toward my legs. I could see both of my arms and my chest. My arms were definitely broken, osmosis was spreading blood throughout the sleeves of my uniform, but I could still move them—sort of. I half-propped myself up again, onto my side, and peered down toward my legs. But when I finally looked downward, in the direction that my legs should have been, all I could make out was thick, black blood and a pile of muddy entrails.

"I am cut in two," I said aloud, unsure whether I was talking to the dying men around me, or to myself.

I ran a bit of an organ through the fingertips of my left hand. I was certain that it had once belonged to me. Where did it fit in this mess? I searched the jumbled human remains that rested underneath me and wondered exactly where this little organ went, but I couldn't complete the puzzle. My mind drifted. Distractedly, I wondered what it was going to be like to die. Certainly, there could be no way to save a man who had been cut in half!

"Oh, God! Oh, God! Oh, God!" The screams filled my ears again.

"I'm hit!" "Johnny!" "Medic!"

Was that me yelling, I wondered? I tried to look for the frantic

American voice, but all I could see was dark red sand, limbs which had been flung from their torsos, bloody men writhing on the ground begging for death to end their suffering, and hundreds of empty sandals.

Lying there, still rubbing that piece of what I believed to be a pancreas between the tips of my fingers, I again contemplated what it was going to be like to die. Was I going to cross over into some other dimension and meet Jesus like I had been taught my entire life, or was it all just going to go black, like slipping quietly into a slumber? A sleep that one never comes back from. *Please don't let this be my final resting place,* I thought. *Not this shit-hole. Not now.*

"Oh, God!" "Oh, God!" the shouts enveloped me.

Am I yelling, too? The agony that lay between my then-present condition and death grew louder as I gathered my wits. Still propped onto my side, I saw more blood drenched men than ever before. Some were missing arms, or most of their arms. Some were scrambling to their knees to beg Allah to save them. Still others were upright, wandering aimlessly, begging for medical assistance while they looked for their missing limbs.

I could do nothing but lie there in the sand, virtually helpless and unable to move. At this point I still believed that my body may be cut in two. Part of me wondered if I had committed some great sin that God felt I must lie there and repent for before I died. I could think of nothing so grave. Then I wondered if I had been left immobile just so that I could properly ponder the inevitable ending. An ending drawing nearer every second.

I heard a faint, but familiar voice calling my name. "Mac!" "Mac!" It was Johnny, my first line leader and close friend. I tried to keep myself together enough to respond to him, but even in the moment I could tell that my brain was not fully functioning. He yelled to me but I could not focus enough to answer. I knew what I wanted to say, but my motor-skills were gone. My mind and body were too disjointed to form words. It was like being a drowning child at the local pool and hearing one's mother yell, "Get out of the water!" The boy may hear her. He may even want to respond; but how could he shout back through all of that water? I was on the sand, but drowning nonetheless.

When the blasts went off they had thrown dozens of men, including me, some tens of feet. When we had all landed I ended up at the bottom of one of the piles of dead and wounded. Johnny pulled the bodies off of me as he continued to shout. The corpses lifted one by one (I believe there were three bodies on top of me), the weight lessened. I could move a little more freely. Then, when one of corpses was pulled off of me, I saw the mangled parts which had blocked the view to my own hips, leave with it.

For the first time since the initial blasts, my waistline was exposed. I was able to see that my hips and at least the upper portion of both of my legs were still intact. I had not been cut in half after all. Great news in the darkest of moments. But, I still could not see below my knees.

Johnny grabbed my body and rolled me over. I realized my legs were still fully attached and fully articulated from feet to hip. The pain was extraordinary, but things were looking up.[9] My friend kept on talking to me as he patched my now exposed wounds. He assured me that both of my legs were still there and that they were not missing any joints. Which I thought I saw with my own eyes, but his reassurance sure didn't hurt anything. He did his best to keep me calm and relaxed. I tried my hardest to tough it out for him.

On every mission I wore Nomex gloves which I had cut the fingers out of early on during the deployment. Because my right hand was so mangled Johnny and Lyle, another soldier who was helping administer first aid, thought it best just to get the bleeding stopped, so they bandaged my hand right over the top of the glove. They had my right hand elevated and bandaged up by the time I saw it, but both the bandages and glove quickly ran through with blood.

There was a three-inch-long gash across the top of my right forearm just above my wrist. It had been opened up so wide that it revealed the bright white bones and my warm and pink muscle fibers which twitched on either side of the wound as it bled.

---

9 I had spent most of my youth running around in the Rockies getting into various sorts of trouble which often culminated in shorts falls off of cliffs, deadfall, or living trees, and the rest I spent riding dirt bikes, bulls, and playing sports. I was no stranger to broken bones, but this was a whole new world of pain.

There were approximately seven holes in that arm and eight more in my left. They were all leaking. Hot, thin-looking blood traced ghastly lines down each arm from shoulder to hand. I had still yet to see what my legs looked like under my uniform, but it was obvious that, even though all of each leg was still attached, the situation was dire. Every time I shuttered, convulsed—or worse yet—was bumped by someone else, I grunted and moaned in agony. Otherwise, I either gritted my teeth to get a handle on the pain, or babbled incoherently:

"I am sorry, Johnny. I am trying not to be a pussy, but this shit really hurts."

"I know it does, bro. You don't have to apologize."

When Z, our medic, finally reached us he looked me over and said:

"Mac, I have got to go help a Marine. He is worse off than you are. I will be back as soon as I can."[10]

His voice was stricken with panic. I heard it, but I felt a deep sense of pride at how well my friend and teammate defeated that trepidation and did his job *right.* Z stood up and hustled over to SGT Cann's side to begin treatment on him.[11]

Z was worried about my future as any close friend would be, but basic Army medical procedure has a very strict rule of progression. A medic is to start with the American who is most gravely injured. Then he or she works their way to the next most badly injured American, and then to the next, and then the next, down to the least badly injured American.

---

10 My last name is McCoy and it seems like it is a sort of tradition that any man of Irish descent in the Army ends up with the nickname "Mac." I apologize if it is confusing, but LTC Mac and Cpl Mac is what we were each called and I want to stay true to that fact, even though I understand that it can muddy the narrative a bit.

11 I just want to reiterate this point, it could have been upsetting to watch a close friend walk away while I was clearly on the brink of death. Especially since he left to go help a warrior who had almost surely already passed away; but that is not how I felt at all. All I remember feeling was a deep sense of respect in the strength of character that my friend had just displayed. He had been forced into an extremely uncomfortable and complex situation — with nearly no time to think it over — and he had demonstrated the courage to put personal loyalties aside and do the right thing. Just imagine the world we would live in if more people had that kind of fortitude.

Once that person is helped, they move on to treat local nationals who have also become casualties using the same progression. They start with the most devastating injuries and working their way to the least so.

While Z was gone Johnny put my head up in his lap and did his best to keep my attention off of my wounds. Every time I started on about when I die, I want you to tell this person that thing and so on, he answered, "Shut up, Mac. You're going to tell them yourself. You are going to make it." It was like a movie scene playing out in real-time.[12]

At that time in my life I was pretty damn homophobic, so there was no way I could have predicted that one day I'd find myself in the middle of this scene, but there I was, half naked, holding hands with another dude, with my head in his lap, lost deep in an emotional conversation.[13]

When Z returned, he told us that SGT Cann, one of the Marine canine handlers I had met up with at the gate, had succumbed to his injuries. A fate that I knew could be only moments away for me.

"Z, do you have any morphine?" I asked, pleading to have the edge taken off of the pain.

"No. They won't allow us to carry it anymore because they are afraid we're going to shoot it up."

"Typical Army bullshit," I laughed.

We talked as Z removed my body armor. The plate which covered my chest had stopped 6 ball bearings from penetrating, 4 of which would have easily penetrated my lungs, or my heart, had they made it through. I wore a civilian model of body armor that my uncle Brad, who, as a

---

12 Perhaps this is because we are a generation raised on TV and movies. Maybe Hollywood's influence was so powerful that rather than be influenced by situations which play out in reality, things work conversely for us. Maybe *we* mimic what we have seen on the screen now. Which should scare the shit out of us all because that could lead to an eerie and dangerous cycle of exaggerated human behaviors. That may play out in ways as of now unpredictable.

13 I lost all my ignorance and ill-conceived notions toward homosexuality when later, while recovering at Walter Reed Army Medical Center, my favorite nurse (the most talented one too) in the Intensive Care Unit I was treated in was an openly gay man. His kind nature and obvious skill at his craft, melted away all of my previous groundless ideas about homosexual men. To put it in a sentence, I had once been an idiot and now, thanks to Matt, I am no longer a bigoted fool.

major in the Air Force, had purchased for himself. Brad had recently returned from a trip to Iraq where his job was to investigate downed aircraft. When he heard rumor that the Army was sending troops to war with Level I body armor, he figured that I should replace my issue SAPI armor with his civilian-purchased Level III plates. "You'll need them more than I did anyway," he had said. No one ever could have predicted how true that statement would prove to be.

Once my armor was removed, Z retrieved his medical shears and carefully made a cut up the inseam of my pants. He looked over each wound as he pealed away my bloody uniform and the temporary bandages that covered it. Johnny still had my head propped up in his lap. I was finally able to see my bare legs with my own eyes.

In an instant the anguish made perfect sense. I looked at all the holes the blast had carved out with amazement. I couldn't believe that neither leg had been ripped from my body and cast aside like had happened to some of the Iraqi men surrounding me. Fear had left me nearly altogether. I knew how bad the situation was, but I had made my peace with death.[14] Z continued on, slowly and cautiously, cutting away my clothing. When he reached the crotch of my pants he said:

"Jesus, dude! You are not wearing any underwear!"

I laughed as much as I was capable of and retorted, "Hell no! This whole damn country is a fucking sand dune. Sand gets in my underwear and gives me a rash, bro."

"Yeah, but what if you get *wounded,*" he laughed.

"Stop it. It is cold as hell right now."

"Don't make excuses. We all know it's because you're Irish."

"Are you going to tourniquet anything?" I laughed.

"We could put one around your neck!"

What are best friends good for other than providing much needed reprieve in the worst possible situations? In that moment, I was glad to have a laugh, and happier still to have had it with my friends at my

14 It wasn't a conscious decision, either. I just felt at peace. It is almost as if millions of years of evolution have hardwired us to reduce our stress levels at the time of death, though the shouts of the dying men around me begged to differ.

own expense.

My clothing all removed, I could finally see the multitude of holes in my legs clearly. Z began to patch what he could, but they were in even worse condition than my arms were. Each leg had more than ten different holes in it, some of which were nearly two inches in diameter. Most were not that big. They were about the size of a small marble on average, but they had gone straight through both sides of my quadriceps.

At this stage the wounds were not pumping out as much blood as one might have expected. It was more like a steady leak. Each time my heart beat they would bubble up and run fresh blood down the sides of my legs. I lay there watching them bleed for a while thinking to myself, *Holy shit...* Saving Private Ryan *really got it right. These wounds look exactly the same as the ones in the movie did.*

It was the 6th of January, and like I had said to Z, one of the coldest days I ever experienced in Iraq. Not exactly ideal conditions to be lying on a stretcher with all of one's clothing cut off. I was starting to feel everything a little more intensely. The torment was escalating by the minute.

On top of the pain heightening, I had begun to shiver. Every time my muscles convulsed; or involuntarily spasmed, my broken bones would rub together inside my body, causing a grinding sound to fill my head, like gravel being smashed under the tires of a truck on a dirt road.

There was a group of soldiers and Marines going around gathering the injured on litters which would be used to load them onto medevac vehicles. When they reached me they found a new set of challenges. My legs were broken in so many places that they were practically crushed and lifeless. My left tibia was broken; my left femur was broken in three places, and my left hip had two fractures of its own. My right leg was only slightly better off, having two femur fractures and one hip fracture. To make things even more complicated, my lower back and some ribs had been broken as well (neither of which we knew about until much later).

There really was no way to load me without further injuring some part of my body, but there was no other choice; alive or dead, I was leaving Ramadi soon. My brothers would make sure of that.

It took several attempts for them to get the litter underneath my body. They would support me where they could then roll me onto my side, legs sloshing around from knee to hip causing the most agonizing pain I had yet experienced. And the return of the sound of my own bones grinding together in my ears. It was a bit like trying to lift an entire plate of Jello onto a single butter knife. It was not going to be an easy task, but it was one with only a one acceptable outcome.

Eventually, after rolling me around several times, they got me onto the litter and carried me over to the last remaining medevac vehicle: a five ton truck.

My litter had been stretched between the middle of the two bench seats which sat on either side of the truck's bed. Someone had welded this large set of stairs to the rear of the five ton truck, presumably to make it easier to mount, but it was causing us huge problems. Z had to climb in the back with me and hold up the rear door and metal staircase to keep them from either falling or swinging open respectively. Imagine trying to hold up a metal object that weighed well over 100 lb. while simultaneously providing medical aid to your fallen comrade—as if things were not already difficult enough.

Loaded and prepared to move, we set out for Camp Ramadi. Fortunately for us, it was a short drive back to post. The base was only a mile or two away, but the road was covered in potholes made by IEDs and the Iraqis' inability to repair infrastructure during wartime.

Because these trucks are constructed to haul thousands of pounds of equipment and troops, their suspension is virtually non-existent when unloaded, which for all intents and purposes is exactly the situation we found ourselves in.

Each time the truck would bounce in and out of a pothole my bones would rattle and rub together. The pain at this stage was so intense that, when combined with my heavy blood loss, it caused me to pass in and out of consciousness; but because of the condition I was in, Z was doing everything in his power to keep me awake.

"MAC!" "MAC! Don't you go to sleep," he yelled.

I moaned a response as best as I could and then forced my eyes open.

Between Z and me were two mortally wounded Iraqi men. One was missing a significant amount of his skull and the other had bandages scattered about his body (I think he may have been missing an arm as well). They both repeatedly attempted to kneel and pray, but they just were not stable enough to do it. Again and again they sat up and tried to remain steadfast enough to recite their prayers, but again and again they failed. Then to get back up they generally used my body as an anchor point, or like a rung in a ladder, they pushed off on me to raise their bodies up.

Z did his best to keep them off, no doubt fearing, as I was, that their using me as a leaning post may cause further complications to my recovery, or, even force one of my then shattered bone fragments to pierce another artery, mortally wounding me. Another risk, given that they were bleeding profusely, was their dripping fluid onto my body. Each drop that mixed with my own wounds threatened me with serious potential infections.

At the time, the only body part that I could move was half of my right arm. The lower half was basically demolished, but from the elbow up, I was still partly functional. Those two wounded Iraqis continued grabbing ahold to lean up to their knees and every time they did, I would summon whatever strength I had left to shove them off of me, but it was no use. I just could not do it on my own.

Though he was heavily occupied holding up that rear gate and staircase, Z did his best to help them off when he saw them leaning over my body. They kept up their struggle for another few minutes, but eventually they both died of their wounds. It was impossible to look at them right there next to me and not wonder whether they were foreshadowing my fate, just as others at the Glass Factory had done before. When we finally reached the rear entrance of Camp Ramadi we ran into a whole new set of problems: our own soldiers' ineptness.

We rolled up only to be immediately stopped by the soldiers who ran it. They would not let us in because we didn't have a convoy number. Convoy numbers were a sort of manifest that had to be sent out before any group of vehicles left their post. The number was linked to a document that had already been sent to whatever base the convoy was headed to. It let the new FOB (Forward Operating Base) know who was in said convoy, why they were asking permission to enter another camp, and what the convoy carried in cargo. We all understood the reasoning behind the convoy numbers, but this was an instance where bureaucracy needed to be overridden by human intellect, and that just was not happening.

Clearly, we were not a convoy because this was anything but a prearranged mission. It was a hastily thrown together single vehicle, trying to get two wounded Iraqis and myself back to the medical facility on base. Moreover, this vehicle was clearly being managed by American soldiers who were wearing Army uniforms and speaking in American English. It should have been obvious to the NCOs at the gate that we were not terrorists plotting some grand infiltration of Camp Ramadi.

Back and forth our driver argued with the gate guards until eventually Z, still standing in the bed of the truck, lost his cool:

"WE DON'T HAVE A FUCKING CONVOY NUMBER!!!"

"I can't let you on without one."

"This isn't a fucking convoy, you idiot!!! We've got a wounded American here!!!"

Z continued to berate the guards for a minute or two. I am fairly certain that amidst the verbal exchanges I heard a threat or two flung about. I won't insult you by detailing which side was throwing the most verbal abuse around, I will only say that I know that were the roles reversed, I would have been much less professional about it.

Eventually, the soldiers at Ogden Gate let their better sensibilities take over and we were allowed to enter our own home, but the struggle to reach Charlie Med field hospital was far from over.

At some point during our time living in the capital of Anbar province a Sergeant Major had thought it necessary to line the streets of our FOB with speed bumps (seriously, you cannot make this stuff up). I am sure that these obstacles had been added because someone thought it may save a life or two by slowing down a few vehicles with privates at their helm; but when your body is shattered and sloshing around inside your skin like a sack full of wrenches, it is hard to comprehend their logic. How could adding a whoop-section between the gate that leads to the most dangerous road in the world and the largest medical facility west of Fallujah, possibly be a good idea? One had to wonder.

I had begun to pass in and out of consciousness so frequently that I was having a hard time telling the difference between reality and whatever dreamworld I was off to in between. In other words, this is the point of the story where my memories become extremely fuzzy. I know I should not have to caveat my own story like this, but I feel as if I must be forthright: the way I remember the next few hours and days unfolding could have factual inaccuracies. That said, I can only tell the story the way I remember it and hope that you understand.

We had arrived at Charlie Med, Camp Ramadi's largest field hospital. The staff offloaded the deceased Iraqis who had accompanied us and then rushed my litter toward the surgery room. However, once they carried me into the medical facility they quickly realized there was another problem: it was already full of wounded Iraqi men. In one side of Charlie Med we went and then right out the other.

Down the road a little way was another aide station which belonged to our brigade's Engineers, so we headed there. Once inside, the first thing they did was to start transfusing blood. In the beginning they only had lines containing a quart or so apiece leading into each arm, but eventually they had to stick an IV into my jugular and start pumping in fluid that way. After establishing a steady stream of fresh blood into me, they fixed as many bandages as they could and rushed me out to the PLZ (Permanent Landing Zone) to board a medevac flight containing several other wounded people, bound for Balad.

While en route to Balad the flight crew decided that because some of us had lost so much blood, an emergency landing in Fallujah was necessary to save lives, mine included. I was passing in and out of consciousness again, my 'grip' on reality, if you could even call it that anymore, was so slippery that it was like trying to squeeze a wet fish. The harder I tried, the worse it became. The darkness that awaited me each time I passed out was becoming more and more welcoming. I was exhausted. All I wanted to do was sleep. To put it into a sentence: I was starting to give up. What will death be like? I wondered again. Everyone always talks about a white light near the end of a tunnel, but I am not seeing shit.

Suddenly, I was jerked back to the world of the living. I slowly and hazily shifted my gaze from right to left. The room was full of medical equipment and tables. I tried, unsuccessfully, to orient myself. I looked down to see why my right leg was in so much pain, only to find that it was because a doctor was strenuously pulling on my heel. He was tugging so hard that it felt like my leg was going to rip off and fall into his lap. Dismayed I watched as he adjusted my foot on his shoulder and then pulled harder.

My teeth gnashed; I cried out in agony "Ahhhh!!!"

My face, all covered in blood and sweat, would wrinkle and contort with each new burst of pain. They gave me something to bite down on. I gritted my teeth into it and tried to muster up every last ounce of salt that I had remaining, but I was nearing my breaking point.

"Braxton! Braxton! Stay with us! I know it hurts, but we have got to stretch your legs out or you are going to lose them."

"Ahhh!!! Okay. Okay." I moaned. Then I passed out again; blood-stained tears running down both cheeks.

I am not sure how long I was out for, and I was not fully awake yet, but the next thing I distinctly remember was the sound of my flesh tearing under a scalpel. The surgeons were slicing the side of each quadriceps to relieve my Compartment Syndrome. Blood and puss practically spewed out as my swollen legs split wide open. I will never forget the way that cutting sounded inside my head. It was reminiscent of a muddy zipper being forced open. Some things stick with you forever; hearing your own flesh being cut apart is one of them.

Total Known Injuries Sustained:

- Multiple Bilateral Femoral Fractures
- Hip Fractures
- Left Humerus Spiral Fracture
- Right Radius and Ulnar Fractures
- Most of the Bones in the Right Hand Fractured
- Right Median Nerve Transected
- Massive Soft Tissue Damage Caused by Dozens of Ball Bearings
- Several Smaller Shrapnel Holes in Face, Neck, and Hands

Injuries Sustained in Action, but Discovered During Rehabilitation:

- Fractured Ribs (Found 9 years later)
- Brain Contusions
- Neck Damage (Found 9 years later)
- Broken Scaphoids in Both Wrists
- Fused Knuckles in Index Finger and Thumb
- Fracture in Lower Spine (Found 9 years later)

CHAPTER THREE

Leaving Iraq

Death stands above me, whispering low;
I know not what into my ear:
Of his strange language all I know is,
there is not a word of fear.

— Walter Savage Landor, *Death Stands above Me, Whispering Low*

The heat of the desert sun nipped sharply at my face. My eyes struggled open. I was being wheeled across a helipad on Camp Fallujah again, this time going the opposite direction, away. I was put en route to the big Air Force hospital in Balad. *I guess I am still alive*, I thought. The question became a common theme throughout the following hours and days.

Overall, my level of agony had lessened. But I was still unsure whether I the pain had dulled, or had just gotten used it. Either way, the small bumps in the landing pad did not seem to sting as much as they had on the way into Fallujah and that change was good enough for me, regardless of the reason it had come about.

I was strapped to a long, rectangular piece of hard plastic. Emergency Medical Technicians refer to them as stretchers, but in the Army we called these things "litters," which seemed more fitting to me because I was feeling like I was about to be permanently discarded. My body jostled a bit as they lifted the litter I was strapped to off of the rolling cart they had used as a vehicle to get me to the helicopter. The roar of the Blackhawk's engines drowned all sound as the flight crew strapped me down inside the bird. As the old cliché goes, I could not even hear myself think, not that I had many critical faculties left anyway.

When next my eyes opened I was being rushed across the airfield in Balad. I saw that the medical soldiers who were caring for me seemed very concerned about something. *What are they wound up about?* I wondered. *Am I running out of blood again? Maybe they're just trying to keep the rotor-wash out of my wounds?*

In Iraq, landing a helicopter, even in the middle of a city, such as the Air Force base in Balad undoubtedly was, stirs up huge amounts of dust and sand. This dust is so fine that it gets into everything—your shorts, electronics, lungs and wounds—even when they're covered up. We called it "moon dust" because its look and texture so closely resembled the dust kicked up by astronauts in the moon landing footage. The moon dust by itself could cause plenty of problems, but I assumed that what was really concerning the medics was bacteria that lived in the sand. A few weeks later we found out exactly why they were so concerned.

I was so broken and exhausted that I could not muster up the strength to move anything but my eyes. I was only partially coherent. My graze darted back and forth. I watched medical instruments and nurses pass by as they pushed me deeper into the hospital. I could tell that they were taking me to another operating room. I heard the doctors talking about it, but I could not make out why I was going to be operated on. The doctors and nurses who were helping me at this stage were warm and reassuring. My mind sluggishly meandered through the possibilities. Then, I was asleep again.

I awoke to the loud rumbling of an airplane engine. I was being pushed across an air strip toward a C-130 medevac flight headed for Landstuhl, Germany. The medics who were escorting me onto the flight line seemed much calmer than some had previously. *I must be stable now,* I thought. Then they wheeled me on board.

The C-130 Hercules is a four-engine turboprop plane designed by Lockheed. It's been in military service since the 50s. Its usual role is that of a transport, but when outfitted with machine guns and cannons they're used as gunships. Spectre is the name the Army gives them when they're doing that job. We just called them "Spookies." Compared with a civilian airliner, the interior of a C-130 looks stripped down and drab.

Purely functional. This one was different, though. It was lined with bunk beds, monitors, oxygen tanks and other medical equipment. Even to the untrained eye it was obviously much more than just your average cargo plane. It was more like a flying infirmary.

The medics lifted me off of the cart and slid my litter onto a bedframe mounted inside the aircraft. Once they felt I was properly secured to it the medic now in charge of my evac signaled something to the crew chief. I had straps running across my arms, legs, stomach, and even my head. I could not move any part of my body except for my eye lids. I was starting to panic a little at the claustrophobia I felt. Soon the oxygen mask which was covering my nose and mouth pumped more pure oxygen into my system and I fell asleep again.

Later, I woke up choking and in sheer terror. I felt like I was drowning, but how? Instinctively I tried to turn my head to one side to get a breath, but I couldn't because it was so tightly fastened to this bed. I wiggled as much as I could, gagging, hacking, and trying desperately to draw air, still unsure of what was happening. Left and right I moved my head, only managing a centimeter or less in either direction. I groaned for help, still too tightly restrained to move.

Help!!! I screamed inside my head.

I desperately needed to breathe. I couldn't hold my breath much longer. *Yes, you can! Toughen up!* My thoughts ran wild.

"Help!!!" I gurgled aloud this time. It was completely unintelligible because my mouth and nose were filled with water.[15]

Fear turned to anger. Inside my head I screamed a series of idle and senseless threats and cuss words. Suddenly, I felt a strap loosen. My head shifted to one side. As soon as I felt cleared I coughed and hacked

---

15 I have always thought that I remembered the water bottle attached to my oxygen mask tipping over and pumping water through my mask, but in retrospect, I think it could have been that I had thrown up inside it. And I had just thought that the machine was pumping in water for some reason. Although, I distinctly recall the nurse saying something about the tank malfunctioning to another crew member. Either way, I assure you that when you are drowning you care very little about what the liquid is, or where it is coming from, you only want to expel it.

out all of the fluids that were lodged in my throat. I was still in a daze, but at least I could breathe. I gasped for air and muttered, "Thank you," to the nurse who had just saved my life. Inside my head, I was calling this flight and all the unwounded people on it every combination of curse words I dream up.

The next time I regained consciousness a full day our two had passed and I was lying in a proper bed, alone in a room somewhere. *Am I still alive?* I looked around trying to figure out where I was. I noticed the pain radiating throughout my body again. *I guess I must be alive. I have to be alive to hurt this much. That or I really must have done something awful during my time on earth. Heaven just wouldn't be heaven if it hurt this much.*

There was an angelic blonde woman in my room smiling at me as she placed a blanket on my bed. It was a quilt crafted out of blue and red fabrics. It had been beautifully decorated with different images of the American Flag and was adorned with several ways of saying "Thank you, for your sacrifices."

"Hi Braxton, I made this quilt for you when I heard that you had been injured," she said.

"Thank you," I replied

"I spoke with your mother today.... I am from Delta.... My husband is stationed out here in Germany...."

I was trying so hard to listen to her, but I was too groggy to follow attentively. Still, I was amazed that she was from Delta, a tiny town on the opposite side of my home county in Utah. I thought her incredibly sweet and I hoped she'd stay awhile, but that is as much as I can recall. The pain was so intense.

"Did I talk to my mom on the phone today?" This time I spoke out loud. I was almost certain that I had, but my world was too murky to be sure.

Later that day Jesse, the other Marine dog handler, who had not passed away in the explosion at the Glass Factory, came to my room to pay a visit.

"How are you doing, man?" he asked

"I'm okay." I said, "Is that your dog?"

"No, it's Bruno."

"Where is your dog?"

"He didn't make it, so they sent Bruno with me."

"Is your arm going to be okay?" I asked. His arm was bandaged up and wrapped in some sort of metallic cage in place of a cast.

"Yeah man, it's good."[16]

I was too delirious to hold any sort of a conversation with Jesse. I was more delirious, in fact, than I had ever been. But I was glad to see him all the same. I am sure he had come at the suggestion of the medical staff who were probably thinking that I was going to die, but it made little difference to me. I was happy just to share the same air as another man who had just come from that hell.

Later on a surgeon came in and told me that they had planned on trying to put rods in my femurs while I was there in surgery, but the doctors thought that it would be best to wait for an infection to clear up.

He explained, as he lifted my sheets and showed my legs to me for the first time since I had left Iraq, that they instead placed external fixators on each one of them. These metal cages were implanted just to get me stable enough to be flown back to Walter Reed Army Medical Center in Washington, D.C. He told me I was headed there that night.

My new semi-permanent home was to be Walter Reed's ICU. The external fixators, which were essentially metal cages that had been screwed into my bones, above and below each fracture, in order to help stabilize them for safer travel, had done their job thus far. As far as I can remember—and I cannot remember much of it—the flight had been relatively uneventful. I had a steady supply of blood, IV fluid, and morphine being pumped into my body which was keeping me alive for the time being.

The oddest part about my then-current state was that I was living in

16 The first draft of this story that I had written right after I left Walter Reed (9 years ago) said that this dog was Bruno, but in truth I am not sure about that. It could have been a different dog entirely. I may have just thought it was Bruno because I was only slightly acquainted with their dogs and Bruno was the one I had been around most.

limbo. My body and consciousness were trapped somewhere between life and death. The space I occupied could be described at its best moments as confusing and at its worst, no longer worth living. One moment my eyes closed and I was completely lost to this world, and the next, they opened to an environment of pain and a sort of temporary dementia. Sometimes hours passed between these openings and closings, but I never felt the satisfaction of real rest. It was almost as if the time spent in between never even existed at all.

This feeling of helplessness and confusion lasted in varying degrees for days—if not for weeks. During this period, I had surgery nearly every morning to clean and irrigate my wounds and change the bandages that swathed my body. From what I understand, the doctors had to put me under for these daily hygiene sessions, because the sheer number of open wounds and their depth made scrubbing too intrusive and time-consuming to do while I was awake. I had a dozen or more wound channels which were "through-and-throughs," a term used to describe a wound that starts on one side of the body and passes through its other side, exiting entirely. Usually on a limb. I also had dozens more wounds caused by projectiles which had penetrated my flesh, but had stopped in something more dense, like bone or thick muscle.

Along with keeping me in a partial state of being comatose, these daily procedures robbed me of the ability to eat or drink water. When a patient has food in their stomach and they enter surgery, it is plausible that they will throw it up and choke to death. Sedation makes surgery possible, but it also causes nausea and stifles the gag reflex. A very dangerous combination of symptoms for a person who has food or water in their system. Choking and suffocation isn't even the worst possibility either, a person could also aspirate and end up drowning or with severe pneumonia. The staff had done a thorough job explaining all of this to me, so I understood the concerns. On a human level, however, this deprivation of what, to one's mind, feels like basic sustenance seems cruel and unusual. Even when it's done with one's best interests in mind.

Within a few days of my being hospitalized in the States my mother and step-father flew out to Washington, D.C., to visit me. It was as nice to see them as you might expect, but I was still only partly functional mentally and totally incapacitated physically. I am sure that in this case, the pleasure truly was all mine.

While my mother was there she decided to order Chinese food. I guess she figured I had too much on my mind to notice the guards were feasting while the inmates withered away. Someone in the group asked for a serving of sweet and sour pork, which was, at the time, my favorite Asian dish. Still on the strict dietary restrictions that my surgery regimen required, I was left only to take in the aroma and wish that I could be sharing dinner with them—or so I thought.

There was a nurse assigned to ICU who I liked quite a lot called "Matt." When someone in my family, I can't remember who, pleaded with him, begging on my behalf for the opportunity to eat some sweet and sour pork, he caved.

"He can have a bite, but if he throws it up you did not get permission from me!"

"Deal!" I responded ecstatically.

From that day on, I was convinced that Matt was both the kindest and the most qualified nurse on staff. I may be a little biased, but you still could not convince me otherwise today.

Despite the medical team's best efforts, I had been stricken with a severe infection which had spread to my blood stream. The disease had most likely originated at the time of the initial injury, but it was impossible to know for sure. There is a bacteria unique to the sands of Iraq, which had been showing up in the blood of many returning wounded service members. Apart from the obvious dangers presented by infections of the blood, this also meant that I would not be having my external fixators replaced by internal hardware anytime soon. Not that it mattered to me in terms of mobility or anything of that sort, but it was another item added to the growing list of health complications we were facing. It also meant another few days in the Intensive Care Unit.

ICU was a tolerable place; we each had a television and a morphine button, but none of us patients had our own rooms. That meant that anytime one person was being checked on the lights had to be turned on for both people. It made sleep, if you were lucky enough to be getting any of it, nearly impossible. My roommate was an elderly woman dying of lung cancer.[17] Day and night she would lie in bed and moan in what must have been the unbearable pain of slow suffocation. Every hour or so, this poor woman would have coughing fits. Occasionally she let out these low, sorrowful groans that would give even the sternest of consciences goosebumps. Most of the time when these fits would happen, I just lay there and listened to her on the other side of the curtain which divided us, feeling horribly sad for her and her situation. Sometimes though, my mammalian roots showed themselves in an ugly way and my temper flared. I got mad at the hospital for putting me in a room where it was impossible to sleep and even angry at her for keeping me awake.

Why the hell am I put into a room with someone who is dying like this?! I said to myself bitterly. *Doesn't anyone realize that I've got my own problems to deal with here?*

I knew how awful it was for me to be so self-centered, but at that time in my life I was very prone to getting caught up in the moment and reacting emotionally. I was also dealing with the slow onset of chronic fatigue and insomnia. When this sad lady coughed and moaned at night, I burst awake in cold sweats after being right back on those streets of Ramadi, surrounded by the dead and dying. Grown men writhing on the ground all around me, wailing and screaming their final words to their families and prayers to their Gods.[18]

Another sleep issue I dealt with was being caused by me more indirectly. Because I was still under intensive care, I was constantly attached to a monitor designed to alert the nurses any time my blood pressure or heart rate dropped too low. It also sounded when my breathing became too shallow. This alarm seemed to go off primarily at night when I—after a great struggle—fell asleep. Over and over again I drifted off, only to be awakened by nurses moments later. This struggle went on for weeks. I was then deprived not only of food and water, but also of sleep.

---

17 Because Walter Reed was an Army hospital it had all sorts of patients in it. The majority seemed to be other wounded men, but there were some elderly patients around too.

18 Looking back now it seems obvious that this should have been the first time that I realized I have PTSD, but it wasn't. I spent another eight years denying that fact.

At what point do we cease to be human? I often thought. I had yet to be introduced to Maslow's Hierarchy of Needs, but it did not take more formal education to notice the loss of my most basic human necessities.

Despite all the drama and sleep loss the world still turned, and the days still came and went. As Robert Frost once said, "In three words I can sum up everything I've learned about life: it goes on." It was no different for me. No matter how difficult my nights were, to what level my pain had risen, or what state I was in psychologically, life went on—and that is a good thing.

One day while my family was still visiting I woke up from a nap, groggy and confused. I was trying to talk to the people around me, but I could not form sentences. My depth perception went next. Suddenly my tiny room in the intensive care ward looked as long as a hallway. I knew something was not right, but I just tried to ignore it. I asked them to move the TV closer so that I could see it better. The televisions in this part of the hospital were all attached to the bedframes. The arms which they hung on swiveled about 180 degrees. The arm also had a joint similar to a person's elbow that could bend, extend and retract. A patient or their caretakers used these features to best position the screen for the viewer.

"Closer, I still can't see it."

"Okay?" my mom responded. She swiveled the screen a bit closer.

"You are hardly even moving it. I need it much closer, not just a few inches closer."

"Braxton, we are moving it a lot!" Her puzzled face was rapidly turning fearful.

"Todd, something is wrong. Go get a nurse!" I overheard my mother talking to my step-father.

"Closer, *please*!" I was catching onto the fact that something was wrong and I was panicking.

"Braxton! It is right in front of you, it can't be moved any closer."

Then I felt real, intense fear for the first time since I was wounded. The kind that seizes up a person's joints when they encounter a charging grizzly bear.

Up until that point I had not really had enough wits about me to understand the magnitude of the situations that I had been in. But by this stage I had realized how close to death I had actually come—and I remembered how dying felt.

"Can you help me sit up straight?" I asked

"Sure," she said as she lifted my torso upright.

"Can you push me a little more?" I asked, "I am not level yet."

This conversation went just like the one about the TV had. She kept incrementally tilting me at my request until they all finally realized that I couldn't tell when my body was level or plumb. By the time I said enough was enough, I was so far leaning to one side that my elbow was touching the mattress. I had been rotated from one side, all the way past the vertical line until I was leaning twice as far as I had been before—only this time in the other direction.

When the nurse came in to check out our situation she was very nonchalant about the whole scene. When the Emergency Room doctor arrived, things were different. He immediately recognized that something serious was going on. He asked me standard interview questions as doctors always do:

"How are you feeling?"

"When did this start?"

"Have you ever had a reaction like this before?"

He then told us that it looked as if I was having a reaction, perhaps even an allergic one, to the nerve blocking agents that they had placed in my legs. This meant that they would have to administer a drug to reverse the original drug's effect. As with the administration of any medicine, it came with its own set of risks. I could have another reaction to this new reversing agent and be much worse off than I currently was, or adding more drugs to my already failing body could cause some unforeseeable change that may be extremely detrimental to my health. We were faced with deciding whether I should risk a potentially fatal outcome or just tough it out and hope for the best. I am almost always for toughing something out, but in this case the doctor made it clear that was not the wisest course of action.

We chose to take the new drug.[19]

A few minutes after the new drug was administered I was already doing better. I was even regaining some of my wits. I was still anxious, tired, and depressed by the rapid and substantial changes in my health, feelings that were certainly being exacerbated by all of the drugs I was taking, but the worst of the nausea had subsided. And even though I could then feel the pain in my legs again, I was still *alive*—sort of.

---

19 I have since had other doctors speculate that this very well could have been a stroke, not a reaction to the nerve blocks at all. Another doctor suggested that this should have been taken as an early sign that the damage to my inner ear was much worse than they had originally thought.

CHAPTER FOUR

Tedium and Terror

Like the experience of warfare, the endurance of grave or terminal illness involves long periods of tedium and anxiety, punctuated by briefer interludes of stark terror and pain.

— Christopher Hitchens

I spent the next few weeks in the same bed, lying around thinking about what my new life was going to be when I—*if I*—got out of the hospital. When I was not caught up daydreaming about what my long-term recovery was going to look like, my mind was on my brothers back in Ramadi. I knew the morale-crushing war that they were living every day and I had begun to feel an enormous amount of guilt at the thought of them facing those trials without me. The thought was only made worse when I considered that they were doing it while I lay safely in a bed back in the States.

During the Indian Wars on the American frontier the notion that there are far worse things than death a person might face was popularly held. I was finding out first hand just how true that idea feels when there is a little distance between the espouser and his inevitable demise. My fear of death was steadily being replaced by a heavy blanket of grief and guilt. I felt grief, as I think anyone would, for the memories of lives lost and my role, actively or passively, in their deaths. I also felt guilty for being one of the people who survived. I could have, *should* have, done more, I often thought.

By this point in the story, my mind had cleared enough to recall the scene at the Glass Factory in detail. I remembered seeing SGT Cann and Bruno confronting the suicide bomber. I remembered Z telling me that he had to go "check on the Marine" who was injured worse than I was. I remembered almost everything from that morning, including the courageous action Bruno and SGT Cann had taken, yet somehow, ridiculously—and unfairly to SGT Cann's heroic memory—I had saddled myself with the guilt of his death. It was not in any way my fault that he had chosen to give his life trying to protect the Marines and soldiers around him, but that is much easier to write now, with the rationale of hindsight, than it was to convince myself of it in that hospital bed.

For what felt like an eternity, and was likely years long, I only casually interacted with the people around me. When my nurses came in to check on me, or to administer the next dosage of medicine, I talked to them and answered any questions they posed, but I was not really there. I looked through them as we spoke. It was the same with my family. My body was present whenever they visited, but my mind was always back in Anbar Province.

At night, I dreamt of the good and bad times that we had had on runs made to TQ (Al Taqaddum Airbase near Fallujah) or Fallujah, or missions we had been on in the city, or the small villages that surrounded it. I dreamt of nights and days stuck on boring missions, and other times of missions that were a bit more exciting, like the first time we took sniper fire, or when SGT Camp and his crew had been shot at with an RPG that had not been properly armed. An enemy combatant had fired at them around midnight, but the RPG never went off when it hit their position because the safety had not been removed. It had, however, punched right through the wall and landed at their feet. For the rest of my life I will never forget listening to Camp tell that story while we stood there, staring at the thing, laughing at how close a call it had been and how passionately he had told the story. Sometimes these dreams were as real as the bed underneath my back, other times they were more like I was a character in a movie, but both kinds drove me awake. Not a night went by that I didn't wake up panting in a cold sweat, my heart pounding, cortisol sending jolts of electricity through my veins. My sleep cycle stayed like this for years after the war. It was not until a decade later that I, and then only partly, learned how to get enough sleep during a 24 hour period.

The physical pain had largely subsided. It was still present, but it was being so well managed by morphine drips and oral pain medications that it had become only a fraction of what it once was. Sleep, guilt, anxiety over potential health complications, and the onset of what I now know to have been PTSD had become the most dominant problems I faced. Which, in a way, is proof that the physical injuries were healing.

I had a TV and nearly constant visitation, but most of the time I just stared at the white walls and ceiling of the room, wasting away. Doctors and nurses came and went. They stopped in and took my blood pressure, or jostled my feet around to make sure I was not swelling too much. Now and then they came in and removed the apparatus that stretched from my ankles to my calves. They were like long white blood pressure cuffs and they worked a lot like a blood pressure cuff too. Except instead of pressurizing only upon request, these filled with air on regular intervals to squeeze the blood out of my lower extremities and promote circulation. But, apart from those frequent interruptions and simple interactions with members of my family, I just lay there, trapped in my body and trying to escape my mind.

Eventually things did start happening again. A nurse came in and said, "Mr. McCoy, we have some really good news for you!"

Desperately needing to hear such a thing, I eagerly waited in anticipation.

"You are getting out of the ICU today!" she exclaimed.

She was right. This was great news. The nurse then informed me that I would be moving up a few floors to the 57th Ward. I was heading to the Neurology unit, but I did not quite grasp the implications of that yet. Namely, that I had suffered neurological damage.

Most importantly to me was that I was getting out of intensive care and I was finally going to have a room of my own. No more constant check-ups at night. No more dying old lady roommate who needed just as much attention day and night as I did, and no more fasting for long stretches. There was a catch though. I was going to be getting a whole new staff of nurses. That meant that I may never see my new friend Matt or the others that had been so good to me again. Eventually I decided that this trade would be worth it, if only for the serenity that having my own door would provide. Not that the decision was ever mine to make.

Later on that day some of the nursing staff came in and wished me goodbye and good luck. Most of them took the chance to point out that this was quite a milestone, a sign that my health was truly improving. Then Matt and another nurse pushed my bed up to the Neurological Ward while some members of my family followed.

When we got to my new place, I noticed a slip of blue paper taped to the doorway with large font typed on it. I could not quite make out what it said. For a little while I wondered what unique piece of information might be on it, but eventually I lost interest and forgot about it altogether. Not until weeks later did I find out that it had said, "Quarantine."

This new room was not exactly a suite at the Ritz-Carlton hotel, but it was a big step up from the ICU. For one thing, it had its own door—not a curtain. And, for the most part, the lights were going to stay off at night when I wanted them to. Some other noticeable differences were that I began to see uniformed Army officers regularly, and some of the nurses on staff introduced themselves as "Lieutenant so-and-so." Usually they would then tell us that we could just call them by their first name. I think most of them understood that in the Neurological Ward there were more important things to focus on than military bearing.

"Neuro," as it was so-called, did seem a much more stable environment, and I was in need of just that. When one is in intensive care, the surroundings and intrusions make one feel as if he is on death's door. For the most part, those of us in ICU were, in fact, at risk of dying at any moment. But as counterintuitive as it must sound, as simple a thing as moving to a new ward can stave off even the most stubborn of pessimistic attitudes, thereby changing the course of one's physical health. I was feeling the benefits of that change. I was beginning to win and I knew it.

One morning after I finished my breakfast, a mountain of a man walked into my room, took the cuffs off of my lower legs and started moving my feet around. It would seem strange to me if someone walked in and did this without so much as a cordial greeting now. But back then, I was so used to such occasions that I hardly even cared that he was there. Then he started asking me to give him resistance as he pulled on the tops of my feet.

"Who are you?" I asked

"My name is Solomon. Now push against my hand," he said with a smile as he applied pressure to the soles of my feet. Begrudgingly, I obliged and pushed back.

"I am your physical therapist, Braxton, I am here to help you get better."

Better at what—exactly? I wondered

Physical therapy was the last thing I wanted to do, but what choice did I have? By the look of this guy, it seemed like he probably knew a thing or two about building muscle. I did all he asked me to as well as I could, but even the small movements he requested were very difficult and painful to perform. I did my best to follow his instructions, irritated but compliant. When he finished up, he wished me well and said:

"That's all for today, I'll see you first thing tomorrow."

"Great," I said. "I can't wait."

Then a uniformed Army psychiatrist came by. He entered the room with a smile, like they always do, and pulled a chair up next to my bed. He introduced himself as "Major Greene."

"Hey, Braxton, how are you doing?"

"I am doing okay, Sir. Does my company need to leave?"

"No." He responded, still smiling, "we are not going to probe too deeply today. I just want to ask you a few questions."

Altogether ignoring the fact that I was quite sure no one has ever said "I just want to ask you a few questions" to anybody who ever really wanted to answer them, I accommodated him.

"How are you feeling?" he asked

"Sore. Other than that I am fine," I responded.

"Good. How is your sleep?"

"It's fine. Sometimes I get woken up for check-ups during the night and that makes it hard, but it's not a big deal."

"Do you feel agitated, or relaxed?"

For the next few minutes, I did my best to make an honest man out of whoever said, "The most commonly told lie is 'I am fine.'"

Finally he asked, "Are you sure? It looks like you have endured a lot of trauma."

I produced a fake smile of my own and retorted, "Yeah, I look pretty good in this gown don't I? Probably, should let the First Sergeant know that I am not going to make it to formation, though."

He looked unimpressed with my jokes, but he smiled said, "Okay," and walked out my door. Whether he was satisfied or dissatisfied did not make a lick of difference to me. We did not talk long and he had left, that was all I cared about.

The next few days went on in the same way. In fact, the redundancy was reminiscent of the Bill Murray movie *Ground Hog Day*. I woke up, watched *The Dukes of Hazard* until breakfast came, then tried to eat—only to be promptly interrupted by Solomon—who had come to apply his daily regimen of torture to my extremities. Shortly after Physical Therapy concluded the Major would return and ask me the same list of questions as he had the day before, and I responded with the same cavalier nonsense as I had previously done.

I always got the feeling that he was a good guy who had just been saddled with filing some daily TPS reports on the soldiers and Marines in our ward. Even looking back now, with the benefit of hindsight, I cannot imagine that the interviewers expected candor from the men in the Neuro Ward, but they asked anyway and they didn't get it.

Occasionally, Solomon and a smaller, much less tolerable Physical Therapist stopped by and dropped off a fresh apparatus designed to re-introduce me to some new skill. A few training aids that I remember are a half-cylinder-shaped bit of plastic, that had been covered in a soft cloth. The outside of this cloth was ornamented with buttons of various sizes, some Velcro attachments, a bit of shoelace string, and a zipper. The idea was that I could wrap it around the cast on my right arm and learn how to use these common fasteners with just my left. Developing these skills would be important for the rest of my life, because even when my right hand came out of the cast, most of the damage it had sustained was permanent.

Another device I was issued was also a half-cylinder-shaped piece of plastic that had been covered in soft blue and white fabric. This one had none of the other's fasteners; rather, half-inch-wide nylon belts extended off of it. The idea was that I could stretch a sock over it with my left hand and then lower the whole thing down to the tips of my feet and pull on the belts until the sock had seated on my foot. It was a novel idea, but I did not have the flexibility or dexterity to use it.

The first fastener-covered unit I did use, though. It helped me adjust to a new life where only one hand would function normally, which is, despite most around me never noticing, something that I still grapple with today.

These new training aids were useful and they did help me pass the time, but at this stage in my recovery, the only lofty goal I had left to look forward to was getting the external fixators removed and moving into a wheelchair. Not more than a month before I had been a young man—a warrior—in his prime. Now I lay in a bed doing my level best to avoid sleep and my grandest physical aspirations were to have the *cages* removed from my legs and to be fitted for a *wheelchair.*[20]

Nearly daily a member of my surgical team stopped by and checked on my wounds. When they finished their inspection, they generally gave an estimation of when I could expect to have the surgery that would implant rods into the centers of my femurs and hip, thereby allowing the removal of the oh-so-hated fixators.

The doctors usually took a few minutes during every visit to remind us just how major of an operation this would be, but I never cared. Getting into a wheelchair and regaining some semblance of independence was all I had to look forward to, and I was ready to make it happen. The perils of the surgery rarely even registered with me. I mean, what was the worst that could happen, I might die during the operation?

Then, on a particularly dreary afternoon, a surgeon walked into my room, looked me over and announced that he had great news:

"Your wounds look good. Your blood looks good. Your body seems to be clear of infection. We have decided to operate tomorrow," he

---

20 When I look back now at the things I used to take for granted most often in my life, I think good health topped that list before I was wounded.

said smiling in a way that seemed to let on that I was is in line for a disappointment.

"The bad news is, we need your stomach empty. No more eating or drinking."

"Starting when?" I asked

"Now."

The last thing I wanted to do was give up eating again, but this fell into what seems to be the most reoccurring theme of this story. Namely, what choice did I really have?

The next morning some nurses whom I had never met showed up and began to push me toward the operating room. When we arrived at the Operating Room they stripped my hospital gown to clean me up for the ensuing surgery, but no sooner had they started than they noticed something was wrong. I had contracted another infection.

The head surgeon came over to me, looked over my wounds and quickly called the surgery off. They instead took a few swabs from different wounds, finished cleaning me up, changed my bandages and sent me back to my room—defeated.

I had come so close to finally getting out of the bed that had become a horizontal prison to me, and then it all fell apart. I was stuck there for at least another week or maybe longer, who really knew?

The next week or so reverted back to the same ol' doldrums, aside from the increased wound cleanings. The bags attached to my IVs which had previously held saline or fresh blood, were now pumping in a heavy regimen of antibiotics. It had turned out that the bacterial infection I had contracted was gangrene. I was baffled when the doctors told me what it was. I had only ever heard of deer and elk, or maybe livestock, getting that disease before this time.

Once, when I was younger, my grandpa shot a spike elk that had been infected and he took the time to show it to me. He told me it likely contracted the illness because another hunter had taken a shot that he should not have, and explained why it would not be a good idea to eat any meat from that area of the animal. That elk was my only point of reference, so all I remembered about gangrene was that it had been a serious infection, caused by a misplaced bullet and that had turned most of that elk's shoulder green. As it happens, it took a similar course with me.

For a day or so my skin turned a horrible yellow color and then eventually a putrid green. Almost like green beans which had been mushed into baby food and then left on the counter for too long.

The doctors eventually explained to me that, whether I had contracted the bacteria from unsanitary hospital conditions, or it had been introduced during the initial injury did not matter much for us going forward. The reality was, that it was unlikely that it had come from the initial blast because I had already been treated with a heavy regimen of antibiotics for other infections. But, the fact was, I had another disease and drilling into my femurs, which they must do to remove marrow and give the new rods a place to rest, was not a possibility. To open up the bones with an infection present was to risk spreading bacteria to the deepest parts of my legs and the highest red blood cell producing areas of my body. This could cost me my legs—voiding all the hard work those heroes in the field hospitals of Iraq had done to save them—or spread the bacteria to my blood and risk my life—or both.

I lay in bed for the next few days a little more beaten down than before. I raised the sheets now and then with my left arm, my only limb that—sort of—functioned, and wondered whether this was finally going to be the thing that took my legs from me. I was physically tough and I was tolerating the pain, but the roller coaster of emotions and the all-around uncertainty surrounding my life was starting to get me down. I was nearing that breaking point again.

I spent most of my time just watching that yellow-green puss ooze out of my thighs. They looked like Swiss cheese that had been aged way too long and the smell radiated throughout the room. It was not exactly a terrible odor, as strange as that must sound, but it surely was not freshening the place up, either.

I thought it smelled like seafood. Another family member, who said that looking at my gangrene infected quads was the closest she had come to puking throughout my whole ordeal, said it smelled like chicken. Doesn't everybody say that? Anyway, I thought it smelled like crab, which prevented me from eating anything that came out of the ocean for a long time after I left Walter Reed.

When the infection had cleared up and I was rescheduled for surgery. I remember not being nervous at all. I was too excited to get those fixators off to be apprehensive about anything. The surgery itself went well, though it took something like 6 hours to complete. From what I understand, they began by removing the fixators that were screwed into my bone in something like 6 places each. Then they drilled a hole through my bone marrow extending from the knee joint, all the way up to the ball joint at hip level. The surgeons then placed the rods in the pre-drilled holes and pounded them in with a mallet of some sort. Once the rods, which were threaded at their ends, were properly seated, they finished by screwing them into the bone with some sort of driver. Next, they removed the spongy vacuum-like machines that had been inserted into the sides of my quadriceps back in Germany. Their primary function was to suck any extra fluid out of my thighs to keep the inflammation under control, thereby negating the possibility of Compartment Syndrome setting in again. Once they had all of the vacs and hoses out of my quads they started closing the wounds with multilayered stitches and stapled over the top of that. All told, it took hundreds of stitches and staples to close up all the shrapnel holes and surgical wounds in my legs alone.

When I finally woke up from surgery, some of my family was there letting me know that they had finally removed the "x-fixes," as we called them, and had put the rods in. The joy in the room was just what I needed to help me battle the anesthesia hangover. I had a new sort of pain to put up with, but mentally I was feeling great. Things were really going my way again.

I was feeling much better. My pain was mostly under control, my family was there visiting, and my heart was full of anticipation at the prospect of finally getting that wheelchair. I was so sick of being locked in a bed I could hardly stand it any longer. I had actually been in a bed for so long that I had developed bedsores. Not small sores either. One was an open wound about three or four inches long and ran straight down the bottom of my spine, just above my tail bone (I still have a scar from that one). Getting out of that bed was important, not just for my morale, but for my physical health, as well.

Some folks who worked at Walter Reed came into my room and took a series of measurements that were to fit me for a chair. They told me it would be coming within the next few days. Life was really looking up again! My legs were patched up and a little less bionic-looking. Most importantly, I was not going to lose them! I was getting a wheelchair! My left arm was healing, my right arm was healing, life was just good.

Emotion filled the room. I was relieved, joyous, and happy. I had made another obvious step closer to going home. Still, I was not out of danger yet, and we all knew it. This was a positive moment, but there was still a long way to go. I could finally see a way out of the hospital; it was so close I could almost touch it, but I was not quite there yet.

That night I woke up to an alarm going off in my room. Beep! Beep! Beep! It was loud enough to be a little annoying, but not exactly anxiety-inducing. The banality of the alarm was quickly supplanted by panic when I realized that I could not *breathe*.

I tried to suck in air but my lungs just would not fill up. I struggled to draw breath, but was totally unable. My oxygen saturation levels were dropping rapidly. My chest didn't really hurt. There was not a lot of pain. I just couldn't breathe. I gasped over and over again.

The alarm had roused the nurse. She came in to check on me. When she did, she found my breathing labored and slightly painful. She thought it may have just been that my oxygen machine wasn't working. She pulled the tube from my face and held it to her wrist to ensure that it was flowing. Convinced that it was, the nurse knew there must be something more serious going on. She signaled for another nurse to run and get the doctor. And, *hurry!*

CHAPTER FIVE

First Steps

"It was now for the first time war appeared to me in its awful plentitude of horrors. I want words to describe the anguish of my soul, excited by the cries and groans and convulsions of the men who lay by my side."

— Dr. Benjamin Rush, Revolutionary War Surgeon

Bright fluorescent lights drifted slowly by my eyes like white lines on a highway. The bed bumped occasionally as its small, hard rubber wheels caught on the edge of an out-of-place tile. The tiny grouted gaps between the squares produced a faint metronomic clicking sound.

Tick. Tick. Tick.

What is happening? I could tell that I was being pushed down a hospital hallway, but why was I not in my room?

"We had to take some x-rays and an emergency CT scan of your chest. You had a pulmonary embolism."

The guy talking to me was a young lieutenant who worked in neuro. I knew him already. He was a nice guy, many on staff were, but sometimes he forgot that the patients didn't have medical degrees.[21]

"What does that mean?" I mumbled

"A blood clot caused a vessel to rupture in your lung. When the

21 Members of my family and I would later have a quasi-friendship with that LT. He would sometimes loan me comedy DVDs to help me break up the monotony of hospital life.

vessel ruptured, your lung collapsed."

"Oh. That can't be good."

"You are okay now, though. We are going to have a surgeon come up and talk to you about your options."

My mother and step-father had returned to the hospital to visit me again. Before they got there I had turned a corner and had become more lucid than ever, but they could have never known that, based on the condition I was in when they finally saw me. But since the last time they had visited me I could hardly function, for them to see me in this condition probably was not as shocking as it should have been.

As promised, a doctor arrived soon showed up to discuss my options. He explained that he thought I needed to undergo another risky surgery to implant a filter in one of my arteries.

I cannot remember how the description went exactly, but the essence of it was that they would enter my body through one of the many holes in my hip made available by shrapnel wounds. Then they would slide a scope-like instrument into one of my major veins called the vena cava, where they were to place the filter. This IVC filter, as it was so-called, was designed to break up blood clots that may have been traveling from my legs to my torso. I was told to think of it like having a tiny tennis racket implanted in there. The face of the racket would allow blood to flow through, but its screen would break up any oncoming clots.

The problem was no one knew for certain whether the clot that caused the embolism had come from my legs, the surgery to implant the rods, or whether it had formed somewhere in the lungs themselves (I had, after all, been struck in the chest by something like 40 lbs. of explosives). The doctors were betting on my legs though, because during one of my CT scans they had found more clots in my legs, which they called Deep Vein Thrombosis. They seemed the most likely suspect. Armed with that information the decision was even easier to make. To me, whether the clot that nearly killed me had originated in my legs or my lungs, did not matter as much as the fact that more clots did exist below my waist line. If this tennis racket filter was capable of breaking those up should they migrate upward, then why not put it in?

Well, the scariest possible complication was that should a piece of this racket break off and travel in up through my arteries it could conceivably hit my lungs again, or my heart next; either place would likely be fatal.

The alternative option was to leave everything as it was and hope that the blood thinning medications I was going to be put on would dissolve these clots without dislodging them first. To me, given all that we knew, it seemed ridiculous not to accept the potential dangers of the surgery. It would be like knowing that there was an asteroid that may hit earth in a year and having a plan that could divert it and save everyone, but choosing to ignore it because the planet once survived the impact at the Yucatan peninsula. Sure the plan would come with risks, but avoidance and hope are not actionable. Though this was considered an "elective" emergency surgery, it hardly seemed so to me. It felt like the only logical thing to do, no matter the risk.

We informed the doctors that I wanted the IVC filter placed and I was abruptly wheeled back out into the hallway toward the Operating Room. My bed had hardly even crested the threshold before I was asked to count down from ten.

The next thing I remember is waking up to good news: no complications.

The surgery went as smoothly as was possible, but I felt like I was becoming a professional laboratory dummy. The peaks and valleys of recovery were wearing on me, but I was still alive. I understood that that fact was thanks only to the miracles of modern medicine and the talents of those on staff at Walter Reed. But I was still tired of living on edge all the time.

What could I possibly be complaining about? I often thought when I grew annoyed at my own somberness.

Shortly after my filter was implanted my mother had to leave again. Luckily for me her presence was soon replaced. My uncle Justin, whom we lovingly referred to as "Juddy," had come out for a visit. Seeing him was a breath of fresh air in an otherwise claustrophobic environment. We talked about all manner of things, such as Utah, baseball, fishing, archery hunting, Scipio (my home town in Utah), mixed martial arts, boxing, and the war in Iraq.

Juddy had been fascinated by war since his youth. He often speculated that had he not been drafted by a professional baseball organization right out of high school, and subsequently started a family, he would have enlisted himself. Many people make claims like that, to the great annoyance of actual service members, but we all know someone who truly would have enlisted had circumstances not prevented them. Juddy was that guy for me.

He asked a lot of questions about the climate in Anbar Province, Iraqi culture, and the fight in Ramadi in 2005 and 2006. I answered each question to the best of my ability, but admittedly, I was no expert. I was just a corporal in the Army, "…ours is not to wonder why."

These subjects tended to bother many warfighters back then. In fact, most guys that I know would have been angry with him. Especially given the environment we were discussing them in and what had brought us to that place. But I had been close to Juddy for most of my life. I was not at all annoyed by this; in fact, I was happy to talk about anything other than my then present surroundings and immediate health concerns.

One of the days he was there he discovered that some information had been kept from me:

"Hey bro, I need to tell you something."

"Okay," I said, expecting the worst.

"Colonel Mac died. Nobody wanted to tell you, because they were not sure whether you were healthy enough to hear that."

"How?"

"He was killed by shrapnel from the suicide bomber that hit you."

"Oh. Thanks for telling me," I said, slightly in shock. It was particularly devastating news. I already knew SGT Cann had passed away, but Colonel Mac seemed impossible. But he was way too far away to have been struck by any significant amount of shrapnel, I thought.

As it happened, he had been quite a ways away, and he had only been hit by a few pieces of shrapnel, but those ball bearings had hit him in the back of the head, killing him virtually instantly. Survival in war is random, I have learned. Life and death among those courageous enough to put themselves into harm's way are almost always determined purely by proximity and angle, rather than by skill or know-how.

Colonel Mac and I were by no stretch of the imagination "friends," or even friendly. But, he had given his life on the same field of battle that killed one Sergeant in the Marine Corps, and wounded several Army Non-Commissioned Officers and lower enlisted men. That fact, as an officer of his rank and status, was a demonstration of depth and strength of character so rare that the Army awarded him a Silver Star for his courage. To lead from the front, not in words alone, but in *action* is a thing uncommon. We were not "friends," but he was a soldier—and a man—that I greatly admired. As far as I am concerned, he died a hero. And I am proud to call him brother of mine.

Learning of the death of Colonel Mac was another psychological set back in a time rife with them. My bout with survivor's guilt was getting more aggressive by the day. I was still having serious troubles sleeping, and my overall emotional well-being while awake was so fragile that even I was beginning to recognize it.

This was roughly the time that I began to use physical recovery as a distraction from mental anguish. I have often heard a phrase, "Fake it 'til you make it." I am not sure exactly where it originated, but I was about to take my turn at that strategy and would so do for years to come. Flagrantly unsuccessfully.

Physical therapy began in the mornings in the same way it had since I started at it: in my bed. Solomon, or the other therapist, would walk into my room and start manipulating my lower extremities this way and that. They would grab ahold of a foot and pull on it. Then they would ask for resistance:

"Push on my hand," I was often told as one or the other held their palm firmly against the bottom of my foot.

Sometimes they showed up with a small medicine ball about the size of a bocci ball. Then they slid the ball under each knee and waited for gravity to make my joints bend. Other times gravity was not quite a sufficient enough force to manipulate the stiffened cartilage, so they had to apply a little extra pressure themselves. Moving my leg joints was especially difficult because I had been bed-ridden for so long, and my body assaulted with so much soft tissue damage, that my legs were virtually locked straight. I am hesitant to use the word "stiff" again here, because the legs were a bit beyond that. This was essentially a living person who'd had rigor mortis set in.

A few times a week they wheeled me, bed and all, into what looked like a large home gym. It had in it weights, treadmills, cable machines, rowers, short wooden staircases, rubberized walking lanes and all manner of adaptive exercise equipment. The scope of the room was a little intimidating at first, but the largest contributor to the performance anxiety I felt was because there were other wounded service members in there. Up until that day I had never had to do therapy in front of any of my peers, only staff members.

This room had a table designed to "teach" my body how to bear its own weight again. The table was a large stainless steel unit. It looked like someone had converted a hunk of commercial kitchen counter top into a massage table and then fixed it with straps and buckles. It was shiny and cold, too. To get me onto the surface of this contraption the therapists wheeled my bed next to the table—which in my mind, now closely resembled the Rack from the days of medieval torture chambers—slid a board underneath my body and then use that board to transfer me from one surface to another. Once properly settled onto the table, they strapped me to the Rack in several places to ensure my stability.

This table was constructed to rotate either up or down on each end, so that the therapist could add whatever amount of gravitational pressure to the patient's body that he or she desired. For me it would be lifting the side with my head up to apply vertical bodyweight to my lower extremities. Pain increased its height at about the same rate as the Rack did. Every five degrees the table rotated the weight of gravity ratcheted up my pain a few notches. I did my best to force my threshold to keep up.

"I know this hurts, but we must get you bearing weight or you can't get into a wheelchair," my physical therapist remarked. She pushed the button on the side of the bed and my tilt continued.

Once I had reached whatever the goal rotational degree was for the day, the therapist paused the table at that point in the rotation and held me there for a few minutes. The goal was typically to keep my skeleton and my heart, dealing with as much gravitational pull as they were able to handle, for as long as they could. Within several sessions I was reaching vertical status. The hardest part wasn't actually dealing with my own session. It was that when I was fully upright I could finally see everything that was going on in the room.

Most of the other men in the room were all missing one limb—at least. The majority of the therapy that was going on was being done in wheelchairs or on canes. Several soldiers were double amputees above the knee. They started each session by wrapping what was left of their mangled nubs in bandages. When their skin was covered they donned a robotic-looking fake leg crafted be an in-house prosthesis and cinched it up. Then they slowly wobbled their way to their feet and took as many steps as they could before falling over. Sometimes they fell all the way to the ground, knocking the prosthesis off, which started the cycle all over again.

There were others there who still had two fully functioning legs, but were missing their arms. Their sessions were somewhat similar to the young men with the prosthetic legs, aside from the location of prosthesis and their struggles had nothing to do with walking. Rather, they needed to learn how to adapt to a world without the use of hands or arms. Watching any one of these men and women struggle was brutal, but the most heart-wrenching sight in the entire room was the soldier who had lost three limbs. He had gone to Iraq a healthy young man just like the rest of us, and for the love of country and family, he had given up all, but one arm. A man simply ceases to feel sorry for himself in the presence of a smiling young man who has only one arm left to go about the world with. Whatever sorrow I had felt over my roller coaster—or my wounds—left me whenever I was in the presence of this guy happily battling his way through a physical therapy session.

After being laid on the Rack a few times I was finally able to bear my own weight again. My knees were bending more, too. Enough to sit even. They weren't able to reach anywhere near 90 degrees, but the hospital decided to order me my first wheelchair anyway. It was an electric number with a joystick control on the left side because only my left hand functioned at the time. Since my legs couldn't bend far enough to allow me to sit in a normal position, the chair was equipped with braces to hold my legs out in front of it.

Finally having a mode of travel that was mostly my own was the first real feeling of sovereignty I had experienced. The only problem was that I could not get from my hospital bed to my wheelchair without help, so it was more like mobility-when-permitted-by-an-authority-figure than real sovereignty. A member or two of the hospital staff, or Solomon, had to come into my room and lift me into my chair. Not only were my legs too weak to allow me freedom of movement on my own, but my flexibility and range of motion were still so degraded by the wounds and sheer amount of time spent stuck in a bed that even if I could have lifted myself, the risk of further injury made the idea of attempting it silly and fanciful. But whether I required assistance or not, I had a set of wheels and that was as big a boost to my morale as I had gotten since before I landed in Iraq.

After Solomon helped me into my chair we would head down to PT. He was a truly huge man. He stood at around six foot four and weighed in at well over 250 lb. He had once been a defensive lineman on a Super Bowl-winning team in the NFL. Bigger even than his stature and his accomplishments in professional athletics was his heart. When Sol came into a room he had a way of brightening everything inside it with just a smile. No matter how ornery I was on any particular morning he could cheer me up. He liked to joke with me:

"Hey McCoy, I know you got busted up pretty good, but damn, is that really as hard as you can push?"

I had fantasies about ripping my foot from his clutches and kicking him in the face with it when he would tease me, but all I could do was push harder and strain a little more when my ego had been challenged.

Our morning PT sessions after the introduction of the Rack shortly became just as predictable as they had been before. The therapist either met me in my room where I did some exercises in the bed, or took me to the big room with all the other veterans. I hated going to the big room because it was impossible to feel sorry for myself there.

This morning, however, was different. Sol showed up early and helped me get dressed into gym clothes, the only clothes I was able to wear at the time. Then he helped me into my wheelchair and led me out of the Neuro Ward into the main hospital, hazing me in his own genial way while we walked.

"Hey man, keep up. What are you, scared or something?"

Every affront to my ego added more motivation; he was well aware of that fact. As we rolled down the corridors of Walter Reed it was obvious that we were not going back to the main physical therapy room with the big machines and the Rack. I had no idea where we were headed. I rolled along behind my new friend. Up ahead about five meters Solomon took a hard left through a doorway in an area I had never seen before.

The walls of this new room were covered in aluminum walkers and metal canes. There were medicine balls, rubber resistance bands and Pilates balls on the floor. In the middle of the room sat a length of parallel bars which formed about a fifteen-foot-long walkway. They were thick bars, similar in diameter to those that accompany steps into public swimming pools. They were set about 30 inches apart so that one could rest one's weight on each side as one walked down the lane.

Sol guided me to a spot near the bars. They were about to become my new best friends and worst enemies. We did a few warm-up exercises using rubber bands and physical resistance offered by the therapist. Then we used the medicine ball to perform some stretches and lifts. Eventually, I said:

"Hey man, when do we get to walk down those bars?"

My remark was said purely in jest, because I had already been told several times that it would be 18 months—if ever—before I was going to be able to walk again.

"You are going to use them right now," he said, obviously seeing through my lame bravado.

"I can't walk, Solomon." I said coldly.

"Yes, you can. I am going to help you."

I was starting to get irritated at him, because I knew I could not walk.

"I can't even *stand*, for hell's sake!!!" I was frustrated and embarrassed by the whole situation. I was frustrated because I thought that this guy I liked and admired assumed I was capable of more than I actually was and I was about to let him down. *Does he not know how badly injured I am?* I wondered. I was embarrassed that I couldn't dress myself; embarrassed that even if I could have, I could not wear clothes that were not several sizes too big because they had to fit over my casts and braces. I was embarrassed by the fact that I could not do up a button on my own underwear or use the bathroom without help throughout the entire process. I was literally unable to wipe my own ass, as they say. Little more than a month before this moment I had been a roughly six-foot-tall, 190 lb. warrior in the prime of his life, proud and full of all the arrogance of youth. But there I was, a few months later, sitting before a man who wanted to help me—deeply wanted to help me—but I just physically could not do what he was asking.

Then there was the fear. Fear that if—by some miracle of the imagination—I was able to stand up and try to walk, I might *fall*. And, if I fell, I would surely lose all of the independence that I had fought so hard to achieve. It felt like an exercise in futility to even speculate about what it would be like to walk again already. Then Sol loosened the braces on my chair, bent down in front of me and said:

"Are you ready?"

I imagine that the standard procedure would have been to have two therapists there, where each could get some sort of grip underneath each arm of the client, but that wouldn't work for me. I had only one functioning hand that was attached to a broken humerus, and one functioning upper arm that carried around a broken wrist and hand, so grabbing onto my arms was a tricky task. Luckily for me though, the people who worked at Walter Reed were used to making much more difficult accommodations than this one would be. And given the size of this particular physical therapist, we were sure to find a way.

I reached out, put what I could of my arms on his shoulders and he lifted me out of my chair. My heart raced as I stood there for the first time. A feeling of anxiety, fear, and triumph washed over me. Though they were hardly supporting any body weight, my legs shivered beneath me. Then we started walking. We only covered a few feet of distance, but I could hardly contain my joy as Sol half dragged me over to those parallel bars. The instant the cold, stainless steel touched the fingertips of my left hand an invigorating dose of adrenaline shot through my body.

Even though Solomon was still bearing most of my weight I had to overcome an obstacle I had not at all anticipated. I don't know if it was because of my brain injury, or just because it had been so long since last I had walked, but I couldn't make my muscles move my legs like they were supposed to. I knew how walking was supposed to be done: you just lift and step out in front of your lead foot, then repeat on the other side. I could have drawn you a picture or described what walking is supposed to look like. I knew how to do it, but I didn't know how to make *me* do it. Each confusing attempt at the process sent intense bursts of pain to my brain that I was not quite ready for, but the torment, mixed with the excitement of discovery kept releasing more of that ever-intoxicating adrenaline. I was experiencing a unique feeling of euphoria, like the way it feels to win a competition in front of a crowd, or get accepted into college. It left me more empathetic to drug addicts, really. This bliss was so pure, so carnal and profound, that were there a way to encapsulate it in a pill, I would surely end up on Skid Row.

CHAPTER SIX

Arlington

"And you and I and all our brothers
will jump astride the wind
and chase Johnny's smile
halfway across the universe, hollerin',
'Johnny, we did it! Johnny, we did it!'
Until we catch up to where his laughter awaits
beyond the farthest moon
of our most dear dream
just one, last breath
ahead of us all..."

— Steve Mason, Johnny's Song

The adrenaline high had long subsided by the time I left therapy the day Sol lifted me to the parallel bars, but the feeling of accomplishment was still very vivid. I felt victorious and empowered in a way that I had not in months. Sure, Sol had done all the heavy lifting, but that hardly mattered to me. I had begun to learn to walk again and had done so in less than one sixth of the amount of time that was predicted. Nothing could make me feel better than that fact, but as had become so commonplace, I just couldn't make the feeling last.

When I got back to my room new aches radiated through my bones. The reality of my situation grew clearer by the instant; this was going to be a long and agonizing process. And at the end of it, whenever that may be, I might not be anywhere near to 100% recovered. In fact, most early projections—optimistically—suggested that at best I may regain

60-70% of my legs' functionality.

That was to say nothing of my right hand which was so severely wounded that my friend and medic, Z, during a visit to Walter Reed, told me that he was sure, "they were going to have to amputate it if I survived the initial medevac." I had, and they hadn't.

When I left the streets of Ramadi the morning I was wounded no one who had actually seen the condition my body was in took my survival for granted. The medics seemed sure I might die. I didn't die, but my recovery at Walter Reed was a roller coaster ride, maybe that led me to expect trauma after triumph.

In my room waiting for me when I returned to the Neuro Ward was my uncle Justin and my little sister Chelsi. Juddy seemed extremely happy, impressed, "at how good I looked compared to when he had last been out to DC". My sister was a little more shocked to see how frail and small I had become since she last saw me, but this was the first time she had been to Walter Reed so that shouldn't have been a surprise. The bewildered look on her face revealed how bad my condition truly was. I cannot say that I blame her, the first time I saw myself in a mirror my levels of depression and anxiousness to get out of that hospital skyrocketed. I was a pitiful sight, to say the least. I felt getting out of that place was the next goal worth chasing.

Our first conversations were mostly casual. I asked them about the flight, how things were back home and how their hotel room was. Somehow, we ended up on the subject of my current health. Like always.

"Solomon helped me walk. Well, I didn't really walk. He sort of dragged me around, but I stood up. I didn't know how to walk, actually. But, I have been getting better since you left last time, Juddy."

They were as excited to hear this as you would expect they would be, but eventually I expressed my doubts about the whole thing:

"That's awesome!" Justin said.

"Well, I still can't walk though. I don't want to make it sound like I did something that I really didn't do."

I was not doubtful out of pessimism necessarily, though it would be impossible to deny that I was becoming increasingly pessimistic about the event; rather, because the pain of the PT session had slowly, but steadily, heightened since I left the workout room. This new pain was causing a bit of reality to set in with it. I was badly injured and this discomfort could easily be a sign that I had overworked my legs and set them back some. The last thing I wanted to do was cultivate false hope.

"It is amazing that you are walking!"

"It is great. The physical therapist is doing all the lifting though. I could never have held myself up. I keep trying to tell you that."

"Who cares, bro? The point is you are already beating this thing."

"Juddy, I might never walk again. And—if I do—it will probably be assisted in some way. I don't want to push around a walker for the rest of my life. I can't hunt elk on a cane! I'll never again feel that icy mountain water roll past my waders as I cast flies at fall browns. I'll have only memories of sliding into a saddle on a crisp October morning, when at dawn you can see your breath and by noon you've sweat through your hatband. I have done my last bow hunt. No more dirt bikes, or bull rides. I basically just started up my twilight years in my early twenties. I am in a fucking nursing home for soldiers right now and I may always be."

I was being a negative, whiney child, there is no doubt about it. But I was trying to explain to him that everything that made me, Me, was gone. Those were not just activities that I liked to do. That was my identity. I hunted, fished, cowboyed, and soldiered. Those were my essence. If I was too broken to do the things that distinguished me, then I was too broken to live as far as I was concerned.

Sure, I had made progress, but now I was paying the dues for it physically. What about every other time I had made hefty progress? The last major milestone I had crossed ended up being followed by a horrific setback. An embolism that easily could have killed me. What else lurked between me and total recovery? The tonnage of the entire situation set in and it would take more than lofty words from a passive observer to change my opinion.

A member of the surgical team which monitored my progress walked in near the tail end of this conversation. He was just there to do routine check-ups and to introduce himself. He was a young guy who seemed very well put together and high-speed. He checked my limbs one by one for circulation and feeling (I had quite a bit of nerve damage as you can imagine). Juddy put a question to him:

"Hey doc, Braxton has been told that he may never walk again. He thinks he is never going to be able to stand in a river to fly fish, or hunt, or hike, or ride his horses again. Can you talk to him?"

I concentrated on him, hoping to read his expressions for tells of lies. He proceeded to give me all the reasons why I may be able to do those things again. He covered every angle and included some caveats, such as, I may have to use a cane to hike, or limit the distance that I traveled, and only fish shallow holes etc.—but, he was telling the truth. Then, at the end of his answer, he said the most important thing I have ever been told, either before, or since:

"Braxton, I think you can walk again, but you are going to have to do it soon. You have too much soft tissue damage to risk allowing your muscles to atrophy any further. If you don't start now, you may never walk again, at least not without the use of a cane, or a walker. Even in everyday activities. It is all up to you."

"It is all up to you." I repeated.

It's all up to me. Even in a situation like this one! [22]

My body may have been badly bruised, but it is one's spirit that determines the outcome of a tragedy, not a doctor's prognosis. That was exactly what I needed to hear right in that moment. I needed decisive language and a kick in the ass. Not some sugarcoated version of what may, or may not, happen. There was probably not anything that young surgeon said which I had not been told before, but I had never heard that truth until right then. The words he said, the order he chose to use, and the conviction with which he said them were as perfect for me as if the Universe had handcrafted the message.

We all know that there are moments in one's life that define them; they are scarce, they don't come around often, but they are the most important moments in our lives. This was one of—perhaps the—defining moment of my life. It was imperative that I capitalize on it now that it had arrived.

---

22 This is the emergence of the idea of Extreme Ownership, sure it's a slight variation of Jocko Willink and Leif Babin's concept, but the core elements are there.

After that I did walk. I took my first totally unassisted step. It was only from my wheelchair to my bed, and it hurt like hell, but I did it. The actual span could not have been more than 24 inches, but the chasm that I covered in my mind was as important as climbing a mountain. The first step is always the hardest, as they say. That old cliché had proved too true in my case.

The very next day while at physical therapy with Solomon I took a full step from my chair to the parallel bars, by myself. Nothing could match the agony of lying in that pool of blood in Ramadi, but those first few steps were very close. The only thing that hurt worse than lifting my legs with shrapnel riddled quadriceps was putting them back down on shattered bones.

Once inside the parallel bars my left arm was my only available support system. Its newly healed spiral fracture in the upper portion throbbed as I used it to steady myself. I wobbled more than walked. Broken as I was, somehow, I made it through the lane. Wobbling on just three broken limbs, the encouragement of the great people around me, and pure western grit.

Walking again, though what I was doing would not pass as walking to any able-bodied person, was the most exciting and inspiring thing I had ever done in my life. It was a deeply visceral thing. One of those accomplishments that you don't need to see another person's reaction to understand its loftiness. I imagine summiting Everest must feel like this. Sure, other people are there, but they don't add much to the experience.

This new growth in ambulatory ability brought with it another change whose ramifications were not immediately apparent. Relying on intravenous medications was no longer a good solution for me, because a person who's using all four limbs to move, can't push an IV tower around too. Since the IV tower had to go, so too did the pain medications it had been delivering.

The docs had long since removed the largest unnatural input, the "Peripherally Inserted Central Catheter," which is just a fancy term for an IV hookup that is implanted in the jugular vein. The removal process was much simpler than one might think. They simply cut the stitches securing it in place and lifted the line right out of my jugular in one smooth upward motion. The feeling of that long, slender tube slithering its way out of my vein like a snake in the damp grass of a creek bed still makes my skin crawl to think of it.

Along with the PICC line I had an IV infusion in the back of my hand. Pulling this one out was far less dramatic. The nurse just ripped off the tape that held it down and pulled it out of my hand. With both lines removed it was time to get me on purely oral medications. When the lines were in I had been taking some drugs orally; these were, mostly, like antidepressants, some meds to dull acid reflux, and some gastral intestinal aides. After the lines came out my handful of pills each day turned into a rainbow-colored shot glass full of who knows what drugs. As much as I hated taking that shot of pills, I did recognize its significance. The signs were obvious.

Oral pills and capsules had fully supplanted the intravenous medications, no detectable allergies had been found, and the doctors determined me finished with surgical procedures for the foreseeable future. That was huge. Then they removed the last tangible tether to my hospital bed: the IV tower. That meant I was more stable than I had ever been. That was even bigger news. No one threw any celebration for the momentous occasion, but being rid of that IV stand felt like a final rite of passage to me, whether we drank to the day or not.

The ominous "800-pound gorilla" that is addiction remained, however. The mainlined narcotics had made me chemically addicted and physically dependent on them, (how could they not?), but they were nowhere near as dangerous as the oral meds. A doctor or nurse had to come in with a syringe and inject those drugs into my IV bag. Now that the middleman was removed and I was in control of the drugs myself, the process of psychological addiction was set in motion.

Physical therapy graduated from walking a few steps each morning, to resistance training with rubber bands and medicine balls. As training became more difficult my independence also increased, so though my daily pain levels grew little by little, the tradeoff made it worthwhile. Then I was issued two metal, four pronged canes to go along with my wheelchair. They came with the strict warning that if I fell I would have them taken away from me and I would be sent back to the Intensive Care Unit. I assumed the threat mostly hollow, but it was not like I was going to run away and sign up for a 5K or anything like that. Even using the canes, I could hardly make it more than ten feet without needing to stop, but that was not important. I had earned a little more of my independence back. That was as big a breakthrough as could have been wished for. I had crossed another real milestone, again. No one offered to drink to it, but I sure felt like they should have.

I had those two metal canes issued to me on a Friday then on that Sunday, with the help of a Vietnam veteran whom I knew well, I snuck out of Walter Reed in a cab bound for Arlington National Cemetery. It wasn't like I actually "sneaked" out of the hospital, really. The team charged with my care had issued me a standard black-seated, user propelled, wheelchair. My friend just pushed me out the doors in that, but we didn't ask for permission to leave either.

When we arrived at the huge, castle-like marble entrance, the cab driver stopped to let us out. My friend helped me into my chair. The first thing that struck me about the place was its sheer enormity. Not just physically, but spiritually. The place is huge and its power overwhelming. *How in the world are we ever going to find LTC Mac's or SGT Cann's grave sites,* I wondered?

My friend wheeled me into the Visitor's Center and we began to look around. The place was full of pictures and documents recording U.S. history and the significance of the cemetery. There was also a gift shop brimming with trinkets and souvenirs. There were books, shot glasses, key chains, flags and replicas of The Constitution for sale. There were people everywhere, too. Lines formed in every conceivable direction and confused patrons filled in all gaps left in the room. Some people were pushing and crowding into us. A few kids kept bumping into my chair, shaking my broken legs and arm. I was angry and ready to get the hell out of that place, but first we needed some help.

We wandered around a bit before one of the friendlier and more professional staff members helped us locate the kiosk that is used to search for burial plots. The only problem was, at the time, I did not know Sgt.

Cann's first name.

Men in the military, especially those who have not been around each other for very long like Cann and I, never call each other by the first name. It is rather common not to know another soldier's full name, really. Thankfully, the designer of the kiosk must have known this and prepared for it, because we were able to search for their names using last name, rank and date of KIA. Once we had matched Sgt. Cann's first name to the rest of the information that I did know, pinpointing his final resting place was easy.

Col. Mac, on the other hand, was not so simple to find. It turned out that Col. Mac was not resting in Arlington at all. He had instead chosen to be buried in his home state closer to his family. Back then, before I had kids, I couldn't understand why he didn't want to be buried at Arlington. Why would a man who had died so heroically in battle not want to be entombed in the most sacred place in America? A man that brave belonged there, I thought. Now that I am a father, I understand why he and his family chose to lay him to rest where they did. No honor is more valuable than the comfort of one's children.

When we were sure we had found the right plot the kiosk printed us out a map and we set out for Section 60 to visit Sgt. Cann and pay our respects.

As we got to the first rows of graves we read a sign that said:

"Welcome to Arlington National Cemetery our nation's most sacred shrine. Please conduct yourselves with dignity and respect at all times. Please remember that these are hallowed grounds"

These are hallowed grounds, I repeated in my head. The signs are all over the cemetery, but it took only one to spur me:

"I want to walk," I said.

"Okay," he responded.

No pushback. No, "It's too far, you'll hurt yourself," or anything like that. Just, "Okay." Then he handed me my canes and lent a helping hand out of my chair.

Some school children on a field trip skipped past us on their way to watch "The Changing of the Guard" at The Tomb of the Unknown Soldier, their teachers constantly checking their volume and their speed as they went by. A sudden wave of pride and new found enthusiasm swept over me as I wobbled to my feet on that narrow cemetery road. My legs trembled underneath me. I saw another sign. It read simply, "Silence and Respect."

As if to encourage myself internally I kept repeating I can do this. I am going to do this, in my head while sliding my first foot out in front of me. I still wasn't sure.

My arms shook as I pressed into my canes to grind myself forward another step. It felt like my bones were going to explode under the force of my body each time I transitioned my weight. We trod on. Slowly.

At some point in the walk we saw McClellan's Gate which has lines taken from Theodore O'Hara's poem "Bivouac of the Dead" engraved in gold on it. The eastern facing side reads:

"On fame's eternal camping ground their silent tents are spread,

And glory guards with solemn round, the bivouac of the dead."

And on its western face:

"Rest on embalmed and sainted dead, dear as the blood ye gave,

No impious footsteps here shall tread, on the herbage of your grave."

The symbolism and power of the shrine only grew as I struggled along those slender asphalt pathways. We made our way by the rows and rows of heroes sacrificed on the altar of freedom, at a snail's pace, but with the same determination they had brought into combat. I was either going to walk the entire way, or die trying.

I don't know how far we walked that morning, exactly, but it was at least a mile from the gate to Section 60 and I trekked every step of it. My arms ached and shook as my quadriceps quivered their way through steps. The rest periods between legs of the journey grew longer as we went along, but I never went back to that wheelchair. For some reason, on that day, I had decided that riding a wheelchair in a place so holy would be an affront to the honor of the men buried there.

When we reached the sign that said: "Section 60," I did not want to stop anymore.

"Braxton, you should probably take a break here. Don't over do it."

"No. I am okay," I responded, sweat pouring from my face.

When we were inside Section 60's boundaries it must have taken us another hour to reach Sgt. Cann's graveside. Along with the slow pace we traveled due to my fatigue and weakening pain threshold, I read nearly every headstone I walked by on the way, each one adding more time and new significance to the journey, but also giving me a little more fuel to feed the desire to remain erect.

Every step was miserable. Pain radiated from my hips to my knees. The agony had grown so immense that several times I thought that I might throw up because of it, but, we never gave up. I trudged every torturous pace of that march out of respect for Sgt. Cann and the 250,000 fallen warriors he lay with.

When we finally reached his graveside and read:

"ADAM LEIGH CANN
SGT
US MARINE CORPS
JAN 25 1982, JAN 05 2006,
BSM W/V
PURPLE HEART
OPERATION IRAQI FREEDOM"

I lowered myself to a knee and wept.[23] Not because of the pain I was experiencing, but because I had the nerve—the flat-out audacity—to complain about it.

These hundreds of thousands of heroes had given their lives to provide me with a safe place to recover and all I had thought about up to that point was how hard my time had been. Whatever I had given in service to my country and my brothers paled in comparison to what they had done. Who was I to feel sorry for myself? Who was I to complain about my situation? I was above ground. There was not a soul laid to rest in that holy shrine who would not have gladly taken my place if they could have.

It became clear to me in that moment that I really did have nothing to complain about. And, every time I did complain, it should be seen as

---

23 As best I could, that is. I was not capable of kneeling in any sense that would be easily recognizable to an able bodied person.

a slap in the face to far better men than I will ever be.

When I had finished paying my final respects to Sgt. Cann and the men immediately surrounding him, I stood up, on both canes and began my long walk out of the cemetery. A brand new sense of urgency to recover. A new found pool of motivation to draw from. I was going to beat this thing. I was going to fight to take back my life again. Not just because I wanted to, but because I had to, because they couldn't.

CHAPTER SEVEN

Drudging Up Ghosts

And fear not them which kill the body, but are not able to kill the soul: but rather fear him which is able to destroy both soul and body in hell.

— Mathew 10:28 (KJV)

I leaned heavily on the yellow, metal fenders of the cab as the driver folded up my wheelchair and placed it in the trunk. My left hand clung tightly to the roof while I shuffled my feet toward the door. My legs quivered. I reached for the door handle. I slid my right hand behind the black plastic lever, cast and all, and tugged. It was no use. As soon as I pulled on the lever my cast slipped out, subsequent momentum of the retreating arm threw my body off balance.

I am so fucking incompetent! I thought to myself.[24]

My motivation was evaporating, but I did not want to give up too easily. I reached down with my left hand to open the door, but without my good hand gripping the top of the car I was off balance again and unable to jerk the door open.

The inner strength and confidence just gained during my walk through Arlington was already fading. The swelling in my legs and the clear sight of my ineptness made it hard to hold onto any sense of pride for long periods of time, no matter how hard-won that pride had been. Still, I did not want to give up, especially after just having realized how

---

24 Though I didn't know it at the time, I am now convinced that these rapid mood swings were as much chemically induced as they were stress related. Mood swings are a very common side-effect of opioid pain relievers.

short-sighted it was for me to complain about my condition when I was still alive. I had no idea what to do. I stood there stuck on my feet, clinging to the cab like a toddler on the edge of a pool hoping to wish himself out of the situation.

It wasn't long before my friend noticed my predicament. He walked over, yanked the door open and helped me inside. Once I was seated the frustration faded.

From the hips down, my body had nearly doubled in size. My knees and ankles looked like they had just undergone surgery. I tried to rub the pain out of my quads as I often did back in my bed in the Neuro Ward, but they were too swollen. Rubbing them wasn't releasing enough pressure to make any difference. Oddly enough, just sitting there trying to knead the pain from my legs did help ease the frustration a bit. I stopped thinking about the things that I couldn't do, like open a cab door on my own, and started thinking about what I had just accomplished: walking some real distances. Distances no doctor who had operated on me had even imagined to be possible. How did I do that? I wondered.

It took me years to get to the bottom of that question. The truth is that the only reason I had walked that far—in that condition—was because I had read a sign that reminded me that Arlington was not about *me*. I didn't care about myself or my future enough to grind through that kind of torment. Self-gratification, nor self-improvement was enough to motivate me. My own ego was nowhere near big enough to carry me through that. I had done it because I did not want to disrespect Sgt. Cann or any of the rest who had given their lives at war. I made that journey because I had a reason bigger than myself. I needed to cling to that maxim.

***

Back at Walter Reed I was becoming increasingly independent. My wheelchair, which I was still bound to, rendered me more mobile than I had previously been. Physical therapy sessions continued to improve the distances I could walk. I no longer needed any assistance getting to and from the bathroom. Only a month before, I needed help standing up from the toilet. Now, I could walk in fifteen to twenty foot intervals.

This increased mobility subsequently led to more frequent and longer physical therapy sessions, which led to more and more improvement. The exponential growth pattern was in full swing, at least until I hit The Law of Diminishing Returns.

The medical team I was assigned to had even decided to add some more Occupational Therapy sessions to my daily regimen. Occupational Therapy is therapy designed to recover basic life skills. The appointments are geared toward cultivating independence. They teach the patient how to navigate everyday life situations after injury. In my case, most of these freshly needed skills were things like learning to open door handles while resting on two canes, showering without help, dressing myself, and even things as seemingly small as doing up buttons with one hand. Everyday life, though becoming more painful physically, was truly on a steady rise toward something better. I was making tangible progress. Anyone could see it.

One morning I left Solomon's PT room and headed back to the Neuro Ward. I had become able to do this on my own every day, another indication that I was healing. When I returned, the nurses in the ward told me that the orthopedic surgeon who had worked on my right hand would soon be by to take the bandages off and inspect my bones.

I was sitting in my wheelchair watching T.V. when after a few taps, the door swung open to reveal an average-sized man in his mid-forties. He had brown hair and toted a clipboard. I could tell he was the surgeon that had been summoned before he even had the chance to introduce himself. Doctors and senior NCOs are the only people I have ever met who knock as a statement-of-entry rather than as a courteous request. Being as there were no senior enlisted men around, the fact was not difficult to deduce.

I greeted him with normal pleasantries and formally introduced myself. He told me that this was not the first time we met, but I shouldn't worry about forgetting our previous encounters. It was common for a patient not to remember meeting their surgeons. I apologized for my rudeness anyway.

Slowly, he peeled the brown bandages away from their firmly established home on my skin. They had been there for more than a month.

I was curious to see what was beneath them. I had not seen that hand since I'd stared up at it from my back in Ramadi.

As the contents under the bandage were revealed, I recalled more hidden memories of The Fifth of January. I remembered looking up and picking a ball bearing out of the knuckle at the base of the thumb. My own blood leaked onto my cheeks. Drip. Drip. Drip. "*You're already dead*," they whispered as they fell. When the droplets hit my eyelids, the chorus changed: "Close your eyes. Just quit. No one could blame you." It had felt like I was seeing a piece of my body that had already reached the other side. Its blood-soaked outline shading the sun from my face made it appear as if it was thrust through the veil of death, and I, whatever constituted the rest of my mortal being, was just lying there on earth waiting to catch up.

The doc unraveled the thin brown cloth covering my wrist. A wound began to emerge—I had forgotten about it. When I was hit a two-inch wide laceration was opened up just above the large bump that protrudes from the end of the ulnar bone. At The Glass Factory the wound had laid bare the bright white bones of my wrist. Now, a shiny pink scar covered the gash. Even after several weeks of healing, the severely stretched skin still revealed gnarly, broken muscle fibers beneath it.

I had extensive nerve damage in my right hand. The constant fluctuation between numbness and feeling as if half of my hand were trapped in vice grips and thrust into a pot of boiling water made that fact obvious enough. But, I didn't know the culprit was in the wrist:

"See, this circular hole on the top of your wrist is where the ball bearing entered your arm. And, on this underside," he said while rotating my arm 180 degrees, "it exited where this large bulge is. It transected your median nerve which controls the half of your hand that your index finger, second finger and thumb belong to. A somewhat strange thing about the median nerve is that it serves only half of your ring finger." He ran the tip of his index finger down each side of my middle finger to demonstrate this. I was amazed to feel his finger tip rub on the outside of mine, but not on the inside.

How the hell does that work? I wondered

He pointed to what looked like a ganglion cyst on the underside my wrist, right at the base of my hand:

"This bulge on the bottom of your wrist is scar tissue caused by the damage to your muscles and tendons as the shrapnel passed through."

I nodded, but I kept my eyes fixed on the disgusting, dead, off-white skin being exposed.

"It is perfectly normal for skin to discolor and peel away in large chunks after trauma like your body has endured, Braxton."

He had no need for telepathic powers here. I am quite certain that my facial expression revealed more information than he could have extracted by supernatural means.

Large chunks of skin were falling away from my hand. They were not thin and dry strips like those shed from snakes, but thick and wet like scales floating away from a rotten fish that's washed up into the shallows. The discarded skin hardly gave the impression that it was once attached to a living being. The hand itself looked more like a prop on the set of a B-level zombie movie. As if its clammy white flesh should at any moment be thrusting through the sod to grab the ankle of an unsuspecting teenage girl who had wandered into the local cemetery on an ill-fated dare.

"Sometimes people with hands accustomed to manual labor lose large portions of their calluses when they're casted for long periods of time." He said, clearly watching my face contort as the under-portion of the soft cast was removed.

I knew he was just being polite. The sloughing away of calluses only described part of this hideous bag of bones. It was also deformed. The bones that make up the palm portion of the hand were shortened and misshapen.

I recognized how silly it was for me to be shaken by the sight of my hand given the shape that the rest of my figure was in, but, I couldn't help feeling like this part of my body belonged to a corpse. The visual was bad in Ramadi, but that day it only looked as if it were dying. This day the hand appeared *dead*. Like it was foreshadowing all that was to become of me if I were to succumb to my wounds. And, though I was doing much better, that fate was still far from out of the question. I still had infection in my body, blood clots in my legs, an IVC filter that could break apart any minute, and no one was addressing my brain injury yet.

Even if I did live through the whole ordeal, I would be doing it without most of the function in my right hand. All that I had ever done in my life which I had found worth doing, whether it be shooting, working, weightlifting, boxing, wrestling, cowboying, bull riding, or even war-fighting, had required not just two hands, but two strong and capable hands. This hand which had once defined me, now looked as if were gone forever. I had not given it permission to give up, yet there it sat crippled atop my wrist, a symbol of not just what could become of me, but of how little control I had over fate. The futility of resistance can be maddening.

I have never been one to try to deny the undeniable. I always thought SSgt Barnes in *Platoon* got a lot of things right. Toward the end of the film one of his subordinate NCOs asked him if he could go home early. The guy was short-timer[25] who was just trying to dodge having to risk his life in one last firefight. "Bob, I got a bad feeling on this one, alright? I mean I got a *bad feeling*. I don't think I am going to make it outta here. Do you understand what I am saying to you?" Red cried. Barnes knew that the requester understood that his absence was going to add real danger to Barnes' platoon. "Everybody gotta die sometime, Red," the grizzled and battle-scarred SSgt replied.

Barnes was right.

I accepted that fact before I ever left for the war. But, now that I had been to the brink and seen the other side with my own eyes, I was more afraid of it than I had ever been before. Somehow, I hadn't been afraid of dying in combat, that felt like a good way to die, but to die in a hospital for no worthy cause—terrified me.

When my entire hand was revealed in all its wretchedness the doc said again: "It doesn't take the body long to break down." He pulled me back from my thousand-yard stare. Jutting out from the left side between the first knuckles of the index finger and thumb was a half an inch worth of exposed muscle. Over time, the muscle had forced itself

---

25 Slang for soon to have his conscripted contract expire. In other words, a "short-timer" is a soldier who is nearly due to rotate home.

through a hole created by a piece of shrapnel. It looked like a pink curvy mass that moved independently of my skin when I pulled my index finger into the back of my palm.

An inch of steel pin extended from the first knuckles of each of my fingers. The metal pins stood straight out from each knuckle for about half an inch and then they shot straight upward for another quarter inch or so. These L-shaped pins sticking out of my hand made it look like it was adorned with the claws of a comic book figure, but these came with no mutant strengths. Instead they were there to help support my lack of skeletal robustness.

"Your bones feel like they have healed enough to pull the pins out. We are going remove them today." The doc said, motioning for the nurse to go and get his tools.

He held up my hand with his left arm and reached out with his right to grab a tool from the nurse. My eyes widened in amazement when I noticed that he grasped a set of common stainless steel pliers.

"You're not really going to grab them pins with those pliers and yank them out? This is a joke, like back when grandpa used to tell me he would pull out any wiggly tooth with his channel locks, right?" I laughed, still not believing what I was seeing.

"Sometimes the best tool for the job is simple and cheap." He said with a smile.

Hard to argue with that, I thought.

Then he reached down with the pliers and took hold of the pin in my first knuckle. His grip with his support hand clamped down on my wrist. He twisted the pin right and then left to free it from its seat inside my bones.

This can't be happening, I kept saying to myself. *Am I really sitting here watching this guy use pliers to twist a pin around inside my bone?*

He wriggled, twisted again, then pulled on that pin until the four inches of steel which had been inside a bone in my hand slid out through the skin.

"Ouch! Shit!" I said aloud.

"That didn't hurt" he retorted. A small drop of blood formed where the pin used to be.

"Well, it did too!" I exclaimed as he dropped the pin onto his little table with a metallic 'clink'.

"It shouldn't hurt at all. Your bones have no feeling in them." The surgeon replied as he wriggled, twisted, and removed a pin from the finger I desperately wanted to gesture to him with.

"You ever had pins removed, doc?"

"No"

"You ever broken a bone?"

"No."

"Then how in the hell do you know what this feels like?"

He stopped responding to me altogether.[26]

About the time he finished pulling the fourth and final pin out of my pinky knuckle he said:

"Would you like to keep these pins?"

"Well, hell yes." I responded.

"You are right, Braxton. I don't know what this might feel like."

"Thanks, doc." A smile then creased my face.

"You'll be starting occupational therapy in the morning after your regular PT session."

"Okay, sir. Thank you."

"I know your OT personally. You're going to love her. She is the best we have."

"Okay. Thanks again, sir."

He smiled as he walked out the door. I was sorer than I had been before, but with the pins removed, I was more mobile than ever.

With the bandages and pins gone, I could finally see my hand clearly. It looked as if it should move freely, but I could hardly make it budge. It felt like I had cement in my joints. I decided to try anyway. The first thing I did after the doc left was use that hand to reach for one of the pins he'd removed. I wanted to inspect the pin a little more closely. It was immediately apparent, however, that this was not going to be

---

26 I am sure he was right. It probably shouldn't have hurt, but it did. It wasn't excruciating, but I certainly was not *enjoying* myself. And, I didn't feel like this guy—given my situation—ought to be calling my pain tolerance into question.

possible because I couldn't feel my thumb, index or ring finger at all. Aside from the nerve problem, the whole skeletal structure of the hand, barring the pinky finger, had seized up due to the blast damage. The forty days it had been cast in a C shape only exacerbated the problem, I am sure. Frustrating as it was to realize that not feeling parts of the hand meant not being able to use them, I recognized that this was a step in the right direction and I did not want to tarnish that notion.

The next day a gregarious occupational therapist called Alicia greeted me after my morning PT session with Solomon. She had light brown hair and was not much older than me. She was a little taller than my then wife, maybe 5' 5", and a little thinner than average. She was fun to talk to. A genuine distraction from the prison-esque existence of Walter Reed. It was nice to have another professional working with me who liked to joke around. Before I met her, only Sol and a couple of my nurses had understood the power of levity.

She led me to a new area of the hospital:

"They tell me that you have done a little occupational therapy already, so you're practically an expert, right?" She asked congenially.

"Ha! Hardly! I know what the words 'occupation' and 'therapy' mean individually, but I have no idea what 'Occupational Therapy' is," I replied, failing to match her speed in my motorized chair.

"Today we are just going to teach you a few stretches and get an idea of where your hand is at now."

"It's on the end of my arm." I said in true cringe-worthy fashion.

She hardly even acknowledged my dorky, dad-like joke, which is exactly the reception it deserved.

The room we went to was different than any I had seen before that time. It was lined wall-to-wall with blue and gray cubicles and tables. They looked more like the workspaces of computer programmers or telemarketers than they did doctors' bays. It wasn't until we reached Alicia's station that the layout began making some sense.

Strewn about her entire workspace in hard plastic packaging were tools for measuring, stretching, holding, flexing and generally moving the human hand. She placed the back of my right hand on the table. Then she reached for a tool that looked like a modified pizza cutter, but in place of the usual pizza cutting blade was a fine-toothed sprocket. She rolled the wheel along my hand in a pattern reminiscent of a palm reading. She was trying to gauge the extent of the nerve damage to my hand and wrist.

"Which fingers do you feel most normally?"

"My pinky."

"That's all?"

"That is the only one that feels the way it did before the explosion."

"Which fingers can you not feel at all?"

"I can't feel my index finger at all. My middle finger and half of my ring finger feel really weird. Well, the middle finger is different too. I can barely feel that one, I should say."

"How about your thumb?"

"Weird as hell."

"Interesting. But, you can feel it though?"

"Yeah. Sort of. It feels tingly when it doesn't feel like it's been lit on fire."

"How often does it hurt?"

"Most of the time. Generally, it feels the same way your foot does when you sit on it for too long and it falls asleep—if the foot you sat on was broken and had a bunch of shrapnel holes poked in it." I said smiling.

"Okay. That's pretty descriptive." She produced a grin of her own.

She brought the pizza cutter out again and stuck it to the palm of my hand and rolled it toward my fingertips.

"As I move this around I will stop periodically and ask you to tell me what you feel. I want you to respond with a number between one and ten. Ten being totally normal and one being not at all normal."

"Roger." I responded to the lady who more and more felt like a road-side gypsy trying to tell my future.

Between my thumb and middle finger my answer ranged between 0 and 3, but on the outer half of my palm the numbers totally normalized. Like I said before, the median nerve controls part of the thumb, all the index and middle finger and the inside of the ring finger. Meaning half of my ring finger felt perfectly normal, while the other half felt like it was on fire—when I could feel it at all. The most bizarre part of this kind of nerve damage is that there is little to no DMZ between the two areas. I could draw a pencil-thin line down the center of my ring finger and accurately separate the normal feeling side from the abnormal one.

When these experiments concluded, we moved on to the stretches. She showed me an array of stretching techniques used to regain limberness in the hands, but the one that really sticks out in my mind is the so-called "Church and Steeple" stretch:

"Okay, now put your finger tips and thumbs together with your hands oriented toward the ceiling and form a pentagon shape. This pentagon is the church. I hope that is not offensive?"

"Not at all."

"Okay. Now push your hands together as best as you can. That is the steeple. The bottom side of your fingers should be touching from tip to knuckle if you're able to form the steeple shape correctly…" She showed me the technique while demonstrating with her own hands, "Now push those fingers together as close as you can and hold it for 20 seconds."

I shoved my hands together. A sharp jolt shot through the back of my right hand and wrist as the fingers approached what is half of normal range of motion.

"Take care to ensure that all of your fingers are moving equally." She said, clearly disappointed to find my index finger not changing from its C shape at all.

"Okay." I said confused.

I pushed again. My head and face started to sweat as the stress increased.

"Make sure the index finger moves too." She said with a smile

"It is fused at the middle knuckle."

"I know it is tight, but it is important that it moves today." She said while reaching across the table to assist me.

"It won't move, because it can't. It is *fused.*"

"Surgically fused?"

"I don't know if it was from surgery or shrapnel, actually."

"Let me see it." She replied, taking the index finger in her right hand

and grabbing the palm with her left.

She pulled on the finger softly at first, but steadily increased the pressure. As she did I said again:

"That finger is fused, doc. Permanently."

"Braxton, I know the tendons are tight and the knuckle is damaged, but if you don't get that finger moving now it may stay that way forever."

"*Well*, it is going to be like that *forever*, because a ball bearing went straight through the center of the knuckle and now it is *fused*—forever."

Then she increased the pressure till her face had turned red and showed signs of straining.

"Keep tuggin' on that thing if you'd like to, doc, it doesn't hurt me at all. I can't even feel it. Break it again for all I care."

"Are you sure it is fused?"

I laughed a little, "Yes, ma'am."

She walked off obviously annoyed. Then she came back about fifteen minutes later, just as pale as your mother's wedding dress and said:

"Braxton, I am so sorry! You were right. I just got off the phone with your orthopedic surgeon and he said that your thumb and index finger both have knuckles which are permanently fused."

"I know." I said smiling again. "Don't fret over it."

She decided that was enough OT for my first day. Before I wheeled off she produced a few printouts with exercises that I was to do on my own. My homework assignment was to improve the range of motion in both my hand and my wrist between our OT sessions. Once she was confident that I understood, she sent me back to my room in the Neuro Ward. And, I sped off laughing all the way back to my room.

CHAPTER EIGHT

Long Road Home

"It's a funny thing coming home. Nothing changes.
Everything looks the same, feels the same, even smells the same.
You realize what's changed, is you."

— Eric Roth

The excitement of additional therapy sessions, which had become sort of pseudo recreation periods for me, wore off quickly and again the days turned into weeks of doldrums. I woke up, ate, went to PT and OT and then returned to my room and awaited my daily chest x-ray and mental health checkup. After all my medical screenings were completed I generally pulled out my little portable DVD player and watched *King of the Hill*, *Seinfeld*, and John Wayne movies. When the day ended a nurse would come in and stick a shot of blood thinning agent into my abdomen. I'd watch the needle prick my belly as I downed a small plastic cup filled with oral medications. Then she walked out and I would try my hand at falling to sleep, usually failing.

The tedium and constant supervision made the hospital feel more like prison incarceration than a place meant for healing. I felt for the first time in my life as if I could empathize with the people of North Korea. There I was, stuck in a building full of supervisors constantly reminding me that I was in the best facility on earth, receiving the best care afforded to any soldier in the history of the world. But, I could not—for any reason whatsoever—come and go as I pleased.

Comedic value put aside, I don't want to be overly dramatic. It was, in fact, true that I was getting better treatment than soldiers could have expected at any time before the Iraq War. It was also true that leaving that hospital had high risks for a patient like me. I understood that all their directives were well-meaning and decidedly in my best interest. To the spirit of a young man born in the Rocky Mountains, however, captivity and total suppression of wanderlust is a sentence as dreaded as death itself.

The view from my hospital bed bolstered the feeling of captivity. Out the window, for as far as the eye could see was nothing but large gray buildings, smog, and housing projects filled with poor, unfortunate souls, dealing with their own forms of captivity. I longed to get away from this boring and ugly urban landscape and see my beloved Rockies again.

This state of constant depression was periodically broken up by the appearances of famous athletes and celebrities of all stripes. Brad Paisley's father once showed up with a t-shirt, some great family stories and nothing but kind words to say about us "wounded warriors." He was polite, down to earth and exceedingly grateful for the sacrifices we, the semi-permanent residents of Walter Reed, had made for him. Johnny Knoxville came to the PT room and talked to just about everyone there. I wasn't at PT at the time, but those who were, spread stories of how funny and easy going he was. They all seemed to think he was as neat a man as has ever graced the big screen. Robert Dennehy and Dennis Farina both spent nearly 30 minutes each in my room talking to me about the Civil War. They even bought me Shelby Foote's masterpiece collection, *The Civil War* as a gift after they left.

Utah Senator Orrin Hatch was a semi-frequent visitor who always treated me as kindly as you would your neighbor. I know he may have had political motivations to do so, but he was the only Senator or Congressman from my home state to visit. And, I'll say this much in the defense of Orrin, he helped me out a lot as the years went by. He helped expedite my VA claim after the VA told me it would take 24 months to review my case. He helped fight an insurance company to get a large chunk of money that they owed me.[27] For years after I had left Walter Reed I received the occasional random handwritten letter from him asking about my family and little old cow-town. If those are actions are purely politically motivated then so be it. My family was better off for knowing him and that is good enough for me.

Professional wrestler Mick Foley was another frequent visitor to Walter Reed. He came more often than any single person that I can remember, in fact. He even bought my then-wife and me lunch one day while we were visiting the Pentagon and kept us laughing throughout the entire meal. Visits like these always brightened our days. Hanging out with a guy like Mick Foley is a lot better than lying in a hospital contemplating mortality.

When these folks take time away from their highly successful careers to show gratitude for what a stranger did on a battlefield half a world away they deserve—at the very least—a nod of appreciation. For the cynical reader, it may be easy to categorize these visits as little more than public relations stunts aimed at improving the celebrities' standing within the broader society. I never saw it that way, and I don't think that is a useful way to view an action like that. The people I listed here came without television crews or cameras, and this happened long before the emergence of social media as we know it today. Their careers gained little if anything from these trips. I cherish people like this—and I feel that we all should.

Aside from these mostly infrequent distractions, must of us just sat in our rooms confused about what each of our futures might hold. In his great work *The Gulag Archipelago,* Aleksandr Solzhenitsyn wrote, "The Universe has as many different centers as there are living beings in it. Each of us is a center of the Universe, and that Universe is shattered when they hiss at you: 'You are under arrest!'" He was referring to inhumane arrests and incarcerations that were widespread throughout

27 This was a TSGLI claim that I had taken out before leaving for Iraq. The company kept denying my claim for reasons that appeared ridiculous. Orrin's office helped us get them to pay out all that was due to us. My then wife and I used that money to buy a little chunk of ground for my horses and a small two bedroom house in my hometown.

communist Russia, but he hit on a point about humanity that few else have managed to articulate without adding a moral judgment: We *are* our own centers of the Universe. Ours are the only eyes, and our mind the only mind we have with which to process the world around us. Those of us in Walter Reed didn't have our worlds shattered by jack boots or Black Mariahs, but we *were* frantically trying to piece the Universe back together in our own way. And, many were doing it without the limbs with which to gather the bits.

One day I was visited by a Command Sergeant Major who informed me that the Army had a new program called Community Based Health Care Organization. The newly founded organization was designed to help alleviate the growing demand on Walter Reed and other military hospitals. The idea was that once a soldier had been granted outpatient status he or she could be transferred to a battalion nearer to their home where they would be able to continue treatment at local civilian hospitals. That way the injured soldiers could heal with the help of their families. Apparently, my name had been thrown into the mix for this new experimental system.

Overjoyed at the possibility of an early exodus, and more importantly—a chance to be back in my beloved cow-town—made each day at PT a race to reach outpatient status. Daydreams of the smell of junipers, the feel of spring rye running through my hands and watching the sunrise over the mountains at home fueled my morning sessions. My sole focus became proving that I was capable of living *mostly* on my own again.

When I went to OT I tried to show them that I had figured out how to use my pinky finger and thumb to do up buttons and manipulate zippers. I demonstrated that I could get myself on and off a toilet using nothing but my two canes. I learned to use what was left of my right hand to brush my teeth and shave. When my mental health care providers came to my room I lied through my teeth and told them I was sleeping just fine, no nightmares at all. I told them my depression had lessened, and was lessening with each passing day. Any problem I was having with my sleep cycle must surely be caused by the narcotics and other drugs they were pumping into me, I said. I was saying and doing whatever I had to say and do to get back to Utah.

Looking back on it now I am ashamed of all the lying, and in some sense, "faking" I did to get out of there. But, I cannot honestly say I would act differently if put back in the same circumstance. In truth, captivity—no matter how well-meaning and benevolent—warps the mind in ways one cannot imagine until one has it inflicted upon him.

When the time finally came to leave Walter Reed Army Medical Center a series of new measurements were taken on my body. These tests were primarily constructed to detail the range of motion in my joints at my time of departure. To add more data to my permanent record, the hospital also took pictures of my scars, and snapped new x-rays of my chest, legs, arms and hand.

When they bent my knees I was startled by how far they got them to flex. The PTs on the other hand, seemed just as shocked at how little flexibility was there. More evidence that my personal bar of success had been lowered dramatically. When bent to their maximum, my knees were able to reach 140 degrees and about 115 degrees, right and left respectively. A knee must reach at least 90 degrees to sit in a chair normally, so I was not even able to place my feet on the ground when seated yet. Luckily for me, my wheelchair was equipped with braces designed to accommodate my lack of flexibility. That made it so this wasn't too serious a barrier to my getting out of the hospital.

I can't remember what the range of motion measurements were in my hips, back, fingers and wrists, but all were far below normal range, and in many ways far below what is considered acceptable. Again, lucky for me it was not considered likely that these numbers would improve much beyond their then current limit, so this, like with the knees, was not going to keep me in the hospital longer.

That stage completed and a stamp of approval won, the next step was to decide what my mode of transportation was going to be. A Special Forces group stationed in Utah had drummed up some Blackhawk pilots who were willing to pick me up at Salt Lake City International Airport and fly me straight to my hometown, which would have been pretty cool. But, there was some apprehension at putting me on a commercial airliner because I had had a pulmonary embolism.[28] That meant the rapid changes in barometric pressure caused by flying could present a danger to my lungs, and truthfully, I didn't want to fly home, either. I was still afraid of flying back then.

When I was a really young kid my favorite movie was *La Bamba*. A film about the life of a 1950s era rock star, Richie Valens, who died in a plane crash at the peak of his fame. If it is true that *Jaws* cultivated fear of the ocean in my generation, then it is no leap to suggest that *La Bamba* primed my air travel phobia. Then, when about four months into my deployment to Iraq we crashed a helicopter, the fear was ensconced in my subconscious.

We were supposed to be conducting a raid on a small island in one of the largest rivers in Iraq. The intel community on Camp Ramadi had gotten word that some insurgents were using this island to store weapons caches and IED materials. Because Ramadi was so dangerous to fly in[29] when a mission called for air transport, that ride usually came in the form of a cargo helicopter, the CH-46 "Sea Knight" flown by Marine Corps pilots. The CH-46 was first introduced to the Navy in 1964. By early 2004 it was phased out of service nearly military-wide, but, it nicely filled the military's need for a low budget aerial vehicle in Ramadi.

We took off in our CH-46 that morning en route for the island. As is standard procedure we locked and loaded our weapons when we were two minutes off the objective. I jerked the charging handle on my M-4 and I let it go again. The bolt slammed forward without making any discernable sound. The roar of the 46's dual engines was all that we could hear. All around me my teammates locked and loaded then gave the thumbs up sign. We were ready to get on the ground and get after it. Then I heard an engine misfire. I looked out the circular shaped porthole across from my seat and saw black smoke billowing out of the aircraft. *That can't be good*, I thought.

---

28 Pulmonary Embolism is a blockage in an artery in the lungs. This was the same clot and PE that had caused my lungs to collapse a few months before. This story is covered in a previous chapter.

29 This is an assumption, but I think a hard one to argue with.

The crew-chief signaled to clear our weapons. *What the hell for?* "We're going back to Camp Ramadi," he shouted in my ear. We all knew something was seriously wrong, but not one face lost its stoic expression. Something about time in combat makes it hard for a man to care about anything, even a potential helicopter crash.

The bird sped back to camp, throwing out black smoke all the way. In a few minutes time we were hovering over the Forward Operating Base's largest landing pad waiting to touch down. The problem was the pilot couldn't land because our artillery pieces were in the middle of a fire-mission. The crew chief called the artillery operations center and told them to cease fire. No one outside of the flight crew really knew what was going on. The crew chief signaled that we should brace ourselves. *Holy shit, we are going to crash.* I laughed to myself. Then we just dropped out of the sky.

From what I could gather what we had done is categorized as a "hard landing." Which is fine by me, I don't want to make more of it than it was. From inside the bird it felt like being in a car crash, but in point of fact, we did hit hard enough to bounce off of the cement pad twice. Which caused the rear gate to fail, forcing us to climb out the gap left between the broken gate and the rear of the helicopter while the bird burned. It had turned out that it was an electrical fire that triggered the original malfunction. The whole wreck was a minor thing. When it was all said and done the worst injuries among us were little more than bumps and bruises. I had a small cut on the bottom of my chin. It had split open when my face skipped off the butt of my rifle on impact, but that was it. After we crawled out of the bird and finished a head count, another helicopter landed on the sand behind the concrete pad. We got on that one without giving it a second thought and completed the island raid.

When the suicide bomber hit me I tasted death for the first time and it weakened my courage for a while. During my time at Walter Reed the crash became a bigger deal in my mind. I worried a lot about aircraft failure after that. The pulmonary embolism I suffered provided good cover for this cowardice, and I was all too happy to use it.

The only issue with this plan was that because of all the medication

I was on the Army wouldn't allow me to drive myself home. Since my wife was already responsible for a large portion of my outpatient care, that was not a serious issue. We simply proposed that they allow her to drive us all the way home, then developed a basic travel plan that they could agree to. I think our proposed itinerary had her driving for no more than ten hours per day, so it was to be about a four-day trip home. We did it a little faster than that.

Once all of the paperwork was submitted and the holdover company approved our travel plan, all we had left to do was buy ourselves a car that could make the two-thousand mile drive comfortable.

The first stop we made was to a Chevrolet dealership in Virginia. I had already had a truck parked at home that I was quite happy with, so this purchase was going to be all up to her. We weren't there for more than fifteen minutes before she had decided on a brand new Trailblazer. Apparently, she had wanted one for some time and it just so happened that this dealership had one exactly like what she'd been looking for. We put about $8,000 down on it—more money than I had ever even seen all in one place—and signed the paperwork. The salesman called it a "hero's discount," but in reality, we, like so many other young suckers, payed almost $10,000 more than the car was worth. Especially after the myriad insurances and fees were tacked onto the deal. Sure, I had just put my terrible negotiation skills on full display, but we were exactly one car closer to getting the hell out of DC, and that is all I cared about.

The very next day I had my final travel orders issued. Some soldiers from the holdover company came out and helped us get all our gear loaded into the vehicle. We thanked them and then left the hospital with high hopes. I was happy to be bound for home, but happier still to think that I may never have to go back to that city again. I was wrong about that. A few years later I would end up back in DC—often.

Less than a few miles from Walter Reed we stopped to purchase a larger road map and to fill up with gas. I also planned to buy a can of Copenhagen because my nerves were already shocked by the traffic, crowds, and rude and aggressive drivers we had to deal with in DC. (Most likely that was just the excuse I gave myself. In all honestly, I am sure it was because I had never really shaken that addiction. An addict looks for any possible excuse to pick up his vices again, it seems to me.) While I struggled along the short walk into the convenience store, wobbling on the two canes I was then confined to, I noticed a couple of young men who seemed to be up to no good. They slid up behind me as I waited in line for my turn with the cashier. They stood closer than social norms generally allow. One of them took another step closer to me and began to talk loudly just to be sure I would hear his insults clearly. They made fun of the loose-fitting basketball shorts and baggy t-shirt I wore. Then, they had plenty of fun with the sight of a "honkey" in DC wearing shorts and a cowboy hat, leaning on his two canes for support.

"Look at this fool."

"Where is your horse, cowboy?" The other boy said.

"What are you doing here anyway, honkey?"

"Don't you know that this is *our hood.*"

My face got hot and my blood pressure rose. I could feel rage boiling inside me. An almost carnal desire to exact immediate and decisive retribution swept over me. Thoughts of whirling around and crushing each of their skulls with my canes filled my mind so vividly that I could almost hear the dull thud of hickory crashing off each of their heads. The metallic odor of freshly spilled blood flooded my day-dreaming nostrils.

"Look at this bitch getting all angry when he can't even walk. What the fuck are you going to do about it, hick?"

What am I going to do about it? I thought to myself. *This isn't an action movie, and I am no John Wayne. They're right. I can't do anything about it.*

The rage slowly melted into depression and shame washed over me as I realized they were right. I was helpless, and in many ways at the mercy of two young degenerates. I couldn't defend myself any longer—I couldn't defend anyone any longer. Had I even attempted to lift a cane and swing it at them I would have fallen straight onto my side. The fall alone would have injured me severely enough that we would have needed to turn around and head back to the hospital to be reevaluated. That's to say nothing of what would have happened had they jumped me while I lay on the ground. Reality set in firmly in that moment. I couldn't defend myself. I was *nothing.* No longer even a glimmer of my former self.[30] As much as it hurt my pride, I had no choice but to ignore them. I asked the cashier for a can of dip and a traveler's atlas, then slowly waddled out of the store without ever saying a retaliatory word.

Back at the car I slumped into the passenger seat, exhausted by the short walk to and from the cashier's desk. I pulled out the atlas and marked the turns of our predetermined route with a pen. I discovered that the entire journey home would take only a few turns. *How didn't I notice that before?* I wondered. The simplicity of the drive, given its over two-thousand-mile length, brought a ray of hope to my otherwise black world. *At least there is no chance to get lost,* I jested to myself.

We hopped on the interstate and enjoyed a relatively benign drive for a few hundred miles. When we reached the mountains (which seemed more like mole hills to me) of West Virginia things became a little more interesting. Wind gusts ripped across the benches and through the passes. Tornado warnings aired on every radio station. We even watched as a tractor trailer was blown onto its side while traveling at 65 miles per hour. After witnessing the truck tip over we decided that we had better get ourselves off the road. We saw a sign for a Christian women's retreat. "I am sure they will let us get out of this storm." I said. My wife pulled in and asked them if we could pay to stay there a night. We just needed get out of the storm for a few hours, maybe a night, she told them. "This is a women's retreat. We can't allow you to stay here. I am sorry," the lady working the front desk responded. Seriously doubting the words "Christian" and "Sorry" in this context, we pulled out and headed for the next closest place to get out of the storm.

---

30 As a reader these rapid mood swings must look like strong evidence that I had some severe psychological issues to work out. Indeed, I see the same thing as I go back through and edit my work, but it is important to bear in mind that I had a brain injury and I was on an array of opioids, antidepressants, and other forms of drugs. The reality is that all of these things were likely at play in a sort of highly complex concert. As the story develops I try to tease out each of these different actors to get to the core of the issue. I think it worth noting this here, because I feel if one is not careful, it may be too easy to be either overly sympathetic for my position, or too judgmental. I spent a lot of time in this story trying to give an honest take on my role in the story, I think it worth noting that here because I want the reader to resist the urge to label my problems prematurely.

Torrential rains covered the highway. At one point we had to pull off onto the top of an overpass because there was so much water in the road that vehicles were hydroplaning and spinning out of control. We waited there for about fifteen minutes before the rains suddenly cleared. It seemed like they passed us as rapidly as they had come on. She drove us back onto the freeway at a slow but comfortable pace and we decided it best to head further down the road, if only to shorten the drive we had to make the next day.

Near Shenandoah we saw a quaint little bed and breakfast set in an old barn on a little farm. That will be perfect, I thought, happy to be surrounded by green fields and trees rather than asphalt sidewalks and concrete buildings. We left that little family inn the early the following day.

We reached Kansas City late the next morning. I think it was around 2:00 am when we finally stopped. The only hotel we could find with vacant rooms was full of prostitutes and they had absolutely no shame in soliciting me, regardless of condition or company. There were drug deals and sexual negotiations going on in every corner of the building. Even though I had spent many nights in Sin City I had never seen such a thing this side of the curtain of film and television. The venue made for an uneasy night's rest, though uneasiness in nighttime hours had become a way of life, so it didn't make much difference to me.

We made it all the way to Denver the next day. Every mile westward drawing us closer to home, and to the peace I thought would come with it. The Rockies finally within reach an excitement that bordered on mania set in as we pulled back onto I-70 headed west that next morning. Even the small resort towns that pepper the Colorado Rockies, most of which were born during the heyday of silver mining, but are now populated by wealthy folks from Massachusetts and ski bums with trust funds, seemed to echo our return to the mountain west. Idaho Springs, Frisco, Vail then Rifle blew by. Each one adding to the exhilaration I felt inside. At some point, I reached down and turned on Chris Ledoux, a musical hero of all small-town cowboys.

Memories of old bull rides, rodeos, and after parties around a bonfire ran through my mind like wild horses. My legs and back ached from being in the car for three days, but a little extra pain couldn't stop the smile from creeping across my face. The thought of old times pounding leather in the mountains chasing cows was just the sort of relief I needed.

"When we were real small boys—I am talking like 7-8-10 years old—Sonny and I used to go down in his living room and watch *8 Seconds*.[31] All throughout the movie we daydreamed about what it was going to be like when we were world famous bull-riders. Inevitably, we'd strip the couches of their cushions and line the floor with them. Then, we'd shove a pillow between our legs, pull our hats down to our eyebrows, wrap up a corner of that pillow in our riding hands, throw our free hand up to the sky and yell "Lets got boys!" at the top of our lungs. We hopped around like that cushion between our legs was the hardest bucking bull that ever lived—Bodacious himself—at least 'til we heard the buzzer in our heads. Then we'd rip off our hats and fan the bull a few jumps before we jerked tail and landed on our feet..."

"You are a goofball." Amy interjected.

I kept on like I hadn't heard her: "...then we would toss our hats across the room and wave to the imaginary fans who filled the make-believe stands."

"That's what you did for fun?"

"Yeah, but mostly just on days that were too rainy or windy to go outside. When we could get outside, we did. Usually we would grab a bull rope, or some bailing twine in my case, I didn't have money for a proper bull rope back then. Then we'd round up his brother's roping calves and pin them in the corner of the pen. One guy would wrap his arms around their neck and the other would slap a rope around its chest and cinch it down as best he could. Then the guy on the calf yelled 'Let's go boys!' so the other guy knew to let go and get the hell out of the way.

"Then the calf would take off on a run, hop a few times, and then take a hard turn and we'd end up face down in the dirt. With nothing to show for our troubles but a scrape on the chin, pockets full of mud and dirt, and grins wider than Montana. Then we'd do it all over again for the other guy.

---

31 A 1994 biographical drama about the famous bull-rider Lane Frost.

"Other times, we just rode the bucking barrel his dad had built for him, but that wasn't as fun."[32]

The sun was setting as we pulled off in Grand Junction, Colorado, for gas and food. I could tell she was tired of listening to my stories, and frankly, I was tired of telling them. I looked back westward. Utah was so close I could just about see it by then. The smell of cedar, sage and red dirt filled the air. I just sat and took it all in. *Almost there*, I thought.

"I want to drive the rest of the way." I said, when she got back to the car.

"Braxton, you can't. We promised the Sergeant Major that you wouldn't drive."

"I am a grown man! I can drive in my own damned state!"

We bickered back and forth for a while. She was right, I shouldn't have been driving, but I wasn't concerned with who was right and who was wrong in that moment. I didn't care whether we had promised the medical holdover company back in DC that I wouldn't do it, either. I just wanted to drive. Obviously, she had reality on her side in this case, but I was both stubborn enough and persuasive enough to win out. We crossed the state line with me at the wheel. Chris Ledoux still belting out songs about leather fists and buckskin mares on the radio.

The night was black as sin. Reflector posts and little white lines slipped by like a giant ruler counting the distance to home. I was restless and ready to just be in my old town again. I longed to speed up time itself. Of course I couldn't do that, but I *was* in control of the vehicle.

---

32 It's hard now while writing this book, perhaps even harder than it was at the time this story took place, not to romanticize the upbringing I was blessed with. Maybe that's because as my pen scratches away at this leather-bound notebook I am sitting in the Teton mountain range looking at a beautiful creek. I am content with my current lot in life, but I miss the old days a bit.

I know full well that these and other memories are the closest I will ever come to the rush of climbing aboard a bull again. I once heard bulls described as 2,000-pound leather bags filled with hate and discontent. How could a guy not yearn for a thing like that? But, as I am sure is obvious to anyone reading this book, a cowboy with one working hand and two busted up legs just isn't likely to do very well making a living on twisters. I suppose, memories will have to do for now. At least until some mad genius invents highly functional cyborg limbs.

"Is that the exit to the cabin?" she asked

"Yes."

My family had some property a few hours east of our town. This obvious sign that we were—finally—almost home added to my anxiousness. My foot sank into the gas pedal. The needle climbed. 80. 90. 100 miles per hour.

"Braxton! Stop speeding! This road is scary!"

"I've driven it a million times."

100. 103. 105. 106. 107 mph.

Adrenaline crashed through my veins. Ice filled my stomach. All distraction left my mind. My eyes fixed on the road far ahead with laser-like focus. The little white lines on the highway blew by. The anxiousness left me. It was gradually replaced by a growing sense of relief and inner peace. I was *alive.* Some kind of primal itch was being scratched. Intensity. Danger was like a wire-bristled brush on the itch I felt.

There was a deep series of depressions in the road ahead. I knew they were coming up. I could see them. I had driven over them at least a dozen times or more. I knew they were going to be a big problem for us, but I couldn't take my foot off the pedal. *I can handle it*, I said to myself.

A man once told me during my very brief career racing motorcycles, "There is no greater feeling on earth than knowing you should slow down, but choosing to hit the throttle instead." The bumps were just in front of the vehicle as that axiom ran through my mind. I mashed the gas pedal to the floor.

"Braxton!!!" She screamed.

I glanced over. She was clutching the door with one hand and clinging to the dash with the other. I could barely hear her, and I wasn't trying to anyway. I could *feel* again. I was *alive* at a time when all the world around me had seemed so *dead.*

My heart raced a little as our shocks bottomed out on the first bump. There was not another car in sight. Somehow, I knew everything was fine. I was sure that I could pull the stunt off. My mind brimmed with confidence. My eyes still fixed tightly on the road as the car rocked back and forth. The front end was only just within my control. There was a turn in the road ahead.

There's a bend coming up, I'll brake hard as soon as the car is stable again. I think to myself.

Butterflies filled my stomach as we lifted out of the last bump. The car swayed left, then right, and then left again.

Shit! I just lost control, I thought to myself. *Don't overcorrect. Don't overcorrect.*

I smashed the gas pedal all the way to the floor hoping a little acceleration would pull us out of the wobble, but even though we'd slowed down some the car wasn't powerful enough to speed us up.

"Eeeek!" I heard her squealing as the car glided back into my control. The steering wheel stopped shaking. I let off the gas pedal and we began to decelerate. I pushed the brake lightly. 95. 93. 90. The turn kept inching closer. Yellow signs off the roadside indicated that the recommended speed limit for the turn is 55. I figured she had seen them:

"Usually you can take a turn at double the speed they suggest." I told her as if that notion were as true as gravitational theory.

The car was now fully under my control. I hit the brakes as hard as I dared to. 90. 87. 85. 80.

We took the turn way too hard. My only hope was to use both lanes of the road to make the bend. I needed to do everything within my power to keep the vehicle out of the gravel shoulders and ultimately out of the bottom of the canyon that highway crests. As we edged closer to the shoulder I remembered the canyon is hundreds of feet deep. *We'd probably starve to death before we hit the bottom,* I thought to myself.[33]

I hit the gas again to try to level out the car and pull us out of the turn. 75. 80. 83.

Euphoria. Mania. Exhilaration. *Relief* filled my body. My spirit lifted

---

33 I got that line from my step-dad. Once we were pushing cows up this steep and rugged canyon near my home town. There's a spot on that particular trail where the pathway cuts across the face of a cliff, so that you've got a cliff above you to your right-hand side and a 500 foot drop to your left-hand side. This part of the trail is so narrow that you have to take the bedroll off your saddle to avoid being pushed off the edge of the cliff to your left, by the bedroll rubbing against the cliff to the right. This one time he looked off there and in an attempt to add a little levity he said, "Don't worry about the fall, you'd starve to death before you hit the bottom." It's been a favorite of mine ever since.

like it had not in months. I just felt, *great!* Finally! It seemed like the more the speedometer climbed the better I felt.

"Pull over! I want to drive! You're an asshole!"

"Okay, I will stop in the next town," I returned calmly.

We hit the last straightaway before the town at about 90 miles per hour. We were getting close to the exit, so I decided to let the car slow back down and cool off. Just as I began my deceleration I saw red and blue lights flashing on the opposite side of the freeway.

Shit! That's a cop. He'll never catch us before the exit. He still has to find an emergency turn around to use before he can get to our side of the freeway. I think to myself.

I smashed the pedal back to the floor for the last few miles before the exit. I hoped to get enough of a lead on the sheriff to give us time to hide the car at a friend's house. As soon as we hit the off-ramp I braked as hard as I dared. I hardly even acknowledged the stop sign at the bottom of the hill and entered the main road rolling along at nearly its speed limit. Once back on the main drag I still sped, but only about seven miles per hour over the speed limit. I didn't want to draw any attention to us before we reached the turn to my friend's house.

After what felt like an eternity, but in actuality was only a few minutes, we slowly rolled into my buddy's driveway. I hobbled my way into his house, hoping the Law Enforcement Officer had not gotten a good look at our vehicle. I told Amy that she could take control of the car the rest of the way home. I didn't care to drive anymore. My heart was still racing. I felt better than I had at any point since leaving Iraq. I felt *alive.* My lust was fully satisfied. I was once again in charge of my own life, and in some sense more importantly, I'd learned that I still had say in the most important question of all: Life—*or*—death.

CHAPTER NINE

Stealing Valor

Character is the common ruling principle in man in the use of his talents and attributes. Thus it is the nature of his will, and is good or bad. A man who acts without settled principles, with no uniformity, has no character. A man may have a good heart and yet no character, because he is dependent upon impulses and does not act according to maxims. Firmness and unity of principle are essential to character.

— Immanuel Kant

Even in the dark of night, the green agricultural fields of home seemed to glow as our headlights shown on the little mountain valley. It was too late to see my family, they were all in bed long before we arrived. For most of our drive I had been communicating with two of my closest friends, Dan and Josh. They had planned to meet us at our house when we arrived. I hoped they were still awake. I sent them another message, "We are just getting to town," it read.

The words, "Welcome Home, Cpl. McCoy!" were written in big block letters across a banner that spanned the two-lane road at the southernmost end of town.

"Home at last!" I belted out through a grin.

The steps to my house had been covered by a homemade wheelchair ramp engineered by my stepfather. My wife went to the door, opened it and carried our bags inside. Another bit of my pride died as I helplessly watched her do our heavy lifting. I reached across my body and jerked the lever which bound the vehicle's door. My right hand was still too weak to perform the task, but I made good use of its heel to rest my weight on while I pried the door open with one of my hickory canes. By the time that I worked myself out of the vehicle and onto my feet my wife had already finished unloading the car and began to pour herself a drink in the kitchen. Slowly, I sauntered my way inside, wobbling like a newborn foal. Once in the kitchen I sat down and asked for a cocktail of my own.[34]

A few minutes later the doorbell rang. My friends let themselves in to spare us the trouble of getting up.

Josh and I were the same age; we graduated high-school together, and we made for a little bit of an odd pair. He had never been much of a cowboy and he didn't do any sports, but because neither of us played football and we were the only two guys the same age in our town, we bonded over a lot of summer nights spent chasing girls or hunting rabbits. He was a little shorter than me, but he was a handsome guy with dark features and an eyebrow piercing. The rarity of a dude who looked like that in our rural area, combined with his uncanny ability to mimic the voice of Aaron Lewis (lead singer of the band *Stained*), made for a real lady killer. Just the kind of guy a young man wants for a friend.

Dan is a little older than we are, but I had known him a lot longer than I had known Josh. My family used to help his family push their cows across the benches to pasture every spring. He was taller than us both and a striking guy himself. After graduating high-school and becoming a wildland firefighter, he even spent some time working as a male model in Salt Lake City. They brought us a bottle of Jack Daniels Reserve as a welcome home gift. We all exchanged hugs and Amy poured a round for the group.

They, like all others who saw me for the first time since I acquired my newest collection of scars, looked shocked at the obvious frailty of my once sturdy frame. The elephant in the room, as was always the case, was my war stories. Like everyone else they wanted the inside scoop in all its gory detail. After a few drinks I was ready to tell them all they wanted to know.

---

34 Because of the blood thinners I was taking I was not supposed to drink very much, but it was generally accepted that one drink a day wasn't hurting anything.

"Did you ever kill anyone?" One of them asked.

"Yeah."

"So, what happened? How did you get hit?" Asked the other.

I started the story with why my team had been at the Glass Factory in the first place. I tried to inform them of the political climate in Anbar and how the arguments at home were shaping the battlefield over there. I gave them as much backstory as I could, hoping to give them enough to gather a layman's understanding of our experiences. Then I got to January fifth and the buildup to the explosion that crippled me and killed our brothers.

I had been descriptive and honest up to that point, but for some reason that I may never fully understand, I started lying.

In the veteran community there is an infamous concept called "Stolen Valor." Stolen Valor usually takes one of three forms. Either a person who has never been in the military claims that he has served in a branch of it, or a person who is a veteran greatly embellishes his service. Usually the types who fall into the second category make lofty claims of combat heroism, or pin medals they never earned to their chest. The third form of this Stolen Valor is a person claiming to have served in a Special Operations Force. This lie comes from both veterans and civilians. My lies could be filed under the second category: I embellished my actions.

I said that I had acted in heroic ways after being wounded by the suicide bomber when I didn't. Maybe it was just the whiskey. Maybe it was insecurity. Maybe it was survivor's guilt screaming in my head that I could have—should have—done more. Whatever the motivation was, exactly, I will probably never know. But, there I stood, in my kitchen, pants down to my ankles; leaning awkwardly on my canes, pointing at the scars covering my limbs and lying about battlefield heroics I never exhibited:

"…and then, as I lay there bleeding and broken, I reached for my shotgun and fired back.… But, I couldn't pull the trigger with anything other than my pinky finger because my hand was so messed up. I had to work the action with only one arm, so I slid the butt-stock under my broken hip and jerked the pump back toward the muzzle with my elbow to reload each round.… As I looked around I knew my buckshot loads had no hope of reaching the enemy in the buildings across the street, but I could hit the closer ones. I fired until my gun was empty. When they found my dead body they were going to find it in a pile of spent brass, I thought!"[35]

Yeah, some big action hero I was.

The lies and embellishments I was telling were chipping away at what was left of my pride even as I spouted them, but really, what did I have left to be proud of? I was a shortened, pasty, frail, and morally-compromised shell of whatever kind of man I had once been. *Pride?* What pride could be expected of a man who is forced to urinate in a plastic bottle next to his bed because he is too weak walk to the bathroom at night?

As the sun crept over our eastern mountains the next morning the booze wore off and my friends were gone. I sat there alone in my home thinking about what I had done the night before. I reached for my medicine bottle, shook out another OxyContin and washed it down with what was left of a drink from the night before.

I hate this person, I thought. *I don't even know who I am anymore.* A few minutes later I grabbed my canes and hobbled to the bathroom hoping to reduce the pain in my stomach. Once inside I couldn't kneel to throw up because my knees still didn't bend far enough to allow it. Even if they could have flexed that far, I wouldn't have been able to tolerate the pain that resting the full weight of my body on them would bring. I leaned over the toilet as best I could and heaved. My head still three feet above the rim, arms straining and quivering to support me. I heaved again.

I picked my black Resistol[36] up off the top of the tank, personal shame prompted me to pull it way down on my brow as I hobbled back

---

35 I want to be absolutely clear about this fact: I was lying and I knew it. But, when I was wounded it was true that my first thought had been that we were being ambushed and I had—only in my mind I think—frantically searched for my weapon hoping to return fire. I only add this caveat because this was the geneses of the story. I took this little anecdotal part of the story and blew it way out of proportion. I later found out that there was no ambush at all. In fact, the only shots fired came from some confused Iraqi Police Officers within our ranks.

36 Virtually the only hat I ever wore.

toward the coffee table in our living room. During all the commotion I was making my wife had woken up and made some coffee. I reached for the cup she had poured me and downed a fist full of pills, most of which had purposes that were still unknown to me.

My mother called about that time and told us that my family was eager to see me, "Grandpa and grandma are here waiting for you too."

When I was a kid my biological father was rarely around because he was in and out of jail for reasons I never fully understood. When I did see him I knew he had a good heart, but he was rarely clean or sober. I had a stepfather but he never liked me very much when I was younger. My grandfather[37] had been much more than a normal grandparent to me; he had been the sole consistent father-figure in my life. I was excited to see him and the rest of my family, so I quickly made ready for the short, four block drive to mom's house.

The familiar sound of the gravel driveway crunching under our tires should have brought the smile back to my face, but it didn't. I didn't really feel much of anything, yet. From the car window I looked upon the beautiful little log home that my mother and stepfather lived in. The yard was dressed up in front with a white wire and wood fence that the pioneers had placed there more than one hundred years before. I remembered being a young teenage boy and rushing to finish that paint job so that I could head off to the hills with my buddies where we might chase deer, elk, rabbits, coyotes, or snakes.

"I am surprised that thing is still white at all," I said, thinking of the poor job I had done in painting it the first go-round. "Todd must have repainted it while I was in Iraq."

Behind the fence sat a row of huge lotus trees which the pioneers had planted back when our lot used to be the local post office. The house was bordered on the south side by several horse corrals and an old tin-covered barn. One pen contained saddle horses, most of which were geldings, my own included. The next had broodmares; some of them

---

37 Both of my grandfathers acted as father figures to me in my youth. The other isn't written about much in this book so I feel it best just to mention one here to keep the narrative clear.

could be ridden if necessary. The next held the colts, and the last few pens kept in our stud horses.

On the other side of the house, the north end of the lot, was the garden, bunk house, horse walker, and round pen. Looking at the round pen and bunkhouse reminded me of how bad off I really was. Only a year before I had been in that round pen helping my stepdad break horses; now I sat staring at it from a car window wondering if I could even walk to it without needing a rest.

The smell of green grass, alfalfa, and horse manure overwhelmed my senses as I opened up the car door. The only concrete in sight was the sidewalk my four limbs now struggled to carry me down, and the porch at its end where my beautiful mother, grandmother, and younger siblings stood beckoning me to join them. Tears filled my mother's eyes as my feet met the plywood wheelchair ramp my stepfather had spent days crafting for me.

As the warm arms of my mother and family all wrapped around me I found myself wishing I could cry too:

"I never thought I'd be home again."

"We love you." My mother managed to choke out through her tears.

"I love y'all too. Where is grandpa?"

A strange look shot across my mom's face.

"He's inside the house," My mother said, turning to walk inside. I followed her as best I could manage.

A few years before I joined the Army, grandpa broke his hip and back when he fell off a scaffolding at work. For years, we all watched him fight the subsequent degenerative back disease that tried to force him into a chair. He valiantly resisted. His strength had motivated me through some of my worst PT sessions. One of my goals was to be able to die saying my grandfather never saw me in a wheelchair in person. In truth, I kept hoping I might hear him say: "I am proud of you, Brack," when he saw that I had followed his lead and refused to allow disability to hold me hostage to my wheelchair. I was eager to get through that front door and show him I was upright.

When I finally made it inside grandma met me with a hug and said:

"Glad you're home, hun."

"Thank you, grandma. I am glad to be home. Is grandpa here?"

"He's over there on the couch." She pointed.

I plopped down beside my childhood hero and clung as tightly as I could manage. His arms felt weaker than they once had, but not a thing could diminish his mountainous stature in my eyes. We sat there for awhile in embrace. I almost felt like a kid who had fallen down and scraped his knees. I just wanted to hear him tell me it was all going to be alright.

"I am so proud of you." He whispered,

"I love you, grandpa. I am sorry." Tears welled up in my eyes.

He told me that he was proud of me just like I had hoped he would, but it didn't make me feel good. I didn't deserve that accolade and I knew it. When he said he was proud of me, he was talking about who I was as a man, not what I had accomplished physically. I knew that. The very night before I had demonstrated lowly character, why *should* he be proud of me? He wouldn't be if he had known that I was the kind of man who lied to his friends.

"Oh, you dummy. What the hell are you sorry for? Knock it off before I kick you right in the ass!" Grandpa responded.

I buried my head into his once broad and muscular shoulder trying to hide my shame. I don't know how long I stayed there, but I would have stayed longer if he had let me.[38]

"I spent the better part of a week building that damn wheelchair ramp and you didn't even use it!" My step-dad quipped.

"I am never sitting back in that goddamn chair again!" I bellowed.

"Braxton!!! Watch your mouth!" Mom yelled.

"Watch it, or I'll sock ya one!" Grandpa joined in.

---

38 Grandpa is gone now. Right now I am still up in the Tetons chasing black bear and enjoying the company of his favorite animal, the grizzly bear. Tear stains dot the pages of this leather journal more numerously than sweat does my pack, but I wouldn't trade this moment for much of anything.

Strapped to my pack is a wooden-handled tomahawk with his dog tags attached to it. I carry it on every adventure. It is heavy, but in some strange way its impractical weight is like a symbol of his memory. It's like having him right here with me while I explore new country and chase new dreams. In some sense, I feel it's the least I could do for him and this is the perfect place to relive this story.

I could never tell whether he was serious when he chimed in like that, but it didn't really matter. We talked back and forth for a few hours. They got me up to speed on the politics of town; the irrigation schedule, the local fishing and hunting reports, the lives of our extended family and the situation at our family cabin. Eventually I had had enough and we decided it was time to head back to our house and process everything.

While we were saying our goodbyes to my little siblings and my mother, out of the corner of my eye I saw my grandma helping grandpa off the couch. This wasn't exactly a new sight, my grandpa had been in rough shape for a long time, but his struggle to stand up was clearly much harder than had been in the past. Then I noticed why everyone had been a little uncomfortable when I brought up being bound to a wheelchair. There, just on the opposite side of my grandma, sat a red motorized chair. The whole thing hit me at once: *That's grandpa's chair*... I was shocked and puzzled.

Like many other soldiers at war, my home-front had changed considerably during my absence. My great-grandmother whom I had been very close to passed away, but she had written me a letter while I was in Ramadi saying she expected to go soon. Her death was not so unexpected. My step-grandpa never seemed to age a day in his life before I left for the war, but while I was gone he developed prostate cancer. The chemotherapy aged him dramatically in just one year, but even this was less jarring than the sight of that wheelchair. Everyone's life has an event horizon, my grandfather's had come earlier than I had anticipated. That was all there was to it. I just wasn't ready for the sight of my hero—the man who had raised me when no one else wanted to—crawling into a chair. It was as if I was watching the rock I had always cleaved to in my weakest moments crumble before my eyes. To make matters worse, the first look at I got at the process was long after the erosion had begun.

While it was true that his physical body had changed dramatically, it certainly did not shake my view of his character, or change the way I loved him. It just signaled that I was going to be on my own for the recovery process.[39] I would always have the memories of his strong

---

39 Perhaps there was something more to it than that. Maybe it was that I knew how

calloused hands carrying me around the yard as a boy, or reaching down to pick the katydid off my nose after it had perched itself there, making me cross-eyed and confused. I remember tugging at his pant leg as if it were a lifeline. He was my lifeline, he always had been. Now, I forced myself to accept that the cord was severely frayed and *fraying*.

---

much better, stronger, and more determined a man he was than I am. Maybe deep down I felt that there was no way I could ever endure my challenges if he had to eventually succumb to his.

CHAPTER TEN

Bulldog

The good NCO has never been short in confidence, either to perform the mission or to inform the superior that he or she was interfering with traditional NCO business.

— William G. Bainbridge

We entered the freeway going northbound on Interstate-15. The new Community Based Health Care Organization (CBHCO) unit I had been assigned to was located about two and a half hours drive from our town. We passed the last hayfield at the north end of our little valley and entered the sagebrush covered flats of an area known locally as "The Low Hills." A big brown sign flew by indicating that we are nearing the local reservoir.

"We ought to do a little fishing this week." I said. Completely forgetting my new limitations.

"You can't, Braxton." Amy answered back.

"Oh. Right."

Another hour up the road we entered the limits of the first big town I had been in since we got home to Utah. At that time I still didn't believe that the psychological trauma of war bugged me much. Mostly I thought the PTSD stuff was an illness rarer than many would have us think. I knew I had a few issues, but I was convinced that the role combat stress was playing in my life was the least problematic of them.[40] Still, every

40 Looking back on this I think that among the many reasons I waffled back and forth on the question of PTSD and its effect on my life is that I wasn't very perceptive

city I had seen since Iraq kind of reminded of Ramadi.

When I looked around my throat tightened a little and sweat beaded on my brow. I became irritable and ornery for no reason that I could understand.

"Do you have to ride that guy's ass?" I said rudely.

"I am *not* riding his ass." She retorted.

"Well, I am looking at the same goddamned road you are and it looks to me like you're awful damned close to that guy. I'd be pissed if I were him."

"I don't need you to tell me how to drive, thank you. You're not in Iraq anymore, you don't get to order me around like I am one of your soldiers."

"I never ordered anyone around over there."

"Seems like it." She said sarcastically

My anger built. Before we started bickering I was just nervous and rude, after the exchange I was anxious, rude and *mad.* I felt like my wife was being supercilious. To make matters worse, I knew she was *right* in the main point. That made it even harder to control the sort of witch's brew of neurochemicals bubbling inside my brain.

Internally I could see no real reason to allow anxiety to take over my critical faculties just because I entered an American city, so why was I struggling for control?

Why the hell am I having an anxiety attack right now? I was never even this nervous when I was actually in Ramadi! What is wrong with me?

What should I say to her now that I knew I was in the wrong? *Nothing*. I bottled my anger and bit my lip. *Screw cities! I hate them and anyone*

---

to the changes in my mood and I didn't fully understand what PTSD is. The image it conjured for me was some overblown Hollywood version of the crazy Vietnam veteran crawling under tables and chairs to hide from incoming fire that is whistling around only in his mind. If that was PTSD, then I don't now, and never did have it. Pull the rest of this footnote up from the next page.

I have since come to find out, that is not an accurate depiction of the disease at all. Since becoming more educated, I found that the rest of this book is essentially a story about mental health problems more so than anything else.

who would choose to live in one.

The gate guard at the front of the army post greeted us kindly when we stopped for inspection:

"How are you doing this morning? I need to see some identification, please."

"Here ya go," she replied, handing him each of our ID Cards.

"Okay. You're good to go. I just have to ask that you put on your seatbelt, Corporal."

"Yeah. Alright." I wanted to hit him in the face with my canes.

My body is already ate up. What the hell is a 10 mile per hour collision going to do to me?

The parking situation in this new CBHCO unit was inconvenient even for an Army installation, but because I was still considered handicapped we got special treatment:

"Look at this! Front door service. Are you sure this is an Army base?" I said to her.

"Corporal McCoy. How the hell are ya?" A deep familiar voice boomed out from behind the vehicle.

"I am rolling along, Top. How have you been?"

It was First Sergeant K., a senior NCO that I knew well. In fact, he had been the guy who approved my request to volunteer for the deployment to Ramadi.

"I have been well, cowboy. I want to introduce you to your new Platoon Sergeant, Master Sergeant Dillinger."

"Hullo, Sergeant." I said extending my hand.

He grabbed my hand and proclaimed:

"Young man. I expected to meet a soldier in a wheelchair, you seen him around anywhere?"

"Yeah well, I am doing my best to stay out of that damn thing, Sergeant."

"He's a grizzly old bastard, Corporal. Most of us around here just call him 'Bulldog,'" First Sergeant K chimed in.

Master Sergeant Dillinger was a short, stocky, combat veteran of the Vietnam War. Usually he paced around briskly with a cigarette on his lips looking for someone's ass to chew. He didn't beat around the bush about anything. If he had a thought, you were liable to hear it, but he cared about the men in his platoon and he played no games—especially the Army's. Later on in our relationship when there was a "mandatory formation" upcoming that he didn't think I needed to drive up for, he simply called my phone and asked me where I was and whether I was okay. Then he told the commander that I was accounted for. Over time I developed a deep admiration and respect for that man, the kind that no rank or ribbon racks can earn.

The two upper enlisted men led me into a small portable building that was designated as the headquarters for this region's CBHCO program. They introduced me to the commander who proceeded to explain the program in detail.

The colonel was younger than the NCOs. His youth brought a certain vibrancy absent in the older enlisted men. He seemed like an excellent guy, but I would be lying if I told you that I cared how many soldiers and how many different states his particular unit was in control of. I just wanted to sign the paperwork that I had to sign and go back to my hometown to hang out with the people I had not seen in almost two years. His exuberance was refreshing and some of it rubbed off on me, but I was ready to move on.

Luckily, as often happens in the military, my platoon sergeant had already distilled his spiel down to the basic components I needed to understand before we ever walked into his office. As the commander talked, I listened as best I could and tried to nod at the appropriate moments, but I was glad I had the Bulldog guiding me through this program. In hindsight, I realize that Master Sergeant Dillinger was everything the Army should, but seemingly does not, value in their Non-Commissioned Officers.

"Cpl. McCoy, this is Sgt. Ramirez, she is in charge of all your leave documents and pay. She's a good person to know around here, but that don't mean shit to you. You will come to me and I will go to her. Understood?"

"Roger, Sergeant."

He continued to brief me as I hobbled around the building:

"Now, this next office we're going to is the civilian psychiatrist. I would get you out of this bullshit if I could, but I can't. Army says it's good for you, then it's good for you. Got it?"

"Roger, Sergeant."

She had a little office filled with certificates and a random collection of trinkets and plants. It's been my observation that most shrinks have the same taste in decorations. Usually I sit in their offices and wonder how much of the decoration is there for aesthetics and how much they put there as a subconscious display of their own chaotic psyches.

She stuck her hand out to shake and introduced herself. Then she started with the same tired line of questioning I had been subjected to every day since I woke up in the ICU:

"How's your sleep?"

"Fine"

"Are you taking your meds?"

"I guess so. I don't have any idea what half of these things are. Doctor says take them at X time, so that's what I do."

"Are you still on Wellbutrin?"

"Is that the big gray one?" I asked my wife

"Yes."

"Yeah. Why? Can I stop taking it?"

"We could consider that. Why do you want to come off it?"

"Because, Doc, I am on enough medication to kill 15 horses. I want to get off of this junk and if that has to be one pill at a time then that is fine by me. Let's get started."

"Okay."

"And, to be totally honest, I feel like I am an asshole right now."

"If you are feeling irritable Wellbutrin should be helping with that, not making it worse. It is more likely that your lack of sleep and PTSD are what is making you irritable."

"I don't have PTSD. I read through my files on the drive to Utah. The doc in DC found me at a 0% for PTSD."

"That 0% is just a projected disability rating. It means the doctors at Walter Reed determined that you do have PTSD, but they found little or no evidence that its symptoms disable you."

"Isn't that what we are talking about here, disability? I am not here because I am able bodied. What is the difference between having no PTSD and having PTSD that has no effect on you?"

This conversation went on a bit longer following basically the same trajectory. I was clearly digging my own grave in this instance, but I didn't realize it at the time. What person actually believes they have a mental health problem in its early stages? Generally speaking, I would say that few who have a mental disorder ever realize it and fewer still recognize it early on.

Master Sgt. Dillinger met me as soon as I left her office and said: "Let's go have a smoke, Cpl."

I settled in on the wooden bench next to my new first line leader. He offered me a smoke. I declined and proceeded to tell him all about how I had quit after my lung had collapsed in the hospital. Instead, I pulled out my can of dip and loaded up my lip with snuff in a sort of demonstration of solidarity. I may have quit smoking, but I still understood the value of vitamin N. I was no spit shine boots, REMF, and I felt it imperative he know it.

"Cpl., I know you have been through a lot of shit in the last year. And, I am old enough to know what that shit is like. I did my time in Nam—"

"Our war wasn't squat compared to yours Serg—" I interrupted.

"Shut the fuck up, McCoy." He cut me off, "I've seen plenty of war, it's all the same shit. Our wars may have been different, but you did your time in the shit. You don't owe me or anyone else a fucking caveat. Understood?"

I nodded.

"What I was trying to say is that this unit is different. This is a medical holdover company. We are not a line unit—but don't get it wrong—this is still the Army. There's enough bullshit around here to pack 10 five-tons. I will do my best to make sure you only eat the shit you have to, but I swear to God, if you fuck with me, I will have your crippled ass on the next fucking flight to DC. Understood?"

"Roger, sergeant."

"I will call your cell phone any time I feel like I want to and if you don't answer it, you had better be dead, dying, or in the middle of a medical appointment. Understood?"

"Yes, Sergeant."

"You'll call me first thing every morning. I will know about every medical appointment on your schedule and if you leave your house for *any* reason—I don't give a shit if you just want to go outside and piss on a tree—you *will* ask me permission first. Copy?"

"Roger, sergeant."

"Alright. Now get that pretty little wife of yours home and let her relax, Corporal. You are free to go."

"Roger, Sergeant."

I had only made it a few steps when I heard his voice call out again: "Corporal McCoy!"

"Yes, Sergeant."

"Welcome home, son. Glad you made it."

"Thank you, sergeant."[41]

41 I can't remember all these interactions verbatim, but I can assure you that the language and the characters are displayed as best as I can possibly manage. Anyone who knew Bulldog would agree that this is a near perfect description of the man he was, even if the exchanges aren't. He was truly a one-of-a-kind character and among the best men I ever knew.

CHAPTER ELEVEN

Outpatient

I was like a man in a boat who when carried along by wind and waves should reply to what for him is the chief and only question 'whither to steer', by saying, 'We are being carried somewhere'.

— Leo Tolstoy, *A Confession*

I started my new regimen of outpatient treatment at a local hospital about an hour's drive north of home. My primary care physician Dr. T and I had a lot in common. He was a fellow hunter and fisherman and he had also grown up in rural Utah, just like I had. Sharing life experiences with the doctor charged with my overall short and long-term care was a welcomed departure from the previously assigned Army doctors who, generally speaking, tended to come from more affluent urban and suburban backgrounds. Additionally, and in some sense in contrast to my stay at Walter Reed, my civilian physician was interested in my personal story as much as my current medical condition. Genuinely interested, in fact. This shift was impossible not to notice and I think it made one of the most influential differences in the upward turn my recovery trajectory would eventually take.

It is not that I loved telling the story of the day I was wounded over and over again—I didn't. I hated it, actually. It is more that there seemed to be something cathartic in telling my story in detail to a person who was not interested in prying open the psychological scars which accompanied my physical deformities.

This particular day the doctor assessed my injuries and ordered new x-rays to be taken. After he finished handing me the paperwork I needed to show the radiologist to ensure the right images were taken, he spent a few minutes going over all the reasons I was going to really like the new physical therapist I would be working with later that morning. This new guy had his work cut out for him if he was to fill the enormous role Solomon had played in my journey up to that point. Still, I walked out of his office determined to remain open minded and ready to begin anew.

The PT room at this hospital was smaller than Walter Reed's, but it was vastly more sophisticated, both in equipment and supporting staff. I hovered around the receptionist's desk waiting for her to finish a phone call so that she could direct me to whichever area was to be mine for the next few hours. She was a pretty and genial woman who looked to be in about her early 40s. Her smile lit up the red hair resting her shoulders. She hadn't yet spoken a single word to me, but she didn't need to. Her positive presence radiated throughout the room. She seemed the personification of the adage, "smiles are contagious." I didn't exactly *want* to be at physical therapy that morning, but my hesitation, perhaps it was really anticipation, melted away in the company of such friendliness. When she had finished her phone call she took my paperwork and cordially informed me that my physical therapist, Chris, would be with me shortly. I thanked her and took my seat in the reception area.

"I don't even know why I am here. We already know that I am about as good as I am going to get." I said to my wife.

I probably said this because I secretly wanted to get out of the pain I knew was coming my way, but I had a decent excuse to hide behind. One of the grounds for my release into the CBHCO program was that I had completed the majority of the physical progress I was likely to make. I don't know why Walter Reed seemed so adamant that soldiers released into this "heal at home" program be near the peak of likely physical recovery, but they had.

"You don't know that, Braxton. Maybe these civilian doctors will be able to help you get even better." She said.

"I guess."

"Hi, I am Chris." A tall, dark haired man interrupted us. I wasn't sure whether he had heard my complaining, but I hoped he hadn't. I took his outstretched hand as a sign that he wasn't dissuaded even if he had. My eyes met his, I reached out with my left hand and shamefully apologized for both my whining and my inability to shake with the traditional hand. He told me not to worry and that he understood. Then he released the grip on my left hand and motioned to an area toward the back of the room.[42]

I stood up to follow him toward the bed that would be our workstation for the day. He asked me why I was there, and what exactly my injuries were. I explained the wounds as best as I could slogging along behind him as we talked. Something about him was different I noticed. He wasn't reacting the same way all the other civilian professionals had. He seemed unfazed by my story and the total amount of damage I'd taken. Where most had seen a sob story, he saw only *a story*. He sat down in front of me in a rolling chair with a round seat:

"This first visit is just going to be an evaluation. I need to understand exactly where you are at before I can design a treatment plan for you."

I was a bit taken aback by his cavalier attitude. *Great. This guy doesn't even realize how big of a deal it is that I am even upright in this condition. The whole medical world thinks I should still be wheelchair-bound; what is his problem?* I thought to myself.

A few minutes later he returned with a familiar looking black plastic box about eighteen inches square. Before he opened the box he poked and prodded at my legs with his fingertips. "You've got a ton of scar tissue built up in your quads." He said.

No shit. I thought.

The areas of my legs he kneaded were swollen and had a reddish tint to them. The nerve damage in my thighs was sporadic. In some places I could barely feel anything, and in others it felt like he was thrusting

42 I was whining a lot at this time, this scene is no exception to that; but it is out of my character for me and I don't know exactly why I became that way. I think it probably had a lot to do with the heavy dosage of opioids that I was on, but I can't say this for certain. Lack of sleep, depression and head injury must have had some causal role as well. But, since I am not a psychologist I will just have to live without a sufficient answer to this question. A thing that I think I can say with certainty, however, is that opioids rob a man of all that he is. Whatever those drugs do inside the brain pervades every aspect of personality and character. A person who is on them simply is *not* himself. Whatever that means.

spear points into my muscles rather than fingers. I knew in the back of my mind that some pain is good. "Pain is just weakness leaving the body," as they say. Still, as much as I tried to hide it I knew the torment must have been showing itself on my face. It felt like I was a supporting cast member in a scene from a comedy movie. I imagined my eyes bulging from my head as the lead character, a sadist doctor, enjoyed his handiwork. I laughed a little at the thought of it, but the laughter only made the treatment more uncomfortable. *That's all I need,* I thought, *is this Bill Murray guy to think I am laughing at him whilst he grinds up scar tissue in my body. He must think I am a crazy person.* Maybe I *was* a crazy person, but I was no masochist.

"Okay. Let's measure your range of motion." He said as he pressed a plastic protractor-like device to the outside of my knee. He said the tool's industry name is a Baseline Goniometer. I can't even pronounce that second word, so I just called it a protractor. It has a disk-shaped center with 360 degree markings around it. Protruding from one side of the disk is a sort of ruler-shaped length of plastic, probably about twelve inches long. It has a black line down the ruler shape labeled "Baseline." Fastened to the back of the main disk is a smaller disk which has another ruler shaped bit of plastic protruding from it about the same length as the first one I described. The only difference being that this bit is covered in dashes which mark both inches and centimeters exactly like a normal ruler.

The way the protractor is used, as I was about to find out, is the baseline is placed on the body part that will remain motionless, in this case, my femur line, while the other arm of the protractor is placed on the part of the body which will move—in this case, the tibia line of my lower leg. The numbered disk placed alongside my knee then became the pivot point. My femur line was then placed at 90 degrees which acted as the base measurement. Then, with the aid of the physical therapist the knee was flexed and the maximum angle reached on the protractor was read aloud and written down by his assistant. He repeated this process three times before moving onto the next step: knee extensions. After he had finished the three extension measurements he calculated the average of the three measurements and filled me in before moving on to the other leg. It was all well and good. Measuring was nowhere near the most painful part of the PT process, but when you're 20 years old and your knee struggles to flex past 90 degrees hearing the results can be depressing.

I started sweating as he pushed my knee downward and then back toward the bed I sat on. *Am I going to hurt like this for the rest of my life?* I wondered. Was my new normal to be doomed to agony at even the most regular of activities? [43] When it hurts just to let one's leg drape over the edge of a bed or chair without any support holding it up, one had to wonder: What does *better* even mean in this instance? *Maybe this is all futile and I should just quit now and learn to live with the disabilities as they stand.* If this is all supposed to be improving my quality of life, isn't it objectively *better* not to hurt? Thoughts of giving up ran through my head as I listened to him call out the measurements to his aide.

"So, did you wrestle for Millard or is that just a gym t-shirt?"

"Yeah, I wrestled for them." I replied through gritted teeth.

"That's a great program. Were you any good?" He asked, smiling.

"No. But, I never lost to a kid from this area." I quipped.

No matter how obvious the joke may have been it probably was not a wise move on my part to insult the man whose job it was to inflict pain on me. Still, it's hard to pass up ribbing a guy I just met. Particularly one as stoic as he was.

"I used to be the physical therapist for the Olympic wrestling team."

"Get atta here! That's pretty cool."

He told a few stories of injuries he treated on wrestlers. Each one was interesting but I couldn't shake the feeling that what he was indirectly saying was: You're being a pussy. And, in truth, I probably was being softer than I should have been. He obviously had a lot of experience, and he must have been very good at his job if the Olympic team used him. I should have felt lucky to have a professional of that ilk working on me, rather than frustrated and annoyed at the pain. I knew all of that. It wasn't as if the thought never occurred to me before, but as all good

43 The answer unfortunately is yes—sort of. I've learned to live with it and ignore it as best I can, but the pain is always there.

caregivers do, he found a way to make that point sink in without ever saying it out loud.

I told myself that none of my behavior was overreaction when taken in context, after all, these little bursts of extra pain may have been slight when considered on their own, but when piled on top of the constant and never-ending aches I endured, they seemed excruciating. I hurt every second I was awake, and nighttime brought me no reprieve. When I lay in my bed at whatever time seemed appropriate that evening, I didn't sleep. What's more, I never *expected* to sleep. How could I sleep when I hurt *so much.*

What had I become? I was being *weak.* I had once thought my mental toughness was as sure as the sun coming up in the morning, but I was broken down again. (Before I was wounded I used to claim that I had never quit in my life and nothing could make me, but I was wrong. I hit many, many breaking points during recovery.) The internal dialogue whirled about my head in an endless cycle. I was being soft and I knew it, but rationalizing the pain was so damned easy to do! I had made all sorts of excuses over the course of the past few months, and although it should have been the last time I made such justifications, it wasn't. My physical therapist caused me to steel my resolve for the day, but the whirlwind of internal dialogue never stopped. I broke again later on that same day, just as I had done the day before.

My mind continued to churn. I heard Chris explain that he was going to use ultrasound to help break up the scar tissue in my quads. *Ultrasound? The machine they use to look at fetuses?* I wondered to myself. At Walter Reed no one had ever mentioned such a thing. How in the world could that work? Skepticism—or maybe it was pessimism—stopped my internal conflict for a moment. I thought there was no way this man was taking the extent of my injuries seriously. *Ultrasound? Yeah, right.*

"We will start using ultrasound tomorrow," Chris said.

The next day I was back at the hospital having my blood drawn to test the level of blood thinners in my system. Due to the deep vein thrombosis and the blood clot which had caused the embolism and subsequent collapse of my lung at Walter Reed, I had been put on a drug called Warfarin. This highly controversial drug is generally used to thin blood. Because of the dangerous side effects of the drug and the act of thinning of a person's blood, a patient on this pill must be tested every day. Which worked out fine for me at the time, because I required daily physical therapy sessions and checkups anyway.

Dr. T had proven to be an excellent physician. Though the treatment at Walter Reed had been decent, this was turning out to be a much better hospital. I was confident that if I could indeed improve my situation, this place would help me do it.[44] During my visit with Dr. T I showed him a few ball bearings that were close to the surface of my skin. He asked me if they were bothering me. I told him they were, so he set up a follow-up appointment to remove them using local anesthetic and a scalpel. If he did it this way he could perform the minor surgery in his office and I could continue on with my normal schedule. The appointment was set for the end of the week. *Finally!* I thought. *Someone in the medical field is listening.*

I left his office and headed to the Physical Therapy room across the hall. At this stage, I was still required to have someone drive me to and from all medical appointments, so my wife was in the hall waiting for me to finish up with the doctor. When she linked up with me I told her all about the future surgery.

The worst part about having shrapnel invade one's body against his will is the idea that some terrorist bastard had *put* them there. It is almost as if I walk around carrying medals underneath my skin that *he* won. Like he could be sitting around a table on the other side smoking shisha with his friends bragging about how many of his ball bearings had hit their intended target: Me. Like I was a walking billboard for terrorist

---

44 Anyone familiar with the scandals at Walter Reed during 2006 may find it odd that I am treading so lightly on the subject. I am doing this for two reasons, 1) there were many good healthcare providers at Walter Reed who were genuinely there just to help wounded soldiers recover. Blaming them for the mistakes of the worst employees would be wrong morally and ethically. I just don't want to engage in that. 2) Because if the reader is interested in learning more about what went on there you can find that information in other places. Adding it to this book would just be a distraction.

success. The only consolation I could come to when this thought occurred to me—I am still not sure whether it is any consolation at all—is that the suicide bomber who had struck me down temporarily was not around to enjoy his successes.

At any rate, my wife seemed just as happy as I was that some of these ball bearings were going to be removed very soon. Part of her excitement must have been knowing that she would not have to listen to me talk about them bothering me any longer, and of course, this meant that I wouldn't be using my pocket knife to whittle at my arm any longer.[45]

I told my good news to Susan, the receptionist, the moment I walked through the door of the PT clinic. "That's great!" She exclaimed from behind her desk. Another much welcomed moral boost from my kindly-natured new friend. Deep down I knew that I really only told her about the minor operation because I expected her to pretend to be happy about it. Even if she was actually mortified by the idea. I needed a pick up and she was always good for one.

"Chris will be with you shortly she said." I thanked her and walked back to an area of the clinic that I had come to think of as my own.

My PT sessions started in the same bed every time because the large bin of hot wax was located next to it. Each affair started by dunking my right hand and wrist in hot paraffin wax. The shrapnel damage to multiple places in the hand had caused a condition called Palmar Fibromatosis, or Dupuytren's Contracture (Don't worry, I can't pronounce those names either). This is where the tissue that covers the palm of the hand—some of which is actually stronger than steel by comparison—becomes shorten or contracted. This can be brought on by myriad different injuries. Burns seem to be the most common cause of the ailment, but in my case, it was caused by a blast injury and then exacerbated by the position that my hand had to be casted in for several months. The idea was that heat

---

45 I still remove small bits of shrapnel from my skin every now and then. Sometimes they fester up and I yank them out with tweezers, other times I have to break the skin with my pocket knife before I can get to them. One of the more annoying thoughts, admittedly a kind of funny one, is that I can feel a ball bearing coming through the skin on my backside right now. So, right now I am sitting on a ball bearing while typing about how uncomfortable they are.

from the liquid paraffin wax would help to loosen up some of these tissues, subsequently making the stretching session that kicked off each PT day more profitable. I knew the drill by this point, and I was the only person then using the wax pot. That's why I knew exactly where to go.

After the wax had sat on my hand long enough to cool down one of the physical therapy assistants would come over, peal the wax off of my hand, and help me through a stretching routine. The wax generally peeled off in large pieces that made it look kind of like a shattered, pink-colored sculpture of a hand—if that sculpture had been crafted by a first grader. The stretching exercises we did were routine. The PTA would first massage the fascia at the base of my fingertips right about where the biggest calluses form. A strange burning sensation radiated through my hand and wrist as they worked the muscles, tendons, and tissues. It didn't hurt or anything like that, but it was a bit uncomfortable. Occasionally, during stretching, the area with the most nerve damage would "light up" (that's how they described it when I could feel something in the damaged region). When this happened it felt exactly like my fingers and hand were actually on fire, so I guess 'light up' wasn't too far from the mark. This burning was often accompanied by a tingling feeling sort of like you had sat on your foot for too long; but even sitting on your foot doesn't do the sensation of nerve damage justice. I have found nerve damage to be the hardest discomfort to describe. How do you describe pain in an area that you can't actually *feel?* It is truly bizarre.

Once the massage was complete we moved on to the stretches. (Much of this felt very good I might add.) We did the same old church and steeple stuff that I had done back in Walter Reed. Then we flexed each finger downward in an attempt to make a fist—I *still* can't close my hand into a proper fist. Then we moved on to another stretch which they called a "Basic Palm Up Stretch" where we turned my palm upward and stretched my fingertips downward and backward. I used the strength of my left arm and hand to force the fingertips of my right hand through the motions. Then they would have me put my upward facing finger tips on the edge of a table and lean my seated body weight into them in essentially the same motion.

Once these and more stretches had been completed on my hand and wrist Chris would walk over and get me set up for whatever lower body mobility treatments and exercises were going to be done that day.

On this particular day we tried the ultrasound Chris had mentioned during our last visit. I had my doubts about the whole thing; but according to Chris ultrasound had been used successfully in physical therapy since the 50s.[46]

"Alright," said Chris, "let's get started."

He pulled a wheeled metal cart over to the bed I was lying in and dipped his gloved hand into some kind of goo. He rubbed this gelatin around the lower part of my quadriceps and retrieved the wand from his ultrasound machine, which looked something like a more sophisticated version of a corded telephone. After pushing a few buttons and twisting a couple knobs he placed the cold stainless steel head of the rubber coated wand into the gel and began working it around in small circles on my thigh.

Ultrasound works by sending high frequency sound waves through the patient's body, causing friction that penetrates up to five inches' worth of flesh and sinew. You can really feel the heat work into your flesh. It felt like it was warming everything in my body all the way down to the bone. A large portion of my femur bones are now made up of surgically placed steel rods. I started squirming a little bit at the new sensation. He asked me whether it was hurting, I told him it wasn't. "It was just feels weird," I said.

He warned me that we needed to be careful not to heat up the rods in my femurs because that could cause some problems. After the area he was working on was heated to his satisfaction he hung the wand back onto the receiver of the machine and began kneading my quads.

---

46 Beth W. Orenstein says that ultrasound was already being used by physical therapists by the 1920s and 1930s. By 1940, like many new technologies both then and now, it was viewed as a cure-all. It may not have turned out to be the cure for all humanity's physical ailments like they thought way back then, but in my own case it worked well. The physical therapist used it for two very specific modalities: 1) to heat up and break down scar tissues, and 2) to deliver topical anti-inflammatory, as well as local pain medications. For our purposes it was a kind of magic cure-all. Source: 'Ultrasound History', Beth W. Orenstein. *Radiology Today.* Vol. 9 No. 24 p. 28.

My legs had so much scar tissue in them that the largest of deposits had formed huge lumps that visibly bulged up through the skin. My leg looked like a pair of peach-colored pantyhose filled with deformed oranges and grapefruits. The lumpy masses protruded in sporadic intervals spanning all the way from knee to hip on both quadriceps. The tumor-esque mass of what my body considered protective tissue was now being slowly crushed, stretched, and broken apart under the force of his powerful thumbs. After a bit of stretching back and forth he made a fist and shoved it into the cartilage-like mass. He rolled his fist back and forth like a baker working a bowl full of dough.

It hurt in a relieving way, like when a cut on your finger gets infected and you drain it by squeezing it forcefully like you would a zit. The pain is sharp and fierce, but somehow you just can't stop doing it, because for some reason, maybe it dates clear back to our primal beginnings, you know that once the infection is cleared the relief will make up for the suffering. This therapeutic destruction of scar tissue build-up is much the same. The pain is immense, but somehow, it feels kind of *pleasurable.* This conflict continues for a few moments longer and then we hear an audible popping sound. My face must have lost a bit of its color because he said, "That popping sound was the scar tissue breaking apart. It may hurt for a while, but later today you should feel some relief." He worked the same area for a bit longer until a few more pieces broke apart. We were finished for the day.

This became my daily routine for weeks. Some people climb into their vehicles in the morning destined for a day of arduous, and mostly thankless tasks, physical or otherwise, but not me; this daily onslaught was my work. And, I think that was the proper way to construe it. It was sometimes annoying, but it was a means to an end—an important end. The lucky part was, PT was never boring.

Still, after weeks of what can only be honestly described as slow, dull agony punctuated by bursts of sharp, oftentimes excruciating muscle, bone, and nerve pain, it became increasingly difficult to appreciate its long-term significance. And even more difficult to see it as a job.

But I got a little limp now when I walk
And I got a little tremolo when I talk

But my letter read from Whiskey Sam
You're a walkin' talkin' miracle from Vietnam
Drive on

The words of Johnny Cash's classic song replayed through my subconscious every time my back hit that PT bed.

CHAPTER TWELVE

Chasing Dragons

"I have absolutely no pleasure in the stimulants in which I sometimes so madly indulge. It has not been in the pursuit of pleasure that I have periled life and reputation and reason. It has been the desperate attempt to escape from torturing memories, from a sense of insupportable loneliness and a dread of some strange impending doom."

— Edgar Allan Poe

Before we begin this next series of chapters I feel I must explain myself. There are a lot of parts of my story that I have shared many times before, be it in print or from a stage, but I have never spoken candidly about opioid abuse until now. I hesitated to add this section to the final book for months. I have kids, do I really want them to know this about me? Not really.

Eventually, I decided that I absolutely had to include it because I know as a matter of fact that I was not the only returning soldier of my generation who developed a problem. Two that I knew personally died from taking opioids and another two have ruined their lives to such a degree that I have no doubt that there are times they wish they had. What weight would the personal oath I swore in Arlington carry if I cowardly avoided the darkest side of my character—especially when I know there are others who were so afflicted? It would be all too easy to cast aside these shortcomings, few could ever know the truth if I didn't tell it. But, in some sense, that would be a much graver sin than the ones put on display in these passages.

On the question of addiction, many of us had little say to begin with.

I didn't choose to be addicted—I didn't even understand the degree to which I was addicted! There was no true "first time" so to speak. I never had an opportunity to debate the potential pitfalls of drugs with a sober mind. The fact is, like with so many other soldiers, my addiction was little more than the tragic side effect of healing. I left Walter Reed taking 100s of milligrams of OxyContin a day. One civilian doctor told me that I had been prescribed dosages in multiples of what he wrote his terminal cancer patients. I didn't choose *that*. Neither did the thousands of other men and women who found themselves in similar circumstances. I did, however, make things much *worse*—and that can't be hung on anyone but *me*.

This caveat to the story is meant to be read as a sort of table setting, not an evasion of personal responsibility. I have learned many lessons throughout my journey, probably the most important of them being: taking ownership of one's failures is the best way to avoid making the same mistakes in the future. If there is a way to rationally place blame on another—or on fate itself—that is all the more reason to look inward for a culprit, because that knave is the only one you can reliably alter.

Amazingly, and much to my appreciation, while the physical therapy sessions gained steam my primary care physician was still just as interested in cutting my daily pill intake as I was. During the time that my physical therapist was using ultrasound technology to break down scar tissue, my primary care doctor had helped me cut out all but about three types of medication. The three that remained were digestion aides, blood thinners and opioids. The digestion aides were needed because narcotics can cause constipation, but they also eat away at the stomach lining which can lead to minor internal bleeding. Since I was on a hefty dose of blood thinners due to my previous bouts with blood clots, there was no such thing as *minor* internal bleeding in my case. Every cut or ulcer was a dangerous one for me and the digestion aides help reduce the risk of sores opening up in my digestive track.

Still, the way I saw it was, if we could get me off of the blood thinners and reduce the opioids, then the digestion aides would be irrelevant and I would be left with only one set of pills to take each day. That is not how he saw it, exactly. He thought it best that I keep both the blood thinners and the digestion aides at their current dosage while reducing the opioids. I then discovered that the idea of cutting my opioids was fine, but actually reducing them was not something I wanted to do. Talking about it was great, doing it was a different matter. I rejected this idea resolutely. I *needed* them, or so I imagined.

The hardest part of managing pain was not dealing with the sharp, often crippling surges, it was the constant aching. In retrospect, I think the most profound effect the OcyContin had was on my sanity. The continual—never ending—dull aches that engulfed my lower extremities, spine and right hand were psychologically torturous. If you've ever been in a situation where you were forced to push your leg muscles far beyond what you had previously thought possible, then you've felt a similar kind of torment. For those of you who like to exercise, just imagine the way your legs feel the day after 'leg day' and you will have some idea of what my legs felt like. The difference being that I felt like that every second of every day—and, the feeling was far worse than the one after a workout. Imagine a leg day that climaxed with a car crash that shattered your bones and poked over thirty holes in your muscles.

My legs cramped up every time I sat, like lactic acid had taken hold and deeply rooted itself. I often begged my body to metabolize the chemical intruder, but it just wouldn't. I tried to wait it out, but that didn't work either. Sometimes I stood up hoping to find relief in motion, but as soon as I did I was beaten back by wobbly, unsure joints and muscles. I forced myself to put one foot in front of the other and walk, but each time I tried I thought that the last step I took was one too far. If I tried to take another I was sure that I'd end up with a face full of carpet. Then I would turn around and go back to my seat, but no couch, no resting time, no amount of stretching lessened the restless, aching, almost itchy feeling in my legs. It wasn't exactly excruciating, but the utter lack of respite was brutal.

Another important difference between muscle fatigue and injury is that, for the athlete, this state can become almost enjoyable in short periods. Those of us who compete in athletics have to develop a slightly masochistic mind to appreciate the payoff at the end of the suffering.

One who reaches this state in a fashion that was self-induced, whether by completing a grueling, predetermined—personally planned—set of Olympic lifts or by being forced into a companywide ruck march, it is generally accepted that the reward will be new muscle growth and a strengthening of the mind that will make the task easier the next time around. In my situation, there was no guarantee that muscles were re-building. There might be no intrinsic payoff. My suffering could have been all for naught. It may have simply been that this pain was my new normal, *permanently.* What's more, my mind did not feel stronger while enduring this onslaught like it used to when I left the weight room; it felt weaker. Often, the pain alone was enough to make me want to give up. What was that about it all ending at the grave again?

All of these thoughts and concerns filled my head while I was talking to Dr. T, but I still wanted to get rid of *some* of my medication:

"Hey Doc, when can I get off of these gall-damned blood thinners?"

"We can talk about that. Why do you want to stop taking them?"

"Well, for one thing, I keep hearing that they're full of rat poison!"

"Many medications can have very adverse side effects, but we have to look at both long-term and short-term effects in a situation like yours."

"I am not going to lie to you, Doc, I have a drink or two every night. I know I am not supposed to. I understand that it is not good for my health, but I am not going to quit either."

"It is *very* dangerous to drink while on blood thinners, Braxton, and it's also against the law for you to consume alcohol."

"Doc, to be totally square with you, I really don't give a shit about the legalities of underage drinking right now. I have done my part for this country, the least it can do for me is let me have my whiskey when I want it. Besides, I will be 21 next month, anyhow."

What I wasn't telling him, though he might have known, is that I was drinking heavily every night. That meant not taking my nightly dose of the blood thinners the way I was supposed to. I guess, I hoped that alcohol ingested in large enough quantities would offset my skipping the second dose of meds. Being that I was drinking at a rate of nearly a half a fifth of bourbon per evening, the blood thinners were a huge concern. In truth, maybe he had even known already that I wasn't taking that medication properly. It must have shown in the blood work, but he had yet to say anything to me about it. Hell, maybe he had already started weening me off the pills and I just didn't know it. He had added a new antacid to my daily cocktail hoping that it would reduce the indigestion I complained about on every visit. Eventually, I pushed hard enough that he finally caved:

"Okay, we will have you weaned off of them by your birthday. Until then, I am going to have to insist that you stop drinking—or at the very least—cut back to just one cocktail per night."

"Deal."

I told him I would cut back, but I knew I couldn't live up to that promise. I said a lot of things I didn't mean during this time. This little black lie was just one among hordes.

That night an old friend from high school came over to visit us.[47] Since he had been over many times already, he was fairly up to speed on my medical woes. I told him about the conversation I had had with my doctor that morning. He laughed and told me I was a bit incorrigible, but that we should throw a little celebration for this much-welcomed milestone in my recovery.

We pulled my pickup truck up to the fire pit in my backyard and called every person we knew that may be willing to party on a weekday. By the time the fire had reached a blaze a few other friends started to show up. Everyone who came had already seen me many times since I had been home so I didn't have to retell my war stories like everyone seemed to expect me to on the first visit. I was always glad not to have to relive Iraq over a bottle of whiskey, at least not in public. We opened the doors of my truck, turned the radio up as loud as it could go and drank the night away. At some point between the drinking and the singing I brought up how much I hated my narcotics.[48]

"What kind of pills are you getting?" The first friend asked.

"OxyContin for long release stuff and Oxycodone for instant relief."

---

47 This person is going to remain undescribed and nameless for reasons that will be obvious. But, for the sake of keeping things very clear, this is not a person who has appeared in this book before this point.

48 Funny thing to say about a substance one isn't willing to give up.

The next time I went into the house to get a shot of whiskey my friend followed me. I leaned heavily into my cabinets as I let go of my left cane to free that hand to fetch the whiskey. I retrieved the bottle from the countertop. Then, because I had to do most things with only my left hand, I slid its base into my hip, then I used my right forearm to lock the bottle down. That made it so I could use my left hand to twist off the cap. I poured us each a shot of sour mash and smiled at him. He grabbed his glass, clinked with mine, and smiled back. Bottoms up.

"Good to have you home, man." He said.

"It's good to be home."

"I heard you out there talking about how sick your pills make you."

"Yeah, they do. I'd rather use whiskey if I had my druthers, really."

"You ever try taking them some other way?" He asked

"What do you mean?"

"Like, crushing them up. You ever tried to crush them up?"

"No."

I don't want to make myself out to be some kind of angel that I never was. I have done all manner of things in my life that I regret, but even though I had tried a few different drugs in my high school days like many other kids, I was still very naive when it came to narcotics. I never would have admitted that to him, though.

"Yeah, I have tried grinding up the white ones and dumping them into my coffee, but I really don't notice much of a difference when I take them like that. Other than it makes my coffee taste like shit." I replied.

"You never snorted those?"

"Nope," I said after a pause, "Show me how you do it."

I had seen it done before, but I couldn't remember how to do it. Again, not that I was going to let him know that and lose face. Whatever the hell that means.

When we got to my medicine cabinet I pulled out the instant release ten milligram pills, but he told me those were weak. I needed to be using the slow release higher dosage stuff. I grabbed the OxyContins, "the good ones," as he had called them and passed them over to him. He took out a dollar bill, a credit card and a lighter from his pocket then asked me for a CD case. I pointed him toward the case of the artist now blaring over the truck speakers outside: Hank III's album *Straight to Hell.*

Fitting enough, I thought to myself as he fetched it from the other side of the kitchen.

I watched as he popped the pill into his mouth thinking that he must be taking that one orally and then "doing" the another one. Soon my fascination at the idea of this guy popping pills and snorting others turned to anger: *is this dude stealing my pills right in front of me?!* I thought. He wasn't. He then spit the pill out of his mouth into a paper towel.

"Once you get it dry, the coating will be gone and you can crush it up."

I continued to observe as best I could as he folded the bill around the pill several wraps deep, like a piece of origami. The dollar was to serve as a simple, but effective cushion and buffer between the pill and his teeth for the next step. He then placed the mint paper pill container he'd created between his molars and bit down, crushing the pill into smaller, more manageable chunks.[49] The next step was to lay the bill down on the cd case and carefully unfold it with the bits of drug still safely within its center. After he had opened it up, presumably to show me what the bits should look like, he folded the dollar bill back over itself one time in the direction that was known in grade school as "hamburger style." Then he grabbed his lighter and rubbed it back and forth over the dollar with even pressure, just like you would if you were trying to copy a set of depressions onto blank paper with a piece of chalk.

When the drug had been ground to his satisfaction he tipped up the bill and rolled it back and forth between his fingertips spilling the ground up contents onto the cd case. Then he took a credit card and cut the pile into two lines of near equal length and width. I knew what the next step was, so I leaned away and retrieved the whiskey bottle again and poured us each another shot. He rolled the bill into a tight tube and pinched it between his fingers.

Liquid courage boosted by the shots we just slammed back did little

---

49 Because I have kids I was a little worried about describing this process in detail, but from what I understand, the FDA has changed the nature of these pills so they can no longer be crushed up like this. Further, the rate at which drug abuse evolves has likely rendered this process antiquated anyhow.

to calm the nerves I was feeling. I knew for certain the act I was about engage in was dangerous and stupid. I thought my heart was going to beat out of my chest. I slipped the rolled-up bill into my nostril, leaned my head over the CD case and slowly inhaled the lines.

The venom spread through my veins like a rattlesnake bite. For a moment I thought I might fall from the barstool I had drug over and made camp on. Within seconds of the initial crash of endorphins and narcotics, euphoria gripped me like a demon's promise: "Don't worry, it will be fun." The drug whispered its deceit throughout my entire body. A putrid flavor ran down the back of my throat. The dragon's kiss.

I felt more nauseous than I ever had before. It must have been written on my face because I heard him say:

"Just go puke, you'll feel better."

Isn't that why we are doing this in the first place, so I don't feel nauseous all the time?! I thought to myself. I really didn't care, the rush was worth the nausea. He was right anyway. After I vomited I felt better than I ever had in my entire life. The devil is Faustian.

I woke up the next morning, picked up the jug of urine I had filled the night before and wheeled myself into the bathroom. Though my consciousness was then mostly freed from the bondage of drugs and alcohol, my conscience was not. The good time had the night before left me with a splitting headache, flu-like symptoms, and more shame. I emptied the jug into the toilet, then my own bladder. I rinsed out the jug, set it on the floor, washed my hands and then wheeled myself into the kitchen.

Though I would never let anyone outside the walls of my own home know it, I still used my wheelchair almost every day. As long as I knew no one was going to show up, or see me through the windows somehow, I took full advantage of the relief and increased mobility my chair brought me. I could wheel around my house at least twice as fast as I could walk and it hurt less. Following physical therapy appointments using my chair also helped me reduce pain and swelling in my legs. The way I saw it, my wheelchair was a necessary evil, but what was left of my pride wouldn't allow anyone else to see me in it.

Rolling around the kitchen before I prepared a breakfast of coffee and oatmeal, I frantically searched the cupboards for my jar of pills. Then I saw them sitting out in the middle of the counter top next to a rolled-up dollar and a CD case. All three were soiled with dust from the previous night's sins. I examined the scene for a moment, remembering how good it had felt when that narcotic dusted the inside of my nose and lit up every dopamine depository in my brain. The memory of other-worldly euphoria and childlike comfort drew my thoughts in like a comet whose trajectory is slowly altered by the immense gravity of a thing much larger than itself. My eyes fixed on the CD case and the white powder. I began to daydream about doctors and family members confronting me about my drug abuse. I thought about how easy it would be to justify it to them in my mind, *The pills do make me feel sick. What business is it of theirs anyway? They're my pills. I will take them however I want to. What am I saying? I could probably end up in jail over this shit. No, I am not doing that anymore.* I grabbed the bottle, slid it between my forearm and torso and set the bottom of the jar on the armrest of my wheelchair. I pushed downward and twisted until the lid popped off. Then I spilt two pills onto the counter and popped them in my mouth. I chased them with water and proceeded to clean up the evidence as quickly as possible. I treated the kitchen as if it had been the scene of some serious crime (perhaps it had been). I wiped down every crevice that may have gotten the slightest pill residue on it. Then I ran the dollar bill under the faucet until I was satisfied that there would be no chalky remains left visible. Once satisfied that even a forensic team would have their work cut out for them in that kitchen, I wheeled myself into the bedroom and woke up my wife so that she could help me get to my appointments.

My desire to continue on was eroding. Many factors were contributing to this, like the impossibility of finding refrain from physical torment. But, my inability to come to terms with the fact that my best friends were still in harm's way living the Hell that was Ramadi in 2006 without me, and my own poor behavioral choices, were the worst of them. Once I had scrawled the timeless military mantra, "Death Before Dishonor," on the walls of my hooch in Iraq. Now, here on the home-front—where that code should be easiest to live up to—I failed, and I continued to fail every day. Over and over the surest form of justification ran through my head: *What does it matter anyway? I am already dead.*

CHAPTER THIRTEEN

Suicide Valley

All that he loves is now become a torment to him. The pin has been pulled from the axis of the universe. Whatever one takes one's eye from threatens to flee away. Such a man is lost to us. He moves and speaks. But he is himself less than the merest shadow among all that he beholds.

— Cormac McCarthy, *The Crossing*

Once I started abusing pain medication my mental health went downhill rapidly, but I didn't care. I felt nothing. Even chasing the dragon became a sort of mundane routine. Doctor appointments, visits with specialists, and physical therapy sessions were too similar to tell apart. The only piece of me that had grown was my opioid addiction. And, it had metastasized.

In the morning I'd wake up, wheel into the bathroom, grind up another OxyContin, and eagerly devour it as if it were cure to—rather than a cause of—my self-hatred. After my usual half-day's work at the hospital, I stopped by the liquor store and picked up a fifth of bourbon. Often times, feeling safely away from the presence of local law enforcement, I opened the bottle the moment I exited the freeway.

Most days I drove right past my house, headed for the nearest solitude I could find. I longed for a place where I could be alone, just me and my thoughts. The mountain range to the east of town filled this role nicely. Though the "East Hills," as most of us good ol' boys tended to call them, reached much lower than the ranges to the south and west of town, these mid-sized geological formations would certainly qualify as mountains to anyone born outside the North American Cordillera. Their peaks rise an average of about 8,000 feet above sea level. The slopes of these East Hills pitched less dramatically than those of the other mountain ranges in the area, but this didn't make them any more verdant, in fact, they are less so. Their sparse grasses betray their position as high-elevation desert ranges. Their sides are thickly covered in sagebrush, junipers, and pinyon pines, providing just the sort of seclusion, and in some sense iconic, landscape I was always looking for. But on this day, I decide to stop at home for a while before driving into them.

I pulled into my driveway and stared through the windshield at the horse pasture behind my house.

My thoughts nearly never left Ramadi. It was almost as if I still lived there in my mind. I had become bitter and angry. I hated everyone and everything around me. *Don't any of these assholes realize we are at war right now? Good men are dying in ungrateful countries half a world away. What the fuck is everyone smiling about?*

The only people I still loved were thousands of miles away and I had no way to talk to them. I suppose I could have sent emails, but I didn't really know how. Even if I would have applied my limited understanding of basic computer function to figuring it out, it would have taken me hours to type a single letter using only my left hand. What's more, there could be no guarantee that my friends had access to email.[50] Who has time to wait for a maybe? In essence, the only lifeline I really wanted to cling to—my brothers—was well outside of reach.

I slid my way out of the truck placing most of my weight on the cane in my left hand and the rest on my left leg. As had become my new normal, pain shot through my body. My hip wobbled. It couldn't handle the redistribution of weight. I let out a short groan:

---

50 During this stage of the war any time a soldier or marine from our base was severely wounded or killed Command would have the internet shutdown for 24 hours. They did this to ensure that the family of the deceased or tragically wounded would hear the news from military professionals, not via an email or phone call. It was a wise policy, my family even benefitted from it in a real way, but it often meant that the soldiers on Camp Ramadi had no access to email or phones for days or weeks on end.

"Fuck this shit!" I yelled aloud, broadcasting my complaint to God, the Universe, and whatever else may be listening.

Once out of my truck I used each of my canes to help drag me up the makeshift wheelchair ramp my step-father had crafted for my house. I must have looked like some kind of medical science experiment gone tragically wrong. I wore a thin, silk like glove to protect the damaged nerves in my right hand and wrist. Each knee was wrapped in a brace made of neoprene and hard plastic. Canes seemed to jut permanently from my palms like a sort of exoskeleton designed to make me a quadrupedal cyborg. Except that the creation that I had become clearly had no superhuman powers. Even the least perceptive of creatures could see that each of the trembling limbs I trudged awkwardly along with posed no threat to anything—other than myself.

I emerged from my home a short while later with my semi-automatic .45 caliber hand gun and fresh bottle of pills in tow. I climbed into my truck, yanked the lever into Reverse and started for my favorite little mountain valley in those East Hills.

During my high-school years my best friend and I had loved to drive up this one particular gravel road and cut fence posts or firewood. Other times, after fresh rain or snow had fallen, we drove up just to test out our four-wheel drives and swap stories. Sometimes we talked about girls we had known, or hunting or fishing trips we relished. We recounted times when we had been fortunate enough to see the other guy crash his motorcycle, or get tossed off his horse. In the past, it seemed the area always brought out the funnier and happier memories we had occasion to share, but now it just served as a comfortable place for me to go and think honestly about my future. Alone.

At the end of this road sat a little valley with an old homesteader's cabin at its mouth. Every time I looked at that rundown shack I thought about how much I envied the family that once inhabited it. The old home-sawed logs acted like a portal to the past. I wondered how they had lived their lives: *Did they stay up here with their livestock year-round, or did they winter back in town? They must have cut those logs from this area, was the valley floor once speckled with pines, or did they cut them from the peaks surrounding the place? How simple was life back then? Did they have to fight Indians for this land, or was it empty by the time they got here? I wonder if the Indians had any interest in this little round haven at all? There was hardly any water. There must have been even less game. Nah, no self-respecting Native would settle somewhere just to till up land. Those people were nomads, their men warriors. That is a life to envy, not sod-busting. What am I? Once I fancied myself a warrior; now I am nothing but a fragile, weak, COB*[51]

As my truck bounced along the road that bypassed the cabin I noticed a trail leading up over the valley's south rim. There's a valley on the other end of that jeep trail where my friend and I used to host some of the largest parties in the county. All summer long we cut big juniper trees and drug them to the middle of the valley and laid them out on an old cement pad in its center. The pad was built to cover an oil well, but no one had ever bothered to open the cap and pump out its contents. We took advantage of their labor and used it as a giant parking lot in the middle of nowhere. We lit huge bonfires with the junipers we had cut and invited every girl within 100 miles to come hang out with us. We never had to invite guys, they always heard about it through the female grapevine and invited themselves.

Looking at that trail acted as another gateway in my mind, this one to a time I had once actually lived. The junipers and sage functioned almost like a veil covering memories and secrets of a happier time in my life. Back when things were simpler. I kept hoping the sun might shine just right on its dusty face and whisk me back there. I daydreamed of a past when my body and mind didn't hurt anymore.

The sun beat down on the cab of my pickup truck, sweat poured out my body, but I hardly noticed it. I had become so accustomed to the climate in Iraq that even in the heat of a central Utah summer I rarely turned on my air conditioner. Most of my bourbon was already consumed. I had been sipping on it throughout the drive. I kept my truck rolling along the trails in the bottom of the first valley for a while, listening to music, wondering if I should climb the steep trail into the party

---

51 "Civilian on the Battlefield." A term we used to describe non-combatants during an engagement.

valley. I decided not to, it didn't much matter where I stopped anyway.

'Death Before Dishonor,' what a fucking joke. I was so juvenile before I was wounded. And, what honor had I left anyway? I lived at the mercy of suffering. A 5' 2" 110-pound girl helps me in and out of the shower. I am a 21-year-old geriatric. This is no life anyway.

I pulled my truck back up to the edge of the valley in front of the old cabin hoping that someone might find me before my decomposing corpse began to bloat. I didn't want my mom to have to deal with that image for the rest of her life. I retrieved my lighter, bill, credit card, cd case and OxyContin. I was ready to get on with it.

I kept pounding whiskey while I crushed up my narcotics. I was anxious to feel the warm blanket of euphoria their imperceptible chains would bring. Lines spread across the cd case placed in the middle of my center console. I rolled up an already chalky bill and snorted the first line. *I feel better already,* I thought to myself, as I chased it down with another swig of bottle I was holding between my knees.

My pistol sat on the passenger seat beside me. I reached over with my right hand, wrapped its two working fingers around the grip and pushed the frame into my thigh to stabilize it. Then racked the slide with my left hand. The gun now made ready, I set it on my lap, muzzle toward the front of the cab:

Never point a weapon at anything you are not willing to destroy.

I took up the bottle again and had another slug. I retrieved the loosely rolled bill and tightened it back into a cylinder. Then I placed it at the tip of my other nostril, leaned over and softly breathed in the last of my respite.

Ahhh.

Calm.

I stared over the dash board at the valley that had once held many of my fondest memories. The world around me slowly closed in. My eyes darkened. I fumbled for the pistol in my lap. I longed desperately for the bite of its cold barrel on the side of my head and the hot leaden delivery it could bring. Every ounce of my soul begged for its one-way ticket to anywhere but the nihilistic Hell I lived in.

***

My eyes opened some time later, a near empty bottle of whiskey on the floorboard and the song, *I Just Got Back From Hell,* by Gary Allen reverberating throughout the cab. My stomach churned, the world spun around me. I threw open the door hoping not to spill my guts inside the truck. I tried to step out, forgetting that my legs were too weak and broken to support me. I put my weight down on my left leg and collapsed onto my injured left hip. Vomit shot out of my mouth as I lay there writhing in agony.

I rolled around covered in my own stomach contents. Blood ran down my cheek from a cut on my forehead. More ran down my left arm from another cut on my elbow. I stopped rolling around and just lay there on my back for a while, staring up at the sun, wallowing in misery. Most of which I had brought upon myself. I was completely alone—just as I had *wanted.*

For a while I stayed right there on the ground using my right hand to shield the sun from my face. I felt sorry for myself. I'd been doing that for months. That's no solution. Once I had stared up at the sun using my right hand in this same way, feeling proud and strong. Now I felt like a coward for trying to finish what Haj had started. I tried to take the yellow way out. I had become too weak to handle the trials that men of war conquered so gracefully for eons before me. I was a disgrace to my family, my team, and my own name, and I *knew it.*

It felt like it took hours to struggle to my feet. I couldn't roll to my knees and just stand up from there like most anyone else could. Instead I rolled to my belly and low crawled in a small circle to the nerf bar under the driver's opening of my truck. I slid my hands onto the bar and pulled my hips underneath me, dragging mud and vomit as I my body slid around.

I once worked for a guy who used to say, "If you're going to do it right, you've got to get your ass behind you!" Which I think meant keep your center of gravity low and under control. I wondered for a moment if I had my ass correctly behind me, *What would Mike say about this position?* I tried to laugh a little as I struggled to my feet. *God, I could use a little of his humor right now.* Legs wobbling like a new born calf I clutched the steering wheel in my left hand and used my right elbow to pry myself into the cab.

When I got inside I located the pistol and unloaded it. I stuck it safely between the passenger seat and the center console. Then I tossed the bottle of whiskey out the open door and leaned back in the driver's seat to rest. As I lay there I saw all the faces of those I watched die prematurely, both friend and foe. I regretted every trigger I had pulled in anger, no matter how lawfully justified they had been. I shuddered at the thought of what my grandfather would say if he could see me now. I wondered how many people at home could see through my charade. Who knew the secrets I thought were hidden safely behind the mask I donned each morning?

My eyes drifted to my gauges when I decided it was time to go home. *Shit! I am almost out of fuel,* I thought to myself, just then realizing my truck must have idled there for hours.

The fifteen-mile drive back home dragged on. My thoughts drifted back to Arlington, the last place in time where I had felt strong and accomplished. I remembered again how it felt to recognize how minor my complaints truly were in the grand scheme of things. My sacrifices were so little when compared to what those Heroes had given. I was kicking away the blanket of freedom and security they provided me. "It is my duty to live for those who can't," I had once said. Who am I to be so selfish? *I was going to throw away my gift of life due to a little suffering?* "Who among them would not gladly trade places with me?" I said to myself, hoping that it would sink in again.

My commitment to those Heroes rekindled. Shame—the right kind of shame—the kind that expedites transformation—washed over me. Not long ago I had stood above their sacred resting places offering whatever small vicarious redemption I could, yet, I had failed at that promise. I had tried to quit my duty in its infancy: *Never again!*

I renewed my vows to them before God and whatever else was listening. I promised never to give in to the darkness again. Now, as I write this today, I wish so desperately that I could tell you *honestly* that I made good on this second oath, but I can't. That was not the last time I failed them, in fact, it was just one stumble among a multitude.

I was starting to feel a little better about myself. I had made a grave mistake, but luckily it hadn't been final. I watched as a semi-truck loaded with coal from a mine located near our mountain property in the La Sal Mountains pass by below me. They roll through my hometown in fifteen minute intervals. When I was a young boy we used wait until dark to climb up to the roof of the only restaurant in town. It was the best place to hide and shoot their trailers with paintball guns. Most times the drivers just sped on by probably never hearing the paintballs splattering against their rigs, but occasionally, the drivers slammed on their brakes. Soon as they did, we took off running through the night hopping fences and praying the cops would show up and make our lives exciting. I rarely see these trucks without thinking of it. I let this one go by safely. A little smile back on my face.[52]

"I have got to get my shit together." I say.

Gravel spun out behind my tires. I had thought the same thing many times before. Hell, this was not even the first time I had said it out loud, but this time I was hoping I meant it—*I didn't*.

---

52 The roller coaster that is PTSD is startling in retrospect, and it must be confusing to see in print. Maybe that is why it is hard to treat, and seemingly harder to define. It's a slippery thing. Some psychologists claim to have it all figured out, but I am not convinced anyone fully understands it.

CHAPTER FOURTEEN

Bright White Dress

It is only those who have not heard a shot, nor heard the shrills & groans of the wounded and lacerated (friend or foe) that cry aloud for more blood & more vengeance, more desolation.

I tell you, war is Hell!

–General William Tecumseh Sherman

Three weeks later I was lying back in the bed at a physical therapy session. We weren't really doing much with my right hand any longer, so I just plopped down, wrapped a pair of cotton and neoprene heating blankets around my quads and waited for Chris to come stretch them out.

"Braxton, how are you feeling this morning?" He asks.

"I am doing well, Doc. Surviving I guess."[53]

"Good. We are going to do something a little different today."

"Alright."

I followed him to the back of the room where the treadmills were located, but I didn't think for a moment that I would end up on one. He pointed at the treadmill. I was shocked, but willing to try. I handed him my canes and climbed aboard the machine. My feet stuck as they drug across the belt. I took ahold of the two hand rails straddling it so I maintained my balance just fine.

This is insane, I thought.

---

53 This was Chris, the physical therapist. I have a habit of calling all medical professionals "Doc".

A lot of time had gone by, many of the injuries were mostly healed, but a number of them had actually gotten worse. Namely, there was a sharp pain at the femoral head, just above my right knee. My inured hand was not getting a lot better either. There was little reason to think it would improve much more, but I wondered what his opinion was. I asked him why the hand still hurt. He told me that even though I have been wearing the gloves they issued me to protect the palm of my hand, I was asking it to bear far too much weight. That burden was slowly crushing a nerve that runs down the middle of my palm, causing not just delayed healing, but creating new damage to the nerve and bones and muscles. I nodded to him in a gesture suggesting that I understood.

He started the treadmill. It was turning at a pace your grandmother could keep up with, which was about all I could do. He asked whether I was okay. I said I was fine, so he walked away for a moment. He had sent an assistant to monitor my progress and to help me up in the event that I fell. *I am fine,* I think. *I don't need any help walking.* The thicker, broader, padded handles which run parallel to one another beside the treadmill offered much more comfort to my right palm. That allowed me to lift much of my weight and walk longer than I normally could. And since I was walking on a treadmill I was not responsible for my own propulsion, so I didn't tire out as quickly. *This is a good idea, actually,* I think to myself. Eventually I realized that I had walked hundreds of yards without stopping to rest—significantly farther than my usual average of 25-30 meter intervals.

"You ready for a break?" I heard Chris's voice coming from somewhere behind me.

Of course I was ready for a break.

"Your gait has improved a lot," Chris said, "How are you feeling?"

"I feel like I am moving better, but the pain is getting worse. I don't really know why."

I didn't want to tell him that I had stopped taking my pain medication altogether. It was a funny thing coming off those opioids for the first time. I felt terribly sick in the beginning, I vomited repeatedly and sweat constantly, but as for the horrendous body aches reported by so many other addicts trying to curb the habit, well, I didn't have that problem.

I think largely because my body already ached all the time, how much worse could it get?

About a week after the drug faded from my system I felt like a thick fog had lifted. The whole world looked different to me. It was as if I had been living with a stigmatism, and quitting the pills was like donning prescription lenses. Everything was just *clearer.* The only emotions I really felt during that time were anger and depression (somehow, I could always laugh when things were funny, though; laughter is a beautiful reprieve), but even they became easier to regulate once the drug was gone.

Chris told me that if pain was my biggest concern, my condition must be improving. I knew he was right. It used to be that pain was the thing I complained most about, but mobility really was the chief problem. When I had first started walking again my legs just would not move. It felt like I was trying to walk in a Jujitsu GI that was sopping wet. I have heard this described by others as trying to walk with heavy ankle weights on, but that just didn't describe my situation adequately. When I tried to take steps, it felt like my legs were meeting resistance from every angle, not just being pulled down by the effects of gravity.

After a few minutes rest Chris said I should get back on the treadmill and try again this time at a faster speed. I reluctantly agreed. He upped the velocity and I did my best to keep one foot in front of the other, leaning heavily on the parallel bars as I went.

The belt was moving under me at what felt like a pretty good clip, probably as fast as a normal individual walks. Then he reached over and sped up the belt again. My palms started sweating making it harder to grip the bars. I forced more weight down on them hoping gravity would anchor me in place as I tried to keep up with the machine. My arms started shaking, it was clear that my upper body had greatly atrophied as well. I wanted to give up, but I was afraid that I would fall. I knew that my legs couldn't support my full body weight or keep up that pace. Something had to give. Chris reached over and increased the speed again. My upper body was convulsing like it was in its final shivers before hypothermia set in. I lifted more weight up with my arms, hardly any was on the treadmill at this point. Chris reached up and increased the speed again. I lifted what must have been *all* of my body weight onto my hands. My feet skipped off the belt. I was not even walking anymore, rather watching my legs bounce off the rolling black belt beneath me almost like I was *jogging*.

Each time one of my feet hit the belt it sent a jolt throughout my entire lower body. It started to feel more like I was trying to hold onto a jackhammer than run. The pain went from dull to sharp and abrupt. My arms were about to give out. I started to get really mad at Chris. I was swearing at him inside my head then. *This guy is an idiot! What the hell is he thinking?!* My shoes were barking every time they touched the belt.

"Why don't you just jog?" I heard him say.

"Because I can't, Chris!"

"Why not? It would be easier to jog." He said.

He was right and I knew it, but I was way too stubborn to admit it. *I wish I would have taken a pill before I came here,* I think to myself.

"I can't jog, Chris, I don't know how." This was the first time I realized that part of the issue was I had forgotten *how* to jog. The idea that I couldn't remember how to jog sounded stupid to me, but somehow I knew it was true.

"Try." He says.

My arms couldn't hold me up anymore. There was nothing left to do but try, so I did.

It rapidly became clear to *everyone* that I indeed could not jog.

Not only could I not handle the pain of jogging, but it was true—I *had* forgotten how to jog. My muscles had lost most of their coordination. Legs awkwardly skipped off the belt. I was basically falling and catching myself over and over again rather than running.

Chris reached over and pulled the bright red emergency stop cable out of the front of the machine. The tops of my shoes dragged the belt to a stop. My upper body was still shaking, barely keeping my body suspended. Chris reached up, grabbed me under the arm and helped me down. I was angrier with him than I had been before, so I didn't want his help. *Don't touch me!* I thought. Unfortunately, I had no choice, I needed his help.

"Okay, that is enough for today." He says.

It would be almost seven years before I jogged again. The next time, however, I did fine. In fact, I eventually ran—and very nearly *won*—a duathlon.

During the drive home I noticed that my leg felt *different*. The head of my right femur was hot, not in a searing way, but in a way that reminded me of standing next to a bonfire in the winter. Heat radiated from the front of the leg to the colder feeling backside. I knew something was wrong, and I knew that I could practically pinpoint the problem area, but I had no idea what the cause of that heat was. Below the leg of my shorts swelling was visible and voluminous. Inflation after PT was normal, but this was not.

The skin around the top of my knee looked pink, almost as if it were showing the first signs of a developing heat rash or staph infection. Maybe it *is* just a heat rash, I wondered.

It was nearly an hour drive back to my house, but it seemed like an eternity. My quads twitched and jerked involuntarily. In Walter Reed I had been diagnosed with Restless Leg Syndrome, which is another "disease" that, to me, seems more psychological than it is physical (which does not make it any less *real*). The exact cause of the syndrome put aside, I was used to these nearly impossible-to-control convulsions. They were nothing new. I decided to try not to make too much of it.

When I got home I hobbled to my kitchen and plopped down into the comfort of my wheelchair. I rolled myself into the living room turned on the TV and elevated my legs. "I can't believe how much this hurts." I said to the empty room surrounding me. The pain kept creeping in. I decided to call my primary care doctor and ask for advice:

"Go ahead and take an extra instant release pain pill. It sounds like you had a hard day at PT."

"Alright. Anything else?"

"Keep your legs elevated and rotate cold treatments in twenty minute intervals," he suggested, "if the pain and swelling doesn't subside by tomorrow morning we will refer you to a specialist."

I thanked him and hung up the phone. The last thing I wanted to do was pop a pain pill. I knew I didn't *need* to take them anymore. I was sure that those little pills were ruining my life one hit at a time, but

I didn't want to say that to him, because I knew that as soon as I did he would stop prescribing them to me. I liked to have them around. I wanted to be in control of the decision, and, like Frodo standing inside Mount Doom, I wasn't quite ready to let go of My Precious.

The debate raged inside my mind as I watched Oliver Stone's classic *Platoon* for what must have been the hundredth time. A few minutes into the movie was the famous first firefight scene. I watched SSgt. Barnes cover his wounded machine gunner's mouth and aggressively whisper "Shut up and take the pain!" In that wounded soldier's bloodied face, I saw my own, like the Barnes' character was talking to me in some sort of philosophical way. I decided I needed to do the same.

Later on came the part of the movie where the troubled platoon descends upon a Vietnamese village and massacres them. I knew from first-hand experience that things like that didn't happen often in war. The picture is rarely that clear. The line between good and evil is not so starkly drawn in violent confrontation.

Once in Iraq I had been posted near a main thoroughfare for a couple weeks. One day while manning my position several rounds smacked into the large concrete barrier I was using for cover. The Northern Cheyenne Warrior, Wooden Leg, once recounted the hum of incoming small arms fire as sounding: "like a swarm of angry bees." These rounds were among the first that had ever been fired directly at me and I can think of no better way to describe them. The buzzing followed a sharp cracking sound when they slammed into the cement wall, but when they missed the wall and were closer to my head, it was a buzzing sound followed by the bark of the rifle's muzzle. The copper jackets ripped away from the projectiles and spattered the ground around me. I looked toward the sound of the rifle's reports, but the only vehicle on the highway was a large truck towing a flatbed trailer. On top of the bed of this trailer was what looked like a wedding party. Most of the men in the party held Kalashnikov's, their muzzles pointing upward, firing celebratory shots into the sky.

"Where the *fuck* are the rounds coming from," I yelled. No one knew for sure.

I trained my rifle on the group and watched them more closely. Then

I saw some of them lower the barrel of their weapons a fire a few more rounds at us. Each widely missed our position—but the next volley might *not*.

I slipped my finger into the trigger guard of my M-4, flipped the safety lever and began to squeeze the trigger. My mouth dried out. My eyes widened, but my focus narrowed. I couldn't see anything in my scope but what looked like a woman in her wedding dress. Everything else was a blur.

I couldn't tell if my heart was racing or whether it had quit beating altogether. The muzzle of my rifle lifted sharply. The stock beat gently into my shoulder. The controlled explosion of my ammunition made no audible noise. I felt a rush of heat flow through me. My pores opened widely, sweat seemed to cover me all at once. Between the jerking of my scope I saw only blank faces holding their weapons—and that *dress*.

I did everything within my power to keep the dress away from the bright red dot I used to deal out my revenge. The truck picked up speed, most of the people on the trailer fell to their knees. I kept firing until I was sure there were no more weapons pointed at me. When the truck was out of sight I stepped back behind the barrier and shook. My stomach churned. *I am going to throw up*, I thought. Then, I felt a rush of excitement, almost ecstasy. I am *still alive.* The feeling soon faded and the sickness set in again. My throat tightened up. It was almost impossible to breath. I felt like a truck was parked on my chest. *Did I kill any of them?* I never found out.

Platoon played on in the background. I found myself identifying with Chris' rage. I never shot at the feet of an innocent civilian like he did, but I knew the *fury* that fueled the dance. The line between good and evil is a myth; in war, there are no superheroes, only men, and sometimes both sides prove it.

I need a drink. I wheeled into the kitchen poured a shot, downed it, then poured myself a glass and wheeled back into the living room to finish the film. After about my fourth or fifth glass, during the final combat scene in the movie, I caved. The instant the opioid hit my bloodstream relief washed over me like a warm sun in spring time. I welcomed my old friend back with arms wide open. I saw his chains clearly this time around, I knew what the demon would do, but the psychological relief was worth the binding. I shackled myself—*Happily.*

CHAPTER FIFTEEN

Bitter Asshole

You will not be punished for your anger,
you will be punished by your anger.

—Buddha

I pulled on my shorts and studied my legs. I already knew there was no chance that I would be able to finish physical therapy that day. My right leg was still pink and swollen. It was too early to reach my doctor's office by telephone, so I just continued dressing and drove the hour north to the hospital.

When we arrived, we informed the receptionist that we needed the doctor to inspect my leg and refer us to a specialist. He looked it over and sent us on our way to a specialty clinic in Utah County.

The CT scans confirmed what we already knew: Most of the fractures in my legs had healed, but there was one which had not. Just above my right knee my femur was still broken. The rod had held the fracture in place much better than a cast would have, but even after more than a year's time the bone had not formed a union. The orthopedic specialist talked about some surgical options, but said none of them really made sense in my case. The most efficient and productive path forward was to stay off my feet and allow the body time to heal. That news made it feel like I was about to start all over again, only this time with an easier beginning.

Winter came early that year. It was bitter and long. Cold winds blew so frequently that it had become common place to hear of a few calves, or even colts freeze to death over the course of the night. Our neighbor who had bred a couple mares to our stud lost the colts to the cold in early spring. Their wet hides froze to the earth before they could stand up. One week in February I checked the thermometer every morning, never once finding it above twenty degrees below zero.

These cold fronts and winter weather kept me shut up inside day and night. In my waking hours, I stared out the window at dark and frigid skies. When I lay down to rest, the freezing world around me was replaced by 130 degree memories and nightmares.

I felt as if my life was constantly on the brink of an unforeseeable, but impending doom.[54] As if to confirm the suspicion, one day in a grocery store parking lot I stuck my cane onto the ground to help support my weight while I slid out of my pickup truck. Unknowingly, I had centered the black rubber tip of the cane in a patch of black ice. When I shifted my body weight onto the cane it slipped out from underneath me and I tumbled from the truck onto the asphalt parking lot. Torment shot from my lower back to the tips of my extremities. I lay there on the frozen ground for a while, unsure whether I could get up on my own accord. Rolling over to attempt it only made matters worse. When my torso twisted, another sharp pain sprung from my lower back. I knew something was injured. I struggled my way back into the cab, never retrieving the produce I had gone for, and drove home. All night I cringed any time I had to move. The next morning I rushed to see my doctor as soon as the clinic opened. He looked me over and then ordered some x-rays be taken of my low-back: I had a new fracture in my lumbar spine.

Depression brought me back to the blanket of the bottle and the brief bliss of medication. My hospital visits were shrunk from five days a week to three, but physical therapy was virtually nonexistent. The only thing that got me out of bed each day was my hatred for the sheets. I did nothing but watch movies, play my guitar, and drink whiskey. Rock bottom is a slower and softer landing than one may think. That's why we

---

54 This dark winter and drug abuse, however ironically, is where I first began to write this book. It has taken many forms since then, most of them not worth the paper they were written on. But, I have changed, and so did the manuscript: both for the better.

keep chiseling away at the bedrock.

Whether it was PTSD, or seasonal depression, or the crushing weight of uncertainty, I could never say. But one thing was for sure: I was alone, just like I had wanted. The drugs destroyed my personality and sapped my strength. The constant, nagging, physical pain was still torturous. Even the drugs stopped providing relief. I had reached my breaking point again.

Depression and sleep deprivation soon took my downward spiral and directed it toward hatred and anger. I hated every single person around me, wife and family included. I never hit my wife, or behaved in any kind of violent way, but I was a complete asshole to her. I often yelled, said things I didn't mean, and some that I did. We were young and our relationship had been rocky since the beginning. The only time we had lived in any kind of peace with one and other was at Walter Reed, and even that was not full-time. I used that history as an excuse to ignore her feelings. I knew I was being harsh with her and I didn't care.[55]

"Don't you see?" I yelled. "I don't give a fuck about you, or anything else! I am sick of all of this!"

Her eyes welled up with tears, "I hate you too!" she screamed back at me, slamming the door behind her.

Watching her walk out the backdoor of our little house felt like the release of a burden, not an added insult. In the back of my mind I knew I was awful. She would be better off just about anywhere other than where I was. Why one would willingly choose to suffer with a person as rude as I was in their house I will never know, but she did. For far too

---

55 My ex-wife and I have a child together. For this reason I have intentionally avoided airing any of her trespasses. Further, this book is about me, not her. I feel I only have copyright to my own life and my own mistakes; that doesn't mean she made none. In defense of her I would say that some of the mistakes she made were simply products of youth and war. To be married so young and expect mature behavior from a spouse is ridiculous. On top of all that, by this point in the story we had suffered more affliction than a normal couple should at any age. It would have taken saintly and super-mature people to overcome them, neither of us were that. We are only human and humans are flawed.

In this story I will air my side of the wrongdoings—and they were many—but no one else's, I hope you can understand why.

long.

She came back after a few hours. Our altercations resumed almost instantly. We fought on an almost daily basis. I often hoped she would leave for good. She had a family back in Minnesota, they loved her, that is where she should have been. Sometimes when she would walk out I wondered if there would ever be another young woman willing to love a crippled wretch like me; usually though, I just plain didn't give a shit. I hated her, and she hated me.

Better to live alone than to live like this, I thought.

The harshness of the winter hit some of its worst in January; so too did our fighting. The first week of the month was the worst. Now that I have had occasion to study a bit of psychology, I realize that much of this was likely due to the fact that January 5th was approaching, the day the suicide bomber detonated his vest at the Glass Factory. The anniversary of my so-called "Alive Day." I hardly felt that way.

When the 5th came around things felt really strange for me. I was more anxious and angry than normal. I hardly even finished my breakfast before I wanted to be drunk. Aside from anger and despair, my emotions usually felt very flat, almost unchanging. My baseline was bitterness and I rarely deviated from it. But this day was different, this day I just felt: sad.

I decided that I wanted to go shooting, so I grabbed a couple of rifles a bottle of bourbon and my cd case. I hobbled around making several trips to the truck to haul all my things. Once loaded up, I turned the ignition in my truck and took the dirt road south of town toward the gravel pits.

Some sad old country song played on the stereo, probably Waylon Jennings, or Chris Ledoux, since that was about all the music I listened to in those days. My mind drifted back to Iraq and the men we lost there. Anguish set deeper than normal.

Fuck it, I thought to myself. I reached for the bottle of whiskey, spun the cap off and let it fall to the floorboards of the pickup. It was almost like I was signaling to God and myself that I had no intention of saving any for later. After swilling a few large chugs off the bottle, I grabbed my AR-15, rested it on the window seal of my driver's side and shot some old swallows' nests out of a dirt cliff.

The rifle lightly bounced off my shoulder. The report of its muzzle echoed in its familiar voice. It was almost as if it spoke what I had hoped it would: "It is all going to be okay".

The smell of burning cordite filled the air around me dragging my mind to unwelcome memories of combat in Ramadi. The comfort it had brought quickly faded to darkness. Suddenly, my trigger felt hot and heavy, like something in my body was begging me to stop. I flipped the rifle's safety lever to its appropriate position and set it back in the truck.

I sat there for minute shaking my head as if the twitch was going to fling bad thoughts from my mind. The whiskey bottle in the cup holder grabbed my attention. I pulled it from its seat and took another chug. Then I saw my pill jar. I reached for it and took one out. Then I pulled out my wallet and crushed the pill. *Just this once,* I thought, *it is my anniversary, after all.*

If there is such a thing as the Christian's concept of the Devil, opioids and alcohol are some the best tools he employs to capture weakened men. The instant euphoria softly whispers its lies to the heart:

"*There are no problems I cannot solve.*"

Addiction snags you at your weakest times like the wolf kills a buffalo. The wolf waits until the bison's gait is crippled, or the snow is deep enough to entrap him, then he pounces. Usually he hamstrings the animal first; then slowly and methodically he gnaws away flesh until his prey expires.

Other times the drug calls like the Sirens to Odysseus. Its lies are sung to you from a distance at first, drawing you in and then dashing your ship and body on the rocks. Modern medicine brings the evil to you in little pink capsules and there is no way to plug your ears. Still, in its carol is *bliss*. Even while you're thrashed about in rough seas.

When I returned home it was about noon and I was already an inebriated mess. I walked through the door, canes and bourbon in tow. The smell of whiskey radiated from my pores:

"Hey Braxton, I have something to tell you." She said.

She must be leaving for good this time, I thought, *she's unemotional. It is for real this time. Am I okay with that? I have wanted to leave her dozens of times, but am I really okay with it? Yeah, I think I am. How will her family take it? Will I remain friends with her brothers? Her dad? No. Maybe they already know that we fight all the time; they must.* Thoughts swirled about my head.

"I think I am pregnant," She said.

"*What*?"

"I am pregnant! Aren't you happy about that?!" She said smiling.

"Of course, I am happy!" I acted as if I were.

I took another shot of bourbon. *Is it even mine?* I wondered.

I wanted to be a father badly, God only knows why. I wasn't fit to be one. Still, I was indeed very happy that I may be fulfilling that wish, but was this really the best time? Was I with the best person for me, or her the best person for her? The answer to both questions was clearly no. Less than a week before we had been fighting nearly every day. We told each other that we hated one and other—and we *meant* it. Each of us had uttered the word "divorce" aloud. Now we were going to have a baby.

But, is it even mine? I wondered again. *Can I ask for a paternity test? What kind of father will I be if I can hardly even walk?*

I stayed there, locked inside my own head, drinking for the rest of the day. The only difference was now I could call it celebratory. I was still living in Ramadi, but the idea of an innocent baby gave me real hope. Maybe this is the answer to the prayers I wish I'd sent.

CHAPTER SIXTEEN

A.V.M.

Children are the keys of paradise.

– Eric Hoffer

The first few months of pregnancy went smoothly. My wife had quit drinking, of course, so she had commanded that I quit as well. It was a good thing for us both. When we were both sober we hardly fought at all. I think it was still clear that this marriage was not meant to last, but for a time—only when we were *each* sober—the marriage was livable. Things were okay at home. I was excited to welcome my first child into the world. If I could have known then how special she would be to me, I may have shook the war much sooner than I did.

Like all expecting parents much of our conversation was fixated on names and what the baby's future might be like. It was going to be so fun to fix up her room, to shop for baby clothes, to read her books, to watch her first steps. I couldn't wait to see her smile, or hear her laugh.

When we finished up Amy's first real ultrasound the conversations became much more serious. I'll never forget the feeling I had when that Radiologist said:

"Oh, there is a little labia."

"What the hell is a labia?" I said stupidly.

"It's a girl, Braxton." Amy said in her typical patronizing manner.

When the ultrasound was finished we walked across the hallway to our doctor's office:

"Looks like it is a girl. I am sure you are both very happy about that!"

The Certified Nurse Midwife said.

"Yes, we are!" I confirmed.

"Everything looks pretty good, but I think we may need to send you to a specialist to check on a few things." The Midwife said.

"What kind of *things*?" I asked

"Well, it looks like she has something going on with her heart—don't be alarmed, though. Ultrasounds are not a perfect scan…and she may have a cleft palate. We need to send you to a specialist to have this all checked out so we know where you're going to have to give birth. We can't operate on the cleft palate here, so you may have to go into labor in Provo where they have surgeons who work on that issue."

Amy cried almost all the way home. Who could blame her? She was ready to welcome a perfect little angel into the world and she'd just found out that her baby might have some serious complications.

I tried to convince her that it would all be fine. Kids are born like this all the time, I said. There's nothing to worry about. Inside my mind, however, I was getting irritated that she was so concerned with the cleft palate when the doctor had clearly said there may be a problem with our baby's heart. It felt like naked vanity to me. A cleft palate is not so life-threatening in the 21st century, why is she so fixated on that?!

Looking back on it now I think she was probably just as worried about the potential heart condition as I was. Her focus on the cleft palate was only because a lay observer can't *see* a heart problem; therefore it is harder to grapple with. Heart conditions lie under the surface of a body, they're in some sense out of sight, out mind. A cleft palate is a visible deformity and the mother must look at it every moment wishing she could give her own flesh to help repair the child's. Earlier in this book we talked about how Aleksandr Solzhenitsyn wrote that each person sees the Universe as if they are at the center of their own. I think this is true of men and women for the most part, but its veracity seems to break down in the case of mothers. If I have learned anything from observing my own mother's life, it is that she very firmly places her children at the center of her Universe; she casts herself in only a supporting role. I am sure this is equally true for most all mothers. Amy was no different.

A month or two later we were at the specialty clinic getting a more sophisticated ultrasound performed on our baby. They immediately confirmed that the baby was a girl, not that there had been any doubt, and that the midwife's initial suspicion at the claim of heart complications was an inaccurate one. Our baby's heart was going to be fine—probably.

We were still going to need special instruments on hand during the labor process, but we could give birth at our local hospital. More good news was that our baby wasn't going to need the emergency surgery on her palate that we thought she might; instead it was only her lip that was cleft. That surgery was not life threatening and could be fixed after she reached six weeks-old. What a relief! Not so for her mother, though. Amy was happy that our little one's heart was *probably* fine, but she was absolutely devastated at the thought of her child growing up with a scar on her face:

"It is just a scar, Amy! The baby will be fine." I said angrily.

"You don't know what it is like to be a girl, Braxton. She'll get picked on her whole life!"

God, she is such a petulant child, I thought to myself. *Why am I still with her?! Don't they say it is better for the kids if parents who hate each other separate?*

I was angry at her for what I saw as childish vanity, but looking back I see that she was right to some degree. School-aged kids are harsh. A baby with a surgical scar on her face probably does become the butt of unspeakable jokes and ridicule. I just didn't see that as the larger of the two problems and I was so inclined to bitterness that most all the positive world fell into my blind spot.

Maybe this is just demonstrative of the differences between the sexes, rather than a case of right or wrong. Males do seem to be more practically minded. We seem to have a tendency to focus on the functional aspects of being; whereas, females seem to have a keener eye for the social world. She saw the would-be scar as an irrevocable ticket to the horrors of adolescent mockery. I saw the harm a faulty machine as important as the heart would cause, but not what psychological torment a scar could usher in. We were both focused on our baby's health, but in different ways. No matter how I tried—and I didn't put a lot of effort into it—I couldn't see her side back then. I saw only childish vanity. I was wrong to see it that way, I think, but that is how I viewed it and I'd be lying if I said it didn't bother me.

We spent the next few weeks at home trying to figure out what we were going to do. Luckily, when the Army retired me I was able to keep the equivalent of Active Duty health insurance, so we didn't have to be overly concerned about the finical burden of surgery. It would cost us thousands of dollars, sure, but it wasn't going to be *tens-of-thousands*. We would struggle, but we could get by, I thought.

That left us only to deal with the emotional bits. I started to notice billboards and ads which talked about babies with cleft lips and palates. I'd never seen them before, but they had always been there. Sort of like when you buy a new car thinking it is rare and then you drive down the highway and see a dozen of them. In fact, it feels like every other car is the same as the one you just bought. Then, in a fashion that was all too typical of myself back then, I wondered what *I* had done to *deserve* such a fate. I decided to stop mentioning it to Amy, but I was still very worried about my daughter's potential heart condition. It terrified and *enraged* me.

I recall a neighbor of ours, a good friend of my mother's, who was diagnosed with breast cancer far too young saying: "God only gives us what he thinks we can handle." I didn't believe that; in fact, I had given up believing in God altogether. The very idea of such an utterance infuriated me. What kind of monster would start a child off in the world that way simply because he thought her *strong* enough to handle it? If there had ever been an anecdotal case against God with real weight, it was this one, I thought.

My wife was a Roman Catholic. Her mother was a deeply devout and wonderful woman. One day I sat on my porch and called her on the phone to talk about it. I tried to convey the way I felt in an honest, but delicate manner. She very calmly answered by saying something to the effect of 'Everything happens for a reason. We may not understand that reason, but God does and you'd be wise not to question that.' Then she went on to tell me that I was probably still just angry about the war and I was using this as a justification to direct that anger toward God. This did not sit well with me back then. Now, when I look back I see just how perceptive she was.

When the day finally came and my wife was going to be induced I knelt down and said a little prayer in the bathroom. I told God I was sorry for all the wrong I was doing in the world and begged that he help my baby be born with a healthy heart, "If you exist at all," I said at the end. After all, she had done nothing to deserve such tribulations.

Had a person met me in the hallway of that hospital and asked whether I believed in God, I would have told him that I believed in a God of the Gaps, or perhaps Spinoza's God. But, that's not how I *acted.* I acted as if I was a true believer, and in hindsight, I think the way a person acts says a lot more than their mouth will.

I stepped out of the bathroom and into the delivery room. An anesthesiologist came and administered an epidural. Then we waited. And waited. Twenty hours later a doctor was in the delivery room putting monitors on the baby checking her heart. Apparently, they had spotted another abnormality during delivery. The scare lasted only a little while. After a few extra tests they found that not only was her little heart beating just right, but her lip was fine too. They speculated that perhaps she had just been squished inside my wife's body in such a way that it made her lip look cleft when it was not.

I watched for a while as my sweet little girl lay on her mother's chest. They had been through a long and hard delivery together. My wife had spent almost an entire day in labor; I could hardly imagine how hard that must have been on her. I was so glad the baby was healthy. It is amazing how much a parent can love a child. I loved her already. I would have happily died for her. I still would. But in that moment, as I sat there watching them, I realized something was still wrong. Not with her—with *me.*

I have previously mentioned other times when I thought that I may have been afflicted by PTSD. Many times my subconscious registered a symptom of the disease that I'd read about or my therapist had mentioned. Who could miss the unwelcomed memories at inopportune times, or the never-ending need to suppress unprovoked anger, or the nightmares, or the illogical moments of panic? I had denied the existence of my illness for many reasons, but the most important was that I did not want to be associated with many of the others I had seen receive VA pensions for the disease. I knew of a guy who had worked a laundromat in Iraq, he got a rating of 80% disability for PTSD. For what experience *exactly*? I wondered. Another guy I heard of had been found 100% disabled from the trauma of answering *radio transmissions* from soldiers in combat! How could a person be so soft that they were damaged by the *sounds* of combat, I wondered bitterly?

During my transition there seemed no less noble an act than claiming to suffer from PTSD. It wasn't just seen as an illness that plagued the weak, it was in many cases an illness *claimed* by liars, whether they were weak or not was unimportant. I had made many mistakes, and acted cowardly and lied many times in my life, but I had no desire to have those descriptors permanently enshrined in my records. At least that was the way I saw it back then.

The problem with the discussion of war and the combat stress that accompanies it is: The discussion is driven by well-meaning but ideological clinicians, and soldiers who are the least likely to have it. I never wanted to look like one of those types. The greatest internal conflict arose when I saw the birth of my child and did not feel the emotions I knew I should have felt, or at least I always heard I should feel. Something was wrong in my head and it was no longer deniable in any honest sense. I had known exactly how I felt when I was angry at God, anger was an emotion I still fully recognized, but I couldn't understand why I didn't feel anything else. I wanted to feel happy. I couldn't and I didn't know *why*.

I it must be that I have PTSD, I knew it then, but because of the stigma attached to the disease I refused to accept it, so I lied to myself about it—for years. I wouldn't recommend lying to yourself. It calls forth monsters.

My wife and I went back to fighting as soon as we started drinking again. She'd sometimes drink a glass of wine a day because she'd read somewhere that it was *good for* the baby if the mother drank a little wine while breast feeding. When she wanted to have a party or drink more she would be responsible and pump enough milk to satisfy the baby while she enjoyed herself. I hated that she did it, but who was I to say anything? I was drinking too. Not that it stopped me from yelling at her about her habits. I wouldn't miss a chance to express my distaste for her.

Once the baby was finished breast feeding we both started drinking again and that led us back to fighting constantly. We weren't overly irresponsible or anything like that. We were not inebriated without someone else, like one of her grandmothers or aunts for example, watching the baby. We didn't put her at risk by any means, but I would never do a thing like that again. I cherish the time I have with my kids too much to waste it on alcohol. I wish I had been mature enough to realize that ten years ago, but I wasn't.

The thing about heavy drinking is it doesn't just affect you while you're drunk. The effects linger. They cause emotions that last long after the headaches are gone. Those types of negative emotions eroded what little relationship foundation we had. Somehow, we made it through the first year of our daughter's life. I got to be there for her first words and her first steps. I got to see her rubbing her first birthday cake all over herself and her highchair. I became used to hearing her little footsteps stumble along our hardwood floors. She became my little friend. But, eventually, I think for the better—for us all—her mother and I divorced.

Watching my ex-wife pull out of my driveway in that Chevy Trailblazer we bought back in Virginia, knowing she was going to be taking my precious little girl 1,300 miles away to Minnesota, was one of the worst days of my life. My heart still breaks every time I think back on it.

CHAPTER SEVENTEEN

Debauchery

My candle burns at both ends,
It will not last the night,
But ah my friends, oh my foes,
It gives a lovely light.

— Edna St Vincent Millay

If you thought that the heartache of divorce and the departure of my beloved child would have caused me to take a long, hard look at myself, you would be wrong. Addiction is often somewhat accurately described as a slippery slope that descends into Hell on earth, or a personal purgatory of a sort, and—it *is* that. But, it's hard to feel the steep grade when you've first begun the declension, because self-destruction can be *fun* (at least in the immediate sense). In fact, the slippery slope is almost impossible to recognize, because hedonism and self-indulgence provide immediate gratification. The rush and excitement and euphoria make it difficult to dig in one's heels and change course—and why would you want to change your lifestyle if you've got no respect for your future? The simple, perhaps sad truth of it is that debauchery can be a plain ol' good time for a while. For about seven years, I lived in Hell and sometimes—*relished it.*

My daughter's visits home were my only reprieve from the perpetual state of heavy alcoholism I thought I loved. I stayed bone sober when she was at my house. I don't think I behaved responsibly around her necessarily because I was striving to be a virtuous parent; rather, it was because I loved her more than the alcohol and drugs. A truth that could not be said about myself. I hated the fact that I was missing so many beautiful milestones when she was with her mom and I didn't want any milestone to slip by me while she was home. Luckily, every fifth week I could get her for two weeks, and honestly, those two weeks of sobriety are probably the only thing that enabled me to get enough work done to keep making my mortgage payments. Even that wouldn't last. Eventually, when she was in school, I only got to see her during her summer vacations and Christmas break, and that's when things really went downhill.

When Amy and I had finally separated for good it was near Halloween time, and it just so happened that one of my old friends from high-school divorced his wife at about the same time. Woodrow and I exchanged text messages about our newly single status:

"I am a free man, pard!"

"Me too!" Woodrow replied.

On our first night out together we went to a bar in a town about an hour away from of ours. From my experience over the years it seems like nearly everyone in my generation goes through a manic phase when a long-term relationship ends. These phases are punctuated by moments of grief, sure; but rather than confront that grief all at once and be done with it, most turn to social events and alcohol (or drugs—or *both*) to cope. Perhaps as a means of distraction. I was no different. In fact, since I was running from psychological problems much deeper than just love-loss, my manic-depressive stage was even more pronounced, marked by higher highs, lower lows, and much steeper gradations than others I have witnessed. I spent my nights trying to drown both love and hate, which at first glance seem opposing emotions, but with further reflection I think they may intersect more often than we realize. Most nights I couldn't figure out whether I loved war and hated my ex-wife, or vice versa.

Halloween night, the first night my old pal and I set out as free men separated from our former lovers, was no exception to that standard mania. We met a couple girls at the bar and spent some time dancing with them before we realized that they were part of a group which included another of our old friends from high-school. Once that connection was established, they invited us over to his house for an after party. I was drunk by the time we got to there, and like would happen so many times afterward, I found myself discussing American foreign policy and my part in the Iraq Campaign with people who feigned interest, but had neither real interest in the subjects, nor any base of knowledge. They were—like many are—little more than well-meaning voyeurs trying to show their 'support for the troops' by fist pumping dead enemy combatants.

Few care about the details, all they want to know is, "Did you ever kill anyone in the war?" *Of course, I did. Many of us did. And, so did you.* My mind wandered off as their shallow questions garnered equally superficial responses. In my head raged the replies I really wanted to scream:

When a country goes to war, its citizens are indirect participants in that conflict. I killed with my rifle, you killed with your ballot. There is a vast disparity in proximity, but less than most like to think in responsibility. My rifle is the tool I wielded. I am the tool you used. The blood on my hands is on your lips. Aloud, I uttered only single word answers.

I "come to" so-to-speak in this memory standing beside an island in my old friend's kitchen. I was telling war stories to entertain the crowd and block further incoming questions. Had you asked me before we left for the bar that night I am sure I would have said, "I don't care what we do, I just don't want to talk about Iraq." Yet, there I was, memories and emotions pouring out of me faster than the whiskey could keep them down.

At some point my old friend Josh, the guy whose island I was leaning on and one of the two men who had welcomed me back to Utah, pointed out that I had not told the story of how I was wounded in Ramadi. This brought me to a point of conflict because when I had first told that story to him at my home the night I got back, I had *lied*. I had exaggerated my heroism in the event, but I didn't want to do that again. I told the retold the story, but I softened my part a bit. I sort of met in the middle. Which is still lying, but it was progress of a kind:

"When we arrived at the Glass Factory that day there were already

1,000 civilian men waiting for us at the gate. Johnny and I quickly decided that we needed to gather some intelligence, but we were not willing to risk any of our guys to do it, so we went out the gate to work the crowd ourselves. Eventually a guy—an Iraqi civilian guy—came up to me and told me that he had seen a grenade with some wires attached to it.

"So, I start thinking there is a tripwire laid out there somewhere amongst this gaggle of civilian dudes. I decided to radio up to my guys and tell them to stay inside because the place was booby-trapped. Then a semi-truck crashed through our eastern perimeter and our machine gunners opened up on it. Civilians were running all over the place then. They were climbing over Texas-barriers, shouting and shoving one and other. Going absolutely nuts.

"Then this high-speed LTC called Colonel Mac came out there with us, and with the help of him, his Personal Security Detail (PSD team)[56], and some Marine dog handlers, we started getting these dudes organized into lines again. Then at some point I heard Sgt. Cann's dog, Bruno, growling and chewing on this one Iraqi dude's arm. And then: BOOM. BOOM. Two *huge* explosions go off and I wake up face down in this pile of blood and guts.

"Once I regained some consciousness I reached for my shotgun and tried to shoot back at the enemy. I mean, I knew I wasn't going to hit anything, but I didn't want to go down without ever having fired my weapon. The problem was I couldn't use my weapon because my arms were broken."

I had not, of course, ever fired my weapon. I never even *touched* my weapon after the blast. I couldn't have because none of my limbs

56 Before I was promoted to Team Leader my original job on this deployment was Point Man on the Interior Diamond of our PSD team. A PSD team is designed to protect high ranking officers, dignitaries and sometimes important cargo. PSD is most easily described as the military's version of the Secret Service, although we were not quite as specialized as they are. It is a conventional force job for the most part, but sometimes it is also done by Special Operators. This causes a little confusion for civilians. They seem to think all PSD is Spec. War. stuff. It's not. I was just a regular guy and a conventional soldier.

worked. They were all shattered, but for some reason, that just felt like a weak story to me. I felt as if the fact that I had never fired back after the explosion meant that I was a coward. And, I couldn't think of anything I liked less than a coward.[57]

I had lied again. Not so blatant and exaggerated a lie as before, for some reason that made it feel a little less badly than it had the first time; but I was still lying, and I knew it. Drunk people often lie, though this was more like a common drunken bullshit story than an outright black lie. And, I was telling this story in front of Josh, my buddy who had heard the grossly exaggerated version the first night I made it back to Utah. I guess, in some way, I felt obligated to him to tell it in a similar fashion. Perhaps that was to protect him. Maybe I thought there could be a person in the room that he had repeated the first version to? I don't know. Either way. I was at fault for the whole thing. No getting around that.

Then there was the Civilian Affect at play. The idea that civilians have been sold a version of war by Hollywood that is so inflated that any honest rendition of the true horrors of combat feels mundane, or even ordinary to them. Like they hear the truth and think, 'Oh, that's not so bad. Maybe even I could endure *that!'*[58] The truth always leaves them with a look on their faces that seems to say, "That's it?"

Then someone asked if they could see the scars on my legs, nearly all of which are on my thighs and hips. I responded by dropping my pants and rolling up my underwear to reveal them to everyone at the party. Severe scarring still draws awe, even when true stories do not.

Right about this time a girl named Jaynee yelled from across the other side of the island, "Shit! I just spilled beer all over my pants!" I heard her and did what I thought any western gentlemen should do: I offered her mine. She wasn't exactly the type of girl one would wish to

---

57 I believe I already mentioned this, but I will say it again because I think it may be interesting to any reader who is curious about human psychology. I never grabbed my weapon after the explosion, *but* inside my mind that was what I wanted to do. My thoughts *were* centered on finding my weapon and helping my friends. It didn't happen, so obviously this was an outright lie; but it had a clear genesis. Why?

58 Which is true! Wars are fought by men, not supernatural beings.

take home to his mother, so she obliged without hesitation. I knew in the moment that this was an invitation of a sort. My venture into nihilism had led me to dispatch with most of my childhood morals, but in this instance drunkenness may have spared us both further insult.

I woke up the next morning on my buddy's carpeted floor, by myself. I was severely hungover and needing a ride home, but aside from the headache, I felt great. Sure, I had been behaving in a way that I was raised to think uncouth, but in the moment—for the first time in a long time—I was enjoying myself. Even if only part of the time.

I wandered down the hallway leading from the living room to the bedrooms and found my jeans next to a bedroom door. I slipped them on and thought to myself, *Thank God, I didn't make any lasting mistakes last night.*

When Josh dropped me off at my house I was glad it was empty. No one was there to nag me about being out all night, or for wasting money at the bar. I was doing my own thing and loving it—at least that is what I kept telling myself. I missed my daughter every day, but I got to see her quite a bit, and who needs to be in a bitter relationship with someone who just drags you down all the time, right? *God knows, I was no better for her.* Being alone was good for the time, but ultimately the endless partying fed only the monster of self-destruction. I mortgaged my future one night at a time.

One such night my cousin Richard came for a visit. He and some friends were going to be elk hunting on a mountain near my home town that weekend, but they decided to swing in for a few drinks beforehand. When they arrived, I drove them to a party that was going on at a friend's place in a nearby town. Being the designated sober driver was a rare occurrence back then, but I knew we wouldn't be at the party long, so I offered.

While we were at the party, unbeknownst to me, one of Richard's friends snuck into a bedroom and molested a fourteen-year-old girl. My phone had a dead battery when we left, but after about five minutes on the charger it sprang to life with a series of text messages. I read them as I was pulling into my driveway:

That son-of-a-bitch touched Charity!!! The first read.

Who did? I wrote back.

That piece of shit that showed up with your cousin!!!

The guy the messenger was referring to was now sitting in my back seat with a despicable grin on his face:

"Hey man, did you touch that girl?" I asked.

"What the fuck are you going to do about it? I am from Rose Park, *bitch*!" He shouted back.[59]

I jerked the hearing aids from my ears for fear that they might be thrust into my ear canal by an incoming punch and slammed my truck in park. I was still walking on a cane at the time, but I could manage without one for short distances, and I could plant my feet more firmly than he had likely suspected. All the years I spent boxing and wrestling in my youth had taught me how to create a strong foundation when my legs were wobbly and weak.

I limped around the cab of my truck to the rear door on the passenger side and yanked it open. He let out a feeble squeal. My knuckles slammed into the center of his face. Adrenaline surged through my veins as I felt his nose crunch under the weight of my fist. He tried to crawl out through the other side of the cab, but the guy seated next to him shoved him out the door. He flopped onto the ground and came up swinging wildly. His punch missed. I grabbed ahold of his hood with one hand and started throwing uppercuts as hard as I could with the other. After about three or four more punches he fell to his knees and crawled away from me. As soon as he could get to his feet he took off running into the dark.

The rest of us walked inside my house. I washed the blood off my hand and asked his friends whether it was likely that he would call the cops over the fight. They all said he probably would.

"Even though he's the one who molested a girl?!" I asked. "Some 'Gangster' he is. God, I hate city boys." I murmured.

I cracked a beer and waited for the County Sheriff to arrive.

An hour later there was a knock at my door. Two sheriff's deputies

---

59 Rose Park is a low-income area of the Salt Lake Valley known for its high crime rate and sporadic gang violence.

entered the house to question me. I told them my story, holding nothing back. Truthfully, I was still so tired of civilian life that I really didn't care what punishment they administered. I didn't *want* to go to jail—who does—but, I was apathetic to the whole thing. Perhaps this helped me out a little bit.

When the questioning was all over the deputies informed me that I was not going to be arrested at that time. My claims had matched the other eyewitness testimonies perfectly; it was clear that I was telling the truth and the other guy was lying. Apparently, he claimed that he was, "jumped by a gang," and that he, "had never even seen a girl that night." Big problem with that: There were several women at the party, some of them had even given statements.

As for the claim of being jumped by a gang? I lived in a town of 270 people, most of which were cowboys and ranchers. There's not a lot of gang activity in the cow-towns of Utah. This was just a case of a weak-hearted coward losing a fight to a crippled person. I guess I would probably want to say I was "jumped" if it were me on the other end of that too. The insult to pride must have been excruciating.

I dodged that bullet, but my good fortune wouldn't last. Eventually, I received a summons in the mail. The kid I hit pressed charges on me after he was tried for the sex crime, and I ended up with an assault on my record. To be square with you though, I would do it again if the situation were the same.[60]

That wasn't my only run-in with the law while I was recovering, either. Sometime later, after a long night at The Stagecoach Saloon, I was arrested and jailed in Billings, Montana, for DUI.

Sadly, jail time wasn't even the worst of it. I once woke up passed out on a concrete sidewalk in Las Vegas. I had gone down there to visit an old friend from the Iraq War and we drank so heavily that neither of us made it back to our beds that evening. Another time in the same city,

60 The official charge may not have been sexual assault. I am lay when it comes to legal terminology and norms. He was convicted of something and sentenced to some time in jail. It was while in jail that he pressed charges against me, I think. I can't remember for sure.

visiting the same friend, I woke up passed out in a parking structure with a cigarette burn on my neck. The evenings, like my descent, always started out in exuberance and ended shamefully. I was not myself, I didn't know who I was. All I knew was I didn't like the man I saw in the mirror, and given the option, I would destroy him. My chief mistake was that I didn't realize there was a cure for my illness: the Truth. Had I only been willing to accept it, I could have been freed of my Hyde much sooner.

Another time, in Washington, D.C., I passed out on the center console of my friend's truck while it was parked in front of my hotel. I had an important work meeting the next morning with a very influential man. At the start of the meeting one of his assistants offered me a glass of water, probably because the stench of the bar we pissed the night away in still radiated from my pores. I took the glass from her said, "Thank you," and then turned my arm over to check the time on my watch, spilling the full glass of water all over his floor. That ended that relationship for good.

There were more girls and more parties than I care to remember—not that I *could* remember them all if I wanted to. My first steps onto the slippery slope were enjoyable. It can be great fun to lose control momentarily, but once on that slope I couldn't keep myself from careening to the bottom. I hardly had control of anything in my life, let alone my alcohol habit. I had ripped the moral substrate out from under my world and descended into nihilism.

Nihilism is not without its benefits though: it simplifies life. The person who goes down its path is led to believe that nothing he or she does matters in any real sense. All the world is relative. The virtue of an action is in the eye of the beholder. There is a problem with nihilism: it leads to depravity and uncontrollable chaos. If nothing matters, then that's that. Why care about health or the future? Unbridled pleasure was the closest thing I could find to happiness. I sought only hedonistic satisfaction—which I think is the logical conclusion of nihilistic ideologies. Nietzsche meditated on this at great length in *Thus Spake Zarathustra* and other works, and he was right, so far as I could see: God was dead, and I no longer knew up from down.

There were two things I still clung to, even in the depths of nihilistic depravity: my daughter, and my dedication to my brothers-in-arms.[61] There is a Canadian professor named Jordan Peterson I discovered while editing this book. He often describes the falls of men as a journey into the underworld, which I think is exactly the right way to picture it. If we accept that the slippery slope leads into a sort of underworld, I think it useful to view this place as if it had its own firmament.[62] We know the truth is above its veil, it's only that the world above is blurry and out of reach. We must slowly claw our way back up the slope into the domain of the living. But the underworld is dark, too dark for our eyes to see. We must have a guiding light to keep us on the right path upward. Most of the world's major religions saw this fact clearly. The notion is instantiated in their doctrines. I had a guiding light, sometimes I even looked through the firmament to see it, but it took too long for me to climb back towards it.

During some of my worst days I volunteered as an advocate and delegate for several prominent veterans groups. Had they understood how negatively my alcohol problem was affecting my daily life they probably would not have used me as a delegate, or as an advocate. I am glad they did not know. Each trip to D.C. where I could represent

---

61 Just to illustrate how warped my mind had become, I used to say that I partied and lived my life to its fullest because I was "trying to live for those who no longer could." I still believe in that philosophy, but I no longer pretend that it gives me license to waste my best days on simple pleasures. I know now that the proper way to orient myself for them is to contribute, to be successful, to give back: to live for something greater than naked *pleasure.*

62 An interesting note on Dr. Peterson is that I became enamored with him because he was saying similar things to what I was, only much better, deeper, and clearer. I had been traveling the country for years speaking about the importance of recognizing your own flaws, for seeing ourselves for what we really are, and for abandoning the hedonistic pleasures for selflessness and honor (he calls it "virtue"). His lectures, I have seen most of them now, are a gift to humanity. If you have liked this book so far you must seek out his *Maps of Meaning* series. I learned some—a fraction of what he knows—through my personal experience descending into and then climbing out of "the Underworld." I consider that a bloody and painful form of cross validation, the kind that not many would wish to pony up for. I paid in flesh, but you don't have to, you can learn from this book and his series.

something bigger than myself, something far more important than my own struggles, gave my life meaning, and kept me somewhat near that pathway upward. I desperately needed help and this was help of a kind.

It's important to note that my life wasn't all bad, either. It rarely is—that is what makes it so hard to crawl back up the slope. I was still making very real physical milestones. I had abandoned the cane altogether. I still stretched every day and did light workouts. My physical body was healing, and aside from the infrequent brushes with the law, I was having fun. No matter how self-destructive that "fun" was. I was, however, greatly neglecting my mental and spiritual health. For some reason, I felt like my mind would heal on its own so long as I was having fun and trying not to talk about the Army with any new person I met. That approach did seem to work for a little while, but eventually it failed too.

I recall one time a veterans summit in Washington, D.C., when I was supposed to do an interview with a local news channel after the veterans group I volunteered for finished breakfast. The TV crew met me in the lobby of my hotel, and after a very brief conversation suggested that we take the interview outside, so that I could put on my sunglasses. I accepted. I understood exactly why they wanted my eyes covered.

The eyes are the lamp of the body, as the Bible suggests, and my sleep-deprived, bloodshot bulbs had become more gray than blue. They opened a window to the darkness I wallowed in, and this reporter had seen it. The most dreadful part was that somewhere buried deep down in my subconscious, in the land of the shadow, was the truth: it was all *my* fault. War, or no war, the problems I faced were of my own creation, and I knew that.

At the same veterans group summit a prominent film maker came to present his award-winning war documentary. I couldn't sit through the screening. For me it was just a little, "too soon," as they say. During the film I wandered out into the hallway and met a fellow veteran and jolly soul named, Robert Stevenson.

He was a U.S. Army Special Forces veteran and Ranger. He went by the nickname, "Ranger Steve." He was a large man, more than six feet tall and easily over 200 pounds. He wore a nice gray wool suit and carried a desert camouflaged backpack filled with some paperwork and a water bladder. Hidden by the jacket was an undershirt soaked through with sweat everywhere the straps of his pack touched his clothing. He asked me why I was in the hallway:

"Hey Warrior, what are you doing out here?"

"Just getting a little air, sir."

"My name is, Rob, but everyone calls me, Ranger Steve."

"Yes sir, I know. I have seen you around for a couple years. My name is, Braxton."

"How long have you been back, Braxton?"

"Couple years."

"How long have you been fighting PTSD?"

"I don't even know."

I had never had another man speak so directly before. Every word he spoke was void of judgment and dripped with empathy and candor. I opened up to him immediately.

"How do you sleep?"

"I don't."

"Most of us don't. Have you always been like that?"

"It's worse now than it's ever been."

"How are your relationships?"

"They're terrible. I got divorced and I can't bring myself to care about a girl beyond a night at a time."

"Your friends?"

"I don't see many of them, but things are fine with the ones I got. We just party most of the time."

"You probably need to quit drinking. Have you tried facing your problems at all? I mean really being open to them?"

I didn't know how to answer this question so I just kept my gaze in his general direction and waited for him to start talking again. He was into some new-age hippie-like ideas, some of which seemed foolish. Some of them did resonate with me, though.[63] I relayed my thoughts to

---

63 This is an aside, but it may be interesting to some:

I had already found some success with one of the methods he suggested. Before

him and invested myself a little deeper in the dialogue:

"Did you ever kill anyone in combat?" His question lacked all the typical voyeuristic elements of civilian inquiry, so I answered honestly.

"Yeah. Only a couple times. Most of them I am really not sure whether they died though."

"How did you feel about that?"

"I don't know. Sometimes good, sometimes worse. Some I am glad are dead, some I don't know. … Sometimes I just don't know."

In my day to day life—almost hour by hour—I waffled between being perfectly okay with killing and abhorring it. I had only done what I had had to do, after all. I never liked doing it, or did I? One time I was really satisfied. I know I am not supposed to feel that way—but I *did* feel that way. *That guy tried to kill me and my friends. He can go to Hell. But what side would I be on if I was born an Iraqi?* I wondered to myself between pauses in the conversation.

Honest soul searching seemed to beg more questions than answers. Most of the time I settled on hating every person who forced me to have to shoot at him in the first place. It was the most convenient way to feel.

---

he and I met I had been going on these short trips that I called "soul cleanses." The ones he did he called, "spirit walks." He had adopted the custom practiced by many Native American cultures where they deprive themselves of food, water, shelter, and most of their clothing for several days and endure a fast and a walk in the wilderness until deprivation prompts a "vision." Scientists would perhaps call these things delusions, but I think that may be premature. The spiritual realm is, in my opinion, under studied.

My version of this practice was a bit tamer. When I went on "cleanses" I deprived myself of food, water and shelter at the outset, but I would take a knife and spend a few days in the woods looking for water and food. I didn't fast unless I failed to find water, or food. I thought that the struggle of searching for nutrients and water had value. Deprivation of sustenance was an obstacle to overcome. A challenge. I liked the triumphant feeling of "conquering" nature. I didn't then realize how framing the world in this way was part of my problem, not a solution to it.

Further, I thought that if a person could stand to be alone with himself with no modern distractions for a few days at a time, he must be doing "okay". I was completely missing the point.

I did gain one thing from these cleanses, though: forgoing basic necessities and modern comforts helped me appreciate my life a little more when I returned to it; and that's not nothing.

Kant was wrong. Sometimes lying to yourself can keep you alive, I thought. There is nothing *truer* than that.

Still, I grieved.

"The Ten Commandments clearly state, 'Thou shall not kill,' right? That always seemed like a pretty hard and fast rule to me. Well, I did kill. Maybe I am damaged because of that."[64] I said.

"People kill in war. That's what war is. The Old Testament is filled with war and killing. Are all those Jews going to Hell because they participated in those fights?" He asked.

"I am not that worried about Hell to be honest. I was just giving you a cultural example. People are good to me in general, but they know I am damaged. Most of these groups treat me like a fine piece of china with a chip in it. They want me displayed on their shelves, but they turn the blemishes toward the wall. I don't blame them. I would do the same thing, but, it is a deception. A self-deception too."

It was also true that our society was doing veterans no favors in this area. It seemed everywhere I turned there was a commercial, a billboard, a song, or a movie telling me that I was broken because I had PTSD. It was like PTSD had become the newest handicap. Going to war, instead of being a selfless act of courage, was a stigma. A sign that one must need special privileges and care.

Ranger Steve could see that I was totally lost and had an answer for me:

"From now on, I want you to introduce yourself like this: 'Hey, I am Braxton and I have had to kill people.'"

"You can't be serious?" I said laughing loudly.

"Try it."

At first glance this seems a ridiculous idea.[65] I was trying to rid myself of stigma not create more ignominy. Upon further investigation,

---

64 Even though it is obvious that my Christian upbringing did me no favors here, I have since learned that the translation may be wrong. It may be that the commandment was, "Thou Shalt not *murder*." That's a distinction with a very real difference.

65 I may be getting this wrong, this may not have been his exact idea, but it was my interpretation of it.

however, the idea becomes clearer. If one feels he is living in a world of self-deception, what better way to destroy those walls than speak the hardest truths to both mankind and the Universe alike! It is a brilliant idea, really, but it won't make you many new friends. And, between working as an Outreach Specialist and partying virtually seven days a week, I was meeting *a lot* of new people. God only knows how many people I frightened during that period of my life. Scores.

As far as girls went, you can guess how many dates the pick-up line "Hi, I am Braxton and I have killed people" got me.[66] It is efficient though. That single line both opens and closes a conversation, and generates fear and intrigue at the same time. Usually, when I would drop this line on some new girl at a bar her mannerly smile would flatten, her eyes would get big and shift left to right, then she would ask if I knew where the restrooms were. Who could blame her for that?

When I said it to men, they generally just laughed awkwardly and then asked a few follow-up questions. Some I answered, some I ignored. I was in a period of true psychological chaos, but with the help of Steve's strange idea I was starting to sort a few things out.

It was also during this time that I began to take the problem of PTSD seriously on a very personal level. I started to read up on the illness for myself and seek—albeit infrequent—help. I went to about five different therapists at the VA before I finally opened up to one a little bit. When I told her about my introducing myself by talking about killing people she hardly reacted at all. She stoically asked how that went over with my peers. I laughed and told her how foolish it had made me look, which she seemed happy about. Maybe she was more interested in whether I had noticed peoples' reactions to that line; perhaps she was trying to gauge my grip on reality. Regardless, she was competent and eager to get me back on track, but I was a terrible patient. I never told her the full truth. I was even somehow convinced that PTSD was *useful*. I thought that it had opened my eyes to the true workings of the world and that hypervigilance kept me safer (this is probably true). I even thought the

---

66 Perhaps this was part of his plan, too. My sex life was not helping me solve any problems. Best just too burn it to the ground maybe?

illness made me more creative and deeper (this is objectively false). I wanted to get myself back on the right track, but I did not want to give up the bits that I perceived as beneficial. Why? I don't know exactly.

One thing she did help me discover was the root of my road rage. She led me back through my memories until we found one that fit the problem perfectly:

"One time I was providing security for an EOD[67] team en route to a prominent Mosque in our area. I was in the gunner's hatch of our convoy's lead vehicle. A bongo truck was in the road in front of us. I shouted and waved at him to move and showed him my rifle, but he crept closer. Usually, when we got a driver's attention he veered of the road as soon as we told him to. Vehicle Borne Explosive Devices were common in Ramadi, so my instinctual alarm bells tripped immediately.

"I retrieved a flare and shot it over his vehicle, but he didn't budge. I grabbed my rifle and fired a warning shot next to his truck. 'Get out of the road!' I shouted again. He ignored me. I fired two more shots.

"When we loaded our magazines, we ensured that every third round was a tracer, I hoped that the bright orange flash would be enough to scare him off the road. It wasn't. He stayed rolling along in front of us. Then I fired a shot into his rear tire hoping it would drag him off the roadside. Still, he persisted. His truck was bouncing and shaking. It looked as if he was doing everything within his power to keep his vehicle on the road in front of us.

"*Okay, this guy has got to feel the blown-out tire! Why the fuck won't he get out of our way?!* I thought to myself.

"I shot his front passenger side tire, but still he stayed in front of us. Now, I was absolutely convinced that either his truck was packed with explosives, or he was trying to pin us in the Kill Zone of an ambush. Our lives were in imminent danger—I did what I had to do. The butt of my rifle tapped my shoulder twice. His rear window shattered and his vehicle crashed into the ditch off the roadside. 'Good! *Fuck* that guy!' I yelled angrily into the void."

---

67 Explosive Ordinance and Disposal

The therapist posited that even though this was a clear-cut case—this Iraqi was obviously trying to do us all harm—the fact that he had never fired a shot at us directly made it hard for me to process the whole thing. When I drove on the roads at home this memory was dredged up into my subconscious and I was left to debate it all over again.

She was right. She helped me with a lot of things and I was making progress; but I just did not want to admit that I had PTSD. I think partly for good reason. I have already addressed the fact that I exhibited signs of Post Traumatic Stress Disorder, such as frequent nightmares, hyper-vigilance, sleep disturbances, anxiety, and the rest of it, but I had also sustained a Traumatic Brain Injury in the explosion. It was never made clear which areas (or how many) of my brain were damaged, because I could not undergo an MRI. The magnetic pull of the machine would have ripped the shrapnel from my body and killed me on the spot. I know of one veteran who had his eyeball destroyed when an MRI pulled shrapnel from behind it that his doctors had not realized was there. I had no desire to become that statistic. Instead, I simply surmised that the damage was mostly to my frontal lobe, the area of the brain that aids in executive function, the area of my life which had changed most since the blast.

It is not like this was all guess work, either. The Army medical teams had found bleeding in my brain, they just never specified exactly where that bleeding was. The blast hit me entirely on the front side of the body and my ability to task-orient myself had changed drastically. It didn't take a neurologist to put those two things together. What else might be the cause of my totally impulsive and obsessive drinking, or my inability to perform executive tasks?

I showed other signs of this type of injury as well. I struggled with light sensitivity. I could hardly tolerate being outside without sunglasses, and prolonged exposure to florescent lights made me nauseous. I also took wildly unnecessary risks—often.

For example, I once entered a Wild Cow Milking contest while I was still walking on a cane. Before the event I wrapped my quads in bandages, put braces on my knees and covered my legs in my thickest chaps[68]. When we got to the rodeo I told my partner (a good friend that I rode bulls with a little bit before my injury) that I was going to have to rope the first cow that came close enough because I couldn't walk more than a few feet past the chutes without something to lean on. The soft, sandy earth of the arena exacerbated the problem. He told me that he understood.

The contestants got the cows running around and I threw a loop at the first one that came close to me. The problem was, the cow I roped was a big jersey with a bad attitude. Once she was on the end of my rope all I could do was hang on, or so I thought. I guess I just didn't realize how weak my legs were, because as soon as she hit the end of my rope I was jerked from my feet and onto my chest. My right hand was so worthless that I hardly hung on beyond the moment I hit the ground. I didn't injure anything physical in the fall, the only thing that was really hurt was my pride and my heart. Things could have turned out very differently though.[69] She easily could have come down the rope and stomped out my life. I never would have been able to get away from her.

I took more than just those kinds of dare-oriented risks, too. My nightlife was one big continuous risk. Drinking, girls, fights, driving, all of it. Bars and clubs are no place for a person who really wants to heal.[70] Nearly everyone there is trying to drown a devil, or themselves. I was no exception. Despite it all, somehow, I felt like I was doing my best to work through everything. I wasn't.

It did not help matters that the VA was disinterested in addressing anything related to my brain injury. To offer a little more proof of this, toward the middle of 2016 I received a letter in the mail saying that my TBI had only been evaluated by a *nurse*. If I was interested I could come back in and go through all new testing. Since it had been eight years

---

68 Chaps made for horseshoeing.

69 It could have been that the cows were already fixed with ropes and all I had to do was catch hold of a rope, but I can't remember now. Either way, the important bits are accurate.

70 "Never look for a wife on a barstool," or some variant of that idea, is a common maxim of American culture, and an accurate one, but not for the reasons most think. The problem person in that scenario is not the potential mate; it's the seeker.

since that initial evaluation, I ignored the letter.

I wish I had taken the therapists more seriously, but I didn't. My party continued.

For years I drank so often that it became semi-regular for me to go on three- or four-day benders. Glasses of whiskey with breakfast were common place during these stints. I couldn't see why I should change. The sunglasses interview with the local station in D.C. had gone fine once the questions started. I looked back on it as if it were just another funny story I could tell to the next girl I met at a party. In fact, when I got home from that very trip a good friend of mine Mikey Mohawk who owned an apparel company met me at my house and coerced me into a last minute road trip to Las Vegas:

"Hey bro, we are going to Vegas!"

"Nah man, I just got back from a month-long work trip. I was in Colorado, Baltimore, Philly, D.C. I need a break," I said as I unpacked my bag.

"What's a better break than a vacation in Vegas? Girls, booze, and you know I have free rooms at the Hard Rock," he said.

I noticed he was throwing t-shirts, jeans, and sweaters into my suitcase as I removed the suits and ties.

"Thanks, but no thanks, Mike. I need some sleep."

With that, he walked outside and drove off. He returned about fifteen minutes later with a soda and a pack of my favorite brand of cigarettes. "You have anything to mix this with? You'll need it on the drive." He went into the kitchen and opened my liquor cabinet. I could hear the soda drizzling down the sink drain as he made room for the Irish whiskey. "Alright, bro. Your bag is packed, I turned your car off and my truck is already warmed up. Let's go."

I woke up that morning in a strange room in an unfamiliar building. I even had to call another friend to ask what city I was in. All I could remember was that we had had a blast the night before.

My life was falling apart. My credit score was tanking, my job was on the rocks, and every close relationship I had once depended on was virtually demolished. I was having too much fun to see it.

CHAPTER EIGHTEEN

I Just Ran!

"I dread it," I confessed, "but I know it will not kill me. I do not want to wait. I want to go on right now. I shall keep my courage from failing by fixing my thoughts upon being a good man."

— *Wooden Leg: A Warrior Who Fought Custer*

Progress is difficult to spot. We descend into chaos with rapidity, but the climb out is arduous and gradual. The ascension can be thought of as steps in a staircase, or rungs on a ladder, but the longer the ladder the harder it is to count its crosspieces. This difficulty to see positive turns in the past is compounded by the fact that mistakes are so easy to spot. Darkness scars deep. Once exposed to its brand, whether it is thrust upon us by happenstance, or we call its forces down on ourselves, its presence is permanently etched on our soul. Once encountered the best we can do is heal the areas around the scarring and look back on the marks as historical lessons—a map for the future. Things aren't so clear with positive change. Healing leaves no obvious such obvious mark. Its process is slow. That's why it's less memorable.

When I thought back on this stage of my life I wondered if I could find a moment, the spark that changed my direction. A singular instant where I decided to learn from my suffering and shift my Universe a little more towards the good. The funny thing is the best example I could find seemed like a modern person would look upon as another example of thoughtless immaturity.

I decided to quit my job over what I had seen as moral corruption within the company. I had heard rumors from other agencies that we worked closely with, but I didn't think much of them in the beginning. The rumor mill is too often a swamp to garner any intellectual respect. As I gained more responsibility inside the organization I became privy to information and found a great deal of contractual fudging. The more I learned the clearer it became that the president was lying outright to our clients all the time. We as a corporation were focused on gaining applicants, not best serving those applicants like we claimed. It was no surprise either. The pathway to this moral failure was logical and obvious; most of the contracts we received were structured in such a way that they paid based on the number of individuals we brought in and trained, not how many we successfully placed in other organizations. At one point I found myself standing before a Medal of Honor winner in Colorado. The President of my company was next to me. He had just finished a presentation where he boasted that our company was successfully fulfilling its goals when it came to veteran applicants %100 of the time. This Medal of Honor winner believed like Carl Sagan did, that extraordinary claims required extraordinary evidence. He asked me flatly:

"What about you, Braxton, do you place every veteran that is assigned to you?"

"Well, speaking only for myself, no. I do not."

He nodded at me, but said nothing. The President shot me a look of disgust, as if I should have lied to this hero because we were doing more good than harm in his mind. I guess he thought that was a good enough reason to lie. The Soviets also thought that the end justified the means, so did Hitler and Mao and a host of other tyrants. The road to Hell is paved with "good intentions." I think that use of the word *good* deserves a second look. My walk through darkness—a lake of blackness that I was still submerged in—had taught me to be leery of any person who thought they knew best, that their plan always wrought more good than harm.

We walked out of that meeting with a new wedge driven between us. My boss knew then that I could not be trusted to back up his lies and baseless assertions. He tried to convince me of the error of my ways over lunch that day, but I was steadfast: "No matter what happens, I am not going to stand before a hero like that and tell a manipulative lie," I said.

The type of lie is worth meditating on for a moment here, because I don't want to give the impression that I thought myself saintly or anything of the sort—quite the opposite. Lies are generally classified as either white or black. Black lies are considered a statement that stands in opposition to fact, whereas white lies are more open to interpretation. I think this framing is lacking the most important element: The individual.

White lies are sometimes told to protect another person. For example, one might tell their child that his or her dog ran away rather than the truth—the dog was hit by a car. We tell this kind of lie to minimize the emotional pain the child feels. He or she might be left with the faint hope that their pet is safe and sound someplace else. The parent thinks this is easier to internalize than the full weight of mourning death. Maybe. I am not so sure this is true. Other common white lies are when we tell a parent that their child is beautiful when we don't mean it, or that a painting they created in an art class is gorgeous when it is truly hideous. We say these things because we hope that encouragement will strengthen the individual and render him capable of handling the full truth at a later date when either his character—or our own—has sufficiently developed.[71] A third type of white lie is a simple "fish story." Fishermen are renowned for exaggerating the size of their catch. Most of the time these lies are told to increase the social currency of the story. They add an element of fun to the whole thing, but like the examples previously mentioned, they stand in direct opposition to the truth: A ten-inch fish is not a fourteen-inch fish, a dead dog has not run away and an ugly thing is not beautiful. Under the most common definition of white and black lies these fall under the category of black lies. But they're not. The common framing is wrong because it ignores an individual's intentions.

A black lie is a lie which is told either to cause harm or to deliver personal gain. A person may tell another person he's ugly just to hurt

---

71 You may object here and say that we lie like this because we just want to avoid conflict. To that I would say, yes, true. But, why do we want to avoid conflict? The only reason we expect conflict, or wish to avoid it ourselves, is because one person or the other has not developed sufficiently to handle truth.

him, regardless of the victim's true physical appearance. A black-hearted parent may call his child an awful name, like "Shit for Brains," not because he actually believes the kid is stupid, but because he wishes to harm him.[72] A husband may manipulate his wife's emotions to get her to agree to allow him to make a selfish purchase, or go out drinking with his friends when he really ought to be tending the children. A bitter ex-wife may try to harm her former husband's reputation at work by telling the boss that he was unfaithful when he wasn't, thereby undermining the boss's confidence in him. We have all seen *and told* malevolent lies like this. We recognize their destructive and evil nature before our lips move, but we proceed anyway because we are imperfect beings.

I did some of these things and had others done to me. In many instances in my life I have been less than good, and worse than bad. I felt you needed to understand my perspective on lying to grasp why I saw this as a clear turning point in my life, but I do not want you the reader to be left with the feeling that I am being sanctimonious. I was in a dark and ugly place, but when I looked into the eyes of a man I admired and respected, I decided that I could not survive telling him a black lie. We meet a lot of people in the darkness of the underworld; not all of them are bad. This man's question, I believe, was an example of a heroic figure stepping down into the darkness to extend a downward hand. He knew my boss was lying—in what business is anything %100 successful?—and he had heard my story. He'd probably walked through the underworld himself. He recognized where I was and offered me the chance to get out, but he knew there was a possibility that I could ignore his hand: "What about you, Braxton…." His eyes had seen the darkness and it was clear that he knew the way out. I took the opportunity to follow him and freed myself—partly—from the underworld.

The path out of Hell is not an easy one. I knew I had to quit my job. I couldn't work for a company like that and maintain any semblance of character. I knew that. The funny thing was Bulldog had come to

---

72 This may actually be done because the parent is made insecure by what he or she knows is a child who is smarter than they are. They wish to beat down the budding youth before he can gain intellectual dominance over them.

work with us when he retired from the Army. He told me after only a month within the company that it lacked integrity, but I ignored him. Back then, I had no integrity and I was making money, money bought pleasure. Pleasure was my god. Why would I forsake my god for an ideal as passé as integrity?

Leaving this company was good for my soul, but not so for my wallet. Financially it was clearly a mistake. I needed to make some money and try out a new venture. My former position had required a lot of travel. While I traveled I sometimes went to open mic events in different cities to try my hand at comedy. It seemed only natural that I should start doing stand-up comedy full time. There's money in comedy, why not work at a thing I enjoy? The problem is, comedy is no way to make a living in Utah, unless you can survive on $500 a month.

Stand-up, while it was not paying my bills, did give me a much needed, fresh, quasi-healthy place to direct my anger. Additionally, most of the comics I met were drunkards, so my excessive drinking habits were seen more as an occupational quirk, rather than a hazard. I quickly rose through the ranks of comedians in Utah. I became a headliner after I won the 2011 K-Town Komedy Competition. Which was no real feat. There were only about ten comedians entered and most were not very good—myself included.

I loved doing stand-up, but you could say that comedy didn't reciprocate the affection. My jokes were a direct reflection of where my mind was at the time. What had been at the outset a healthy place to direct anger, soon became a portal to my own despair and negativity. While it had helped that I had restored some integrity to my being, I still had many other moral flaws to work my way through and my bits were exposing that.

I wrote a lot of jokes about God, the Bible and atheism. I hated God, or at least the idea of God[73]. After all, what kind of creator would make a world then fill it with suffering and war? Why watch mothers wheeze their last breath under the weight of a building crumpled by explosions? Why sit idly by while small children starve to death, their

73 I now see contempt for God as a sign of wanting to deflect responsibility.

bellies distended? Why cancer? Mosquitoes and parasites? Shouldn't such a God *deserve* rebuke?

Beyond atheism and biblical contradiction, I wrote about drugs, alcohol and meaningless sex. I once wrote an entire bit about school teachers abusing their relationships with students. I focused on all kinds of things that I had been raised to believe—and did believe—were abhorrent. I even joked about things that some see as trivial, but had deep roots in my upbringing, like hunting, fishing and the out-of-doors. I had been led out of the darkest parts of the underworld, but I was still completely lost. I didn't know it on a conscious level, but now that I have grown as a man, I think it possible that I was keenly aware of what I was doing *subconsciously*. I had forsaken my moral foundations for immediate gratification and pleasure for years. In its absence, all that had grown was my social status, self-hate, and contempt for mankind and the Universe alike. I had stepped onto the slippery slope years before and I had become nothing but an unrecognizable moral degenerate because of it. Someone I would have loathed before I left for the war.

Somewhere near the tail end of my time doing stand-up I met another person who indirectly helped me find my way out of Hell: a girl. She and I dated for a few years, but neither of us really had ourselves together. Still, just her presence and her belief in me helped aim me toward something better, something greater. I started to cut way back on my drinking, but I struggled to shake my demons. She had a son who was a few years older than my daughter, and after a while he moved in with us. Having him around really helped me get my act together. He gave me a reason to stay sober during the daylight hours even when my daughter was gone. Being responsible for his meals and his home and potentially his future led me to quit doing stand-up altogether and go back to school. But, her boy was having a few behavioral issues, nothing outrageous, just normal kid stuff. I decided that enrolling him in sports might be a good way to help the situation, so I put him in a baseball league.

When the first pee-wee baseball season ended, I felt his coach had not done an adequate job teaching the proper life-lessons that go hand-in-hand with sports, so I signed him up for wrestling that fall.

It turned out that his new wrestling coach would be my communications professor the next semester. On the first day of class his coach recognized me. He had been an official back when I wrestled and later helped coach at my high school. He remembered seeing me around at a few tournaments and knew that I had come from a highly successful program in southern Utah. When the class started he all but told me flat out that my grade would be affected if I did not help coach his little league wrestling program. I guess he thought that my wrestling lineage could bring something new to his team. I happily accepted. I loved wrestling and thought it among the best ways to build character. Plus, I had gotten a large part of my life sorted out and started really progressing again. I was in a good position to help, and I like mentoring youth. I see it as the best thing a person can do after they overcome trials. Particularly self-inflicted hardships.

When his first wrestling season ended, I signed up to coach his spring baseball team. I found that coaching kids helped me more than it helped them. Sure, I had largely started getting my ship righted before I started coaching, but I found that the better I got, the more problems I realized I had had. Being responsible for those kids and witnessing their nearly unbridled sense of joy gave me a reason to believe the world was still largely good, even when a person attempts to deny it.

Spring rolled around and our baseball season was fully underway. We were doing some batting practice at a community park near my house. It was hot and sunny. We were tired and getting dehydrated. Most importantly, both he and I were starting to lose focus.

"Alright, bud. Let's get a few good ones in to end on." He nodded from the batter's box.

My legs were aching, they always did, but there was a sureness in my footing that had never been there before. I noticed it when I was teaching boxing lessons a few years earlier, but I had figured that that was just because I was doing something that I was familiar with. I had guessed that my body had quickly remembered how to anchor and pivot even after my brain had been rattled. I never really considered that my legs may have actually been regaining functional strength. After all, one of the muscles in my right quadriceps had been completely severed. Even my optimistic physical therapist thought that it would never recover. Could I really be edging closer to normalcy?

I flipped a pitch to the little batter. He hit it softly in the air. I lightly trotted to it and reeled it in. Another pitch. He hit a hard ground ball a step to my right. I fielded it with ease. Somewhere in my subconscious the thought rang, *Dang, that felt good.*

I served him another, this time he hit a hard ground ball about three steps to my left, my glove hand side. I sprinted to it and scooped it up with a spinning motion. A smile as wide as Montana creased my face.

"Holy crap! You just ran!" His mother shouted.

"I know!"

I couldn't contain my excitement. I started charging every ball he hit, even the ones I didn't need to. A rush of love filled me. I had forgotten how good it felt to be (somewhat) capable and I likely never would have run toward that ball if I hadn't been tired and losing focus. The lack of attention allowed my subconscious mind to unshackle the chains my conscious mind bound my legs with.

On the next pitch he ripped a line drive over my head, I tried to jump for it. Nope! I still can't jump.

"Well, I guess basketball is still out of the question." I yelled, grinning widely.

We called it quits and I immediately grabbed my phone out of my ballbag. I sent out several text messages that read: "I JUST RAN!" In all caps. The few war buddies who received it called me later that night demanding to hear the full story. When I reiterated it to one of them, he cried.

CHAPTER NINETEEN

Grandpa

He that walketh with wise men shall be wise…

— Proverbs 13:20 (KJV)

As I mentioned before, the individual moments of growth are hard to spot. This is why I think fiction is so powerful; it gives the author the opportunity to develop a character in reverse. The writer knows what the protagonist will become in the end, so he or she creates easily visible situations of clear character development—they're often huge and easy to spot. Real life isn't quite so dramatic, I'm afraid. It's wrong for an author to go back and say, "Now, this is the exact moment in time where I changed for the better! This is where I found the existence of a supreme reason to be." Life isn't like that, and even if it were like that, there is no way we could remember every little thing that helped facilitate proper orientation before the singular event that spurred the most dramatic shift. The best we can do is get close.

I pointed to a moment earlier where I did the right thing, and refused to lie to a hero, even though that decision was going to cost me money. Then I quit my job, that was a good thing too; but then I did some stupid things like telling jokes about abhorrent subjects on stage. The real complexity arises when you notice that my doing standup actually cast a light on how sick I truly was—and that is what made me want to repair my moral foundations. So, can the sinning be seen as all bad? Yes, I think so, but like I said before the good decisions are harder to spot so we have to give ourselves a little bit of a break when we go back through our own histories. Easier said than done.

When I thought back on this little league season I knew there were some turning points in it, but I couldn't remember them specifically. I decided to start coaching in the first place because I noticed my girlfriend's son was not getting the big lessons from his coach. I stepped in and tried to help him. Perhaps that was itself the moment. If we offer to mentor youth and our ethics are at least partly developed we know we must lead by example. We cannot ask the children we lead to do things that we are not ourselves willing to do, so in my case, I started coaching and that forced me to hold myself to a higher standard of conduct all the way around. Therefore the decision to coach youth sports was an actual life-altering moment for me; but that couldn't have been the only instance where I got life right, so-to-speak. I don't want to leave you with the illusion that it was.

There were myriad moments within the course of coaching that boy's wrestling team and his baseball team that helped me grow; it would be impossible to point them all out and any attempt to would miss some that were just as important as any I could mention. It will have to suffice to say that his sports seasons and my starting college to help him in the future gave me a new objective purpose each day and created for me an iron clad schedule.

I think waking up at the same time and performing the same routine likely helped me shed as much baggage as any bit of philosophical inquiry or character-defining moment did. Still there was another defining moment of a sort that I must address. It happened near the end of his baseball season at about 4:00 P.M.:

"Grandpa was just rushed to the hospital by ambulance." Read a text from my mother that would alter my course forever.

I called her on the phone to get the details and to comfort her if there was some way that I could. She was clearly anguishing. What can a son say to a mother who was witnessing her rock wash away?

We had all known that the day was fast approaching, but nothing can prepare a person for the actuality of something like that. My hero, the architect of my moral and ethical foundation—the cowboy who had raised me when no one else would—was dying.

I was driving our vehicle at the time. I sat, eyes fixed on the road, wondering when the full weight of it would set in. I never really felt it until I walked up to his open casket and saw his hair, done specially by my grandma, the love of his life and *his* rock.[74]

That night sitting on the balcony of my apartment in West Jordan, Utah, staring at my tomato plants, I wondered what I would do in a world without him. I wished to be away from the bright lights and noise of the city, sitting by a morning campfire drinking coffee with him again. I knew I had long since begun to rediscover myself, but could I stay properly aimed without him? I had started hunting and fishing again. I went back to my roots. I read a little Jung and became convinced of the importance of symbols, not just in a sociocultural sense, but personally. I had begun to wear my cowboy hat in public instead of only on the weekends when I was away from the prying eyes of onlookers. Still, though this was a positive step backward, I had not truly returned *home* yet. And, I didn't know exactly what that meant. I only knew that the answer lay somewhere in my history, somewhere in my roots. I think it is true that clothing does not make the man, but it is a display of what is inside his heart. A cowboy hat may have been a trivial thing, but before I had descended to the underworld I had worn it with pride. It was a symbol of honor, hard work, and a respect of heritage. I had been so closely attached to that symbol that I'd worn one nearly every second of my life before I strayed. As a boy it was no strange event for my mom to remove a hat from my head as I slept. My hat was the first thing my ex-wife brought to me when I was in Walter Reed recovering. I wore it nearly all the time after that. It was not a fashion statement, but a symbol of all my grandpa believed in.

I thought a lot about all that my grandfather had taught me as a boy. He thought there were concrete skills and lessons required of a man from the west[75] and he made damn sure I learned them. I remembered

---

74 Grandpa was a Marine, but he was no fan of the buzz haircut. The funeral home had done his hair, but when my grandma and her daughters looked at it they felt it was wrong. He always wore a perfectly combed pompadour, somewhere between James Dean and Chief Joseph, two characters he always admired. Grandma fixed it before anyone else saw him.

75 By this I mean the Rocky Mountain West.

his knuckles pressing into mountain mud to show me how a mature mule deer buck's weight causes depressions much different than a young buck, or a doe does. He showed me how to read the difference between an elk track that had just slid down a wet, muddy hillside, and one who was on a dead run. He tied his own flies for catching trout out of our mountain creeks, rivers and lakes—all of which require different flies and weights of flies by his estimation—and he made sure I could do that too. He taught me how to skin an animal by showing me how he did it, but he only let me practice on the lower legs of the elk and deer he killed.[76] He taught me how to trap and how to clean fish and game. He spent time on more abstract things like what it really means to be a Man. That's a much harder concept to pin down on the page.

On one deer hunt when I was about ten years old he handed me a raw liver from a buck he had just killed. He told me that taking a large bite out of it was the only real rite of passage to manhood. When the metallic tasting, fleshy substance filled the entirety of my mouth and thick, warm blood ran down my cheeks and neck, he let out a deep belly laugh. I realized that the joke was on me. He was trying to teach me two lessons there. One, that no single physical act makes a man, and two, not everything an authority figure tells you is worth believing: sometimes you're just the butt of a joke.

Earlier in my life, when I was about six years old he had pulled a similar trick. We were camping in the deserts of southern Utah when he told me that a pile of mule deer excrement was some unfortunate soul's lost marble stash. I filled my pockets with the newly found treasure. When my pockets were stuffed he said, "I'll bet you can carry a few more marbles in your cheeks." It didn't take long to discover that was a lie—those were not, in fact, brown marbles. If his goal was to teach me that it is wise to question everyone—even one's idols—then I can still taste that lesson on the tip of my tongue twenty-five years later. Because of that, because of him, and because of the journey I have been on, I was becoming a Man mostly worthy of the title. My only wish is that I would have gotten back onto the right path before I lost the chance to

---

76 There is still nothing harder to skin (that I am aware of) than a frozen mule deer leg.

show him. Forever.

When I was about ten years old I stumbled onto a wounded badger. It had been run over by a four-wheeler. I had seen the movie *Legends of the Fall*, a popular movie at the time, and I had decided that this would be a great time to have my Tristan moment.

In the film, Tristan, played by Brad Pitt, is the middle brother of three who get tangled up in a love affair and the First World War. At the film's end, Tristan fights a grizzly bear who had scratched him up in his youth. This badger was no grizzly, but for a boy my size, it would do. I wanted my grandfather to be proud of his boy; what other kid could kill a badger with a knife, after all? As I inched closer to the animal its hissing and gnashing of teeth became increasingly ferocious. It was wounded, but it was not paralyzed. I questioned my courage. Deer horn handled knife in my hand,[77] I attempted to "Cowboy Up," as we said back then. It bluff-charged a little and repelled me in a way that I felt even the mighty Tristan could empathize with. I retreated to my own four-wheeler and decided that this would be a job best done with other instruments. I crept nearer to the badger, knife in one hand, large rock in the other. I hurled the rock toward it. The stone struck its back and it charged me again. As quickly as I could manage I grabbed a large stick from the ground and walloped it over and over. When I was convinced that it was, if not dead, at least incapacitated, I jammed my knife between its ribs. I tossed it onto the rack of my four-wheeler and drove back to camp.

I parked the quad and then walked up to him, a vanquished foe nearly half my length in tow. I saw a smile creep across his oft stoic face. His teeth shown as brightly as if I had drug in the ferocious grizzly Tristan battled.

"How'd you get that thing?" He asked.

"With a stick and my knife." He patted me on the back and walked over to the skinning pole, never saying a word about the obvious tire track across its back.

He skinned it right there in front of me, I didn't pay attention as well as I wish I had, but he did make me a neckless from its claws, just like

---

77 A knife he had made me himself.

the grizzly claw neckless mountain man Chris Lapp had worn. I gave him half of the front claws as a gift. I don't know what he did with his half of the trophy, but I wore my half to school that fall. My elementary teacher reprimanded me for "bringing such a disgusting thing to class."

"It would be different if you were a Native American!" she exclaimed.

"But, my grandpa is a Navajo!"

She accused me of lying, which makes sense because I don't think there are a lot of freckled Navajos running around, but I didn't think I was lying. My grandpa's hair was black and thick, his face was as dark as boot leather, and right there on his fireplace, hung among his most prized possessions, like one of his father's rifles, was a ceremonial eagle feather given to him by a Navajo man and friend of the family.

Life lessons with grandpa weren't always painless, however. I recalled a time when I had taken my younger female cousin Sherell out for a ride on my grandma's four-wheeler. A little way into the ride she decided that she wanted to drive, so I pulled off to the side of the trail and let her. A few minutes later she took a turn down a short, but steep hill at a local gravel pit. Apparently, the day before, one of the folks working road maintenance on the mountain had taken a scoop of gravel out from the base of the little hill leaving a three-foot high cliff at its bottom. Unknowingly, we plummeted off the short ledge and flipped the machine onto its back. She was flung off to the side, but when it crashed to the ground I ended up pinned underneath. A couple of my other cousins who had been riding on other quad-runners rushed over and helped get me out from under the one trapping me. My leg was broken in the fall.

When we returned to camp with a twisted four-wheeler rack and a scratched up granddaughter, grandpa was as mad as I had ever seen him:

"What in the hell happened?!" He yelled.

"We wrecked." I said.

"Grandpa, I was driving," Sherell interjected in an attempt to clear my name.

He didn't care. I was with her and despite my injuries I should have known better. He was right. I was on the mountain all summer with him. I knew that the road crew sometimes took scoops of dirt from that spot.

I should have checked before we went down the hill.

"You could have gotten her killed, Brack!" He yelled at me.

I spent the rest of that weekend helping him fix that quad with a broken leg. Of course, he didn't know my leg was broken, he just thought it smarted.

No one knew about the fracture until I got hurt again while playing summer baseball later that year. When I got my leg checked for the baseball injury the doctor said I had only sprained my ankle this time, but there was a freshly healed broken tibia that had not been properly casted. That was by no means my only undiagnosed childhood injury, but it was a memorable one.[78]

I went to bed that night a little drunk, nothing out of hand, but definitely not sober. I kept dreaming of my grandpa, wishing I could ask him some advice on what to do with my current relationship. I knew I couldn't stay with this girl, she and I were just too toxic, but I felt in some way obligated to stay. I wished I could just sit down over some coffee and explain myself to him, but that chance was gone. No matter what death bed advice I had hoped he would bestow on me, it wasn't meant to be. I was on my own.

A couple days later my girlfriend and I were back in my hometown at the church where his funeral would be held. The hallways were lined with pictures of him and my grandma, the love of his life and his best friend. He believed that family was the most important thing in life. There were dozens of pictures of him and his brothers, his kids and his grand-children, to prove it. Tables sat on either side of the doors to the chapel where his service would be held. Each was decorated with his prized belongings: his fly-fishing pole, flies that he had tied, and his hunting knife.

On one table, atop a rack that held his recurve bow and leather quiver filled with wooden arrows, rested his brown cowboy hat. If it is true that you can tell the character of a man by the company he keeps, then I

---

78 It would be easy to read that story in a way that made my grandpa or my mom look kind of bad, but that just wouldn't be fair. Had either of them really known my leg was broken they would have rushed me right to the hospital, but they didn't know. It is events like that that in my mind forge real character.

think it equally true that you can tell the type of man by the possessions his company believes he values.

I stood staring at that hat for a while. I remembered asking him if I could wear it around our deer camp when I was a young boy, he dropped it on my head and smiled. I spent the rest of the afternoon walking around with that hat like it was a crown fit for a King of kings.

My great-uncle John, grandpa's younger brother, came up to us while I was daydreaming and asked how I was doing. John was a Combat Controller in Vietnam; he had seen more than his share of fighting. I knew intuitively that the question was meant to get at something deeper than how I felt at present. I respected him more than I did most others who posed the same question, so like with Ranger Steve, I answered it honestly:

"Getting better—I *think*."

"How long have you been back now?"

"About seven years or so."

"Give it ten and you will be fine," he said. "You may be a mess for those ten years, but you'll be okay after that. It will always be there, it doesn't go away; but one day—all of a sudden—you'll have it under control."

"Okay. Thank you."

I listened to him intently, but I thought he was wrong—he wasn't.

It was time to go into the small room where grandpa's body lay. Front and center sat a wooden casket fastened to a litter. It was bordered by wreathes and flowers. Grandpa had always loved wildflowers. There were a few rows of metal folding chairs lined out facing the front. I sat in the back row hoping not to draw any more attention than was necessary. Then the host called the children and grandchildren up to the casket to pay final respects. Reluctantly, I walked up and put my arm around my mother. She was sobbing uncontrollably. Between gasps for air she whispered, "Aren't you going to go say goodbye?"

"No. I'd rather this not be the last image I remember him by."

She grabbed my hand and dragged me up to his body. Up until that point I had hardly shed a tear. Grandpa never thought men ought to cry anyway. I tried to keep my composure. When I saw him lying there, hair perfectly combed, body dressed in his Sunday best, I broke down in a way I never have before, or since.

The flood of grief and despair twisted my face. I felt like I had been struck by an avalanche of emotion. It seemed as if every little bit of anguish I had collected throughout my lifetime welled up at once. I raised my black cowboy hat up to cover my face and wept. This was a different kind of pain than I had ever felt before. The kind that a person only encounters when he knows he failed another that he loved and revered.

For years after I returned home from the war I had lived less than two blocks away from grandpa and grandma, but I seldom visited them. When my mother asked me why I wasn't going to see my grandpa more often I always gave the same selfish, pathetic excuse:

"It's just too hard for me to see my hero withering away in a bed. I don't want to remember him like this."

I think the full gravity of my selfishness hit me in that moment. It should never have been about *me*. What an ignorant wretch I was. As for the excuse that I had been using to avoid the situation? That was only half true anyway. The whole truth was: Yes, it was hard to see him like that, but I was running from everything in my life after the war. I was running from my emotions, from responsibilities as a man, and from my own mind. My mistakes—as happens to us all when we fail—were too often thrust onto the people I loved most around me. Sure, I was paying for them too—but so were *they*—and they had done nothing to deserve it.

I failed a man that I loved more than life itself. My selfishness had hurt him when he needed me most and it was too late to make up for it. All I could do was weep, and that is all I did.

CHAPTER TWENTY

Lord, Give Me a Wind in my Face

The mountain is the means,
The man is the end.
The idea is to improve the man,
Not reach the top.

— Walter Bonatti

It wasn't long after I carried my hero to his final resting place before the girl and I broke up. We had differences that were simply irreconcilable. I had felt as if she had violated my trust in an unforgivable way, and she felt like I was too quick to anger, too unforgiving and old fashioned (among many other things I am sure). I suppose two things can be true at the same time. This wasn't like when I divorced my daughter's mom; in this breakup I harbored little or no ill will. I was just ready to move on and so was she.

I grew a lot through that relationship, but I still had a multitude of mental health problems. It seemed as if the faster I sorted them out, the less compatible the relationship was with my trajectory. I still thought her a good person then, and do today. I wish her only good things, which I guess was, and is, a manifestation of some real mental progress.

When she and I were split for good I moved in with my good friend and medic, Z. He lived in a huge house with a couple buddies. The home sat on a hill overlooking the Salt Lake Valley and had a full wet bar in the basement. If I was going to be forced to stay in the city, I figured it would be best that I at least surround myself with friends and a good view. Maybe that would make things more bearable.

Both of the friends he lived with were fellow combat veterans. This may seem like a trivial detail, but it is difficult to explain how useful and powerful it is to be surrounded by men who you never have to explain yourself to. I was still slightly heartbroken over the latest breakup, but the problem of full transition to civilian life loomed larger than that. I was finally beginning to realize that I needed to take a more proactive approach to the whole thing. One day Z and I were having a drink together at our basement bar when I brought up the subject of PTSD:

"What is the deal, bro, do we all have PTSD, or is it bullshit?"

"Maybe."

"You think we all have it then? I feel like my mental health has improved a lot. Not as much as my physical health has, but I think I am getting better. The only thing that still bugs me is that I feel like I gave everything I had to the Army and they just dumped me as soon as they felt I no longer served any purpose."

He instantly recognized that I was being whiney and complaining about a thing that was not just in the past and out of my control, but completely trivial.

"Well, suck it up. You're a civilian now."

"No shit. You are right. What the hell am I complaining about? I am not even 30 years old and I am retired. What's not to love about that?"

Of course, there is the whole issue of the shattered bones, shrapnel-filled body, and the rheumatoid arthritis that I had picked up along the way, but still, I am *alive.* What's not to love about that?

I sipped a little more scotch and tried to think through all the reasons I really missed the Army. Most guys jump right to the camaraderie aspect when they list their reasons for wishing they could go back. I felt that way too, but there was something more, something much deeper. Brotherhood is powerful, but as Winston Churchill famously said, "Nothing in life is so exhilarating as to be shot at without result." I missed the *action*. The few times I actually felt like I was doing my job. I missed the feeling of righteous combat. The sting of battle.

I recalled the first time I was ever shot at by a sniper. The intensity of a single accurate shot buzzing by one's head sends a shiver down one's spine that reverberates throughout life. I missed *that* feeling. I missed understanding my purpose.

Nihilism was an enemy of mine and I knew from first-hand experience that combat is its worst enemy. You can try to tell yourself that nothing matters, but try clinging to that notion when you watch young men rush to an aid station to give blood to dying soldiers they have never met—and will never meet. Try convincing yourself that everything is meaningless and that you'd be better off ending your own suffering while enemy fire is bearing down on you. They say there are no atheists in foxholes, I think that is wrong. What they should say is there are no nihilists in foxholes. Even the suicidal person shrinks at the wrong end of *someone else's gun.*[79]

I missed the challenge of forcing myself to respond to incoming fire. I missed knowing that I was not a coward like I had become in civilian life. I never ran from combat, but I had run from responsibility at home and that dishonored me. It was almost as if I wished I could go over and fight again just so that I could come back and *transition* properly. To come home with my head held high like I should have done in the first place. As if another chance at war was the only way to restore my Honor.

I also missed training. I loved the feeling of conquering a particularly difficult work day. The kind of satisfaction that one only gets when he thinks it improbable to overcome the challenge before he begins. That reminded me, *I did run awhile back. Maybe I can run a full mile now?*

I decided to call up my old friend and first line leader Johnny. I knew he had been running marathons and triathlons since he returned from Iraq. Surely, he would love to be there when I ran my first mile since the suicide bombing crippled me. I called him up.

"Hey bro, I want to run a mile."

"Can you run now?" he asked

---

79 Suicide is a choice, the nihilist may logically find himself wondering whether he ought to kill himself since life has no meaning, but he certainly does not want someone else dictating the time and circumstances.

"Well, I don't know. I ran about 90 feet a few times."[80]

"Okay. I know of a few trails, but are you sure you want to run a mile?"

"I can run a mile, Johnny."

"I don't doubt that you can do it. I am asking whether you *should* do it."

I knew I could run a little bit, and I knew I was mentally strong enough to push myself through a mile no matter what happened, but I didn't have a good answer for him. In fact, I was reasonably certain that it was *not* a good idea to try to run that far, but I didn't care. I just wanted to try. Whatever comes of it will come of it I thought:

"It doesn't matter. Let's do it."

Because I was already working as a motivational speaker at the time I decided to ask another veteran friend of mine, Casey, to come film the run. I knew my friends, family, and those who follow me online would be interested in seeing how far I had come. I also thought it would be embarrassing to have folks who didn't know that I had once been told I may never walk again see us filming a simple mile run (Ego). We decided to meet up at a track near Johnny's home in northern Utah. He knew the trail systems there well, so he set us up at a time where we were unlikely to encounter other joggers.

We met Johnny in a parking lot near an asphalt bike path that borders the interstate. No other cars were there. I could not have been more relieved. Casey and I got out of his car, walked over to Johnny and exchanged hugs.

"You ready for this?" Johnny asked.

"I think so."

We walked through the paved parking lot to the track. We were to begin the run in a concrete tunnel bored through another path that crossed over the top of the freeway. I stood there in the shadow of the overpass wondering how my body was going to hold up. I knew I could run the mile, but I was still nervous about the aftermath of it all.

---

80 On a baseball field the bases are set 90 feet apart. That is why I could say 90 feet with certainty.

"How fast do you want to run this thing?" Johnny asked.

"I don't know. It's been awhile. What's a respectable mile time? Nothing fast, but I don't want to be slow either."

"Alright. We can do that."

It was easy to put all my faith in Johnny. Not just because I knew he was running marathons and was a naturally calculative guy, but because we had fought together. Combat builds a form of trust that binds tighter than blood. I trusted him completely. I knew we could get through that mile together and that's probably why it went so smoothly.

The run itself was uneventful, and I know by now it must be getting tiresome to read about the pain aspect, so I will spare you. Suffice it to say—it hurt. All of it. My knees, hips, quads, and back all felt like they were falling apart right there on the spot, but we made it through. The swelling that normally fills my quadriceps throughout the day poured in within minutes of beginning the run. Aside from that, nothing happened that was unexpected. We finished the mile loop in about seven minutes and thirty seconds. I was proud of the pace, but something else struck me after we finished: My ego was *the* problem.

I had discovered that *I* was the root of most of my psychological problems years before this and I had taken some measures to get better. What I hadn't realized, was the role ego was playing in *all* my suffering. I started to look back at every ill-advised decision I had ever made, every argument I had ever been in, and the grudge against the Army that I had held. Nearly all of them could be traced back to arrogance.

For years I longed to reenlist, to have the chance to prove myself again—that was ego. I was angry at the Army for describing me as "Does not meet retention standards." That was ego too. I felt like if they had just given me time to heal I could have gotten strong enough to chase my career goals within the military at some point. It took me eight years to get to the stage that I was at then, running a single mile. By *definition* that does not meet retention standards—Ego!

How could I expect the Army to hold onto me for a decade in the hopes that I might one day be *almost* healed enough to fill a combat role again? That's a pathetic grudge. The Army's job is to be combat effective, not pander to the dreams and will of wounded young men. My ego had blinded me to that fact, and my blindness had led to resentment and anger. Those emotions do nothing but destroy from within and wreak havoc without. My weaknesses—however valiantly won—would not make a team more combat effective. My crippled form would only diminish the integrity of a team. I would be a liability on a battlefield, not an asset. Finally, I had realized that and let go of the weight I had carried for years.

"What frustrates you most about the Army letting you go?" Casey asked.

"It's not about the Army. It's not their fault. It's about how they all said I couldn't, when I knew that I *could*."

"And others just *won't*." Casey added.

"I don't know about that."

I was finally done with the dream of reenlistment, or a return to combat. I was going to suck it up, because Z was right, I am a civilian now.

From that point forward my life began to morph rapidly. When I was a younger man I thought courage, strength, and tenacity were the traits that made a man worthy of the title, but by exercising each of those traits at different times during and after the war I realized they were not enough. They are important—highly important—but they are not sufficient enough to make life worth living. I realized that what grandpa had been trying to teach me all along was that a good man and a good life are made of balance, growth, and selflessness. If those three things are a person's substrate everything else will take care of itself.

Strength is important, but it must be balanced with caring. Selfishness—as hard as it may be to spot—erodes the purveyor, the victim, and all those caught between. If a person is focused on growth, no matter the challenge, he or she will always come out better than they were before the impetus. A mindset of growth helps us internalize our mistakes and craft better strategies for the next bout with trouble—if we can do it without crushing our spirits under the weight of our own self-judgment, that is.

This is not to say that emotions ought to be coddled. Quite the contrary, in fact. When we as adults focus on growth this means that we must own our mistakes, not push them to the side. Surviving the day is not the goal: being content is. A person focused on growth understands that he or she will fail along the way and that what is truly important is how well he or she performs the next time a similar situation arises. Have you learned from failure? That is what matters.

As Oscar Wilde is said to have written, "Experience is simply the name we give our mistakes." That's inarguable in my estimation. Experience is the best way to frame failure, but it requires that the person has the courage to accept that he made the mess in the first place.

The jog I had run with Johnny was only a mile in distance, but it had crossed chasms in my mind. I had many times before thought it was time for me to do "better" at civilian life, but it had taken me eight years to find the way. Eight years to discover *how*. The lesson sank in not a moment too soon.

Once this new-found realization was deeply anchored, like all things truly transformative, it took time to implement effectively. Rare is the occurrence of a true Saul on the road to Damascus moment. Meaningful change takes time, and the person always vacillates a bit while in practice. I didn't get it all right immediately—and I don't have the game down yet—but, I have been growing ever since.

I decided to quit smoking cold turkey. It was difficult, but by no means excruciating. I limited my drinking to a couple of drinks a week (aside from the occasional social gathering at the house) and started each day at 5:00 A.M.—this latter bit being the key to squashing low-key alcoholism most abruptly. A person who gets up at 5:00 A.M. after a long night of drinking either feels horrible and wants to crawl into the shower and pray that God will end their suffering, or they feel great. In which case, they are still drunk and the hangover will set in soon. Then they'll crawl to the shower and beg for a merciful smiting.

The change in my habits helped expedite what was already the most rapid physical change my body had gone through since Walter Reed. Every morning I stretched out and then ran a mile. Soon that turned into two miles. I was lifting weights in my garage every morning and doing a thirty-minute workout at night. I couldn't exercise enough to satisfy my lust for health and vigor. Once my body was strong enough to endure a little hiking, I set out looking for the teacher who had taught me the most valuable lessons in my youth: the Mountain.

I sought solitude deep in the mountains above the Salt Lake Valley, not for reasons of self-destruction or pity like I did when I first returned, but because I was genuinely ready to learn again. Sitting atop a mountain peak, or watching a heard of elk graze in a grassy meadow made me feel at peace. A peace that made me feel closer to my grandpa. The closeness I felt to grandpa helped me reflect, to take real time for introspection—I think of that now as a form of prayer. Looking across those huge, snow covered peaks provided a sense of wonder that I had long since lost sight of. It was hard to look on something so miraculous and not be awestruck. It made me remember what it was like to believe in a designer, God as the ultimate scientist.

The mountains themselves seemed filled with my grandpa's voice. Some days when I had an archery deer tag in my pocket I would let a buck track take me through knee-deep snow drifts. The frigid winter winds ripped through my clothes and covered my body in tingly gooseflesh. Years before, when the wind blew I was always frustrated and angry at Mother Nature—like she cared at all about my feelings. I cast blame as if the wind itself was directed right at me, like it was meant to destroy whatever recreational plans I had for the day. Ego. Now, when the wind ripped across the slopes I recalled an old cowboy poem:

Lord, give me a wind in my face.
A wind with ice in its teeth.
A wind in the mountains, too high for the fog.
A wind to stab me awake to the issues of life.
If we live and nothing ever happens,
Well, it is a curse to our souls.
Always, always if we're alive, something's gonna happen;
if not then we're dead in our boots;
stuck in the slush and the muck and the mire.
So Lord, give me a wind in my face
to blow the fog from my brain.
A wind that cuts like a knife.
And, give me the strength to pull my feet from the miry bog.

Lord, Give Me a Wind in my Face

The will to walk up the pathway too high for the fog.[81]

Each mile up those blustering ridges cut through my delusions. The mountain is indifferent to our existence. We are nothing but another speck upon its rims, no more or less important than the rocks beneath our feet, or the deer we chase. Ego is no currency in the wilderness, that's a lesson we can all stand to learn.

I could have kept complaining about my minuscule position in life like I had done in the past, but what good would that do? None. The mountain is a microcosm of real life. We matter only to the extent that we make a difference for others; our experience is most meaningful only when we strive to make *being* itself more tolerable for the people around us—regardless of how wronged or tormented we may have been in our own lives.[82] I felt alive again. In a healthy way. In a purposeful way.

I remembered that grandpa once shared his deepest wisdom with me. He told me he felt closer to God watching fish rise to take flies on a mountain lake than he ever had in a pew. I did too. Always. Even when I had done my best to ignore that still small voice.

I rediscovered God, or at the very least you could say that I had rediscovered *meaning* (but I think that's a distinction without any real difference) in the vastness of the wild. The indifference of the Rockies humbled me—humility and truth set me free.

It was almost as if grandpa, back in nature, had come to guide me through my healing process when I was ready, after I had given up the idea that I was a victim of circumstance. I was not a victim of anything, giving up that delusion sparked the new change.

Often times we are the source of our own suffering and that means we can end it too. That suffering, or failure, or experience, as Wilde said, would help shape us if we let it. There are things to learn from pain, things we can learn from suffering—things that we cannot learn in any other way!

---

81 From what I can gather this poem's original author is an unknown cowboy who worked the early days of the western frontier. But I was first introduced to it by The Bar J Wranglers when I was a young boy.

82 This is another one that I am certain that I got at least partly from Dr. Peterson.

The mountain was my means, grandpa was my Socrates, experience, old and new, my manual.

CHAPTER TWENTY-ONE

Forbidden Mountain

There are only two mistakes one can make along the road to truth: not going all the way and not starting.

– Buddha

I had been doing public (usually motivational) speeches off and on since I returned from Iraq. Most of the time I felt like a fraud. I could stand up on stage and tell the story of how I was injured and subsequently told I may never walk again, often to tearful and sincere crowds of business executives and corporate employees; but deep down, I always felt like I wasn't well enough to be sharing "wisdom" of any sort. Overcoming physical wounds is hard—very hard. I knew what it took to do that, but resiliency of the body isn't a higher-order problem. I didn't lie to these crowds. I never claimed to have overcome *all* my problems—only the physical ones, and those only partly. I tried not to imply that I had all the answers. Still, I felt like speaking in the manner that I did was somehow wrong.

This feeling left me when I started working out and hiking again. Finally, I could go to these corporate events—usually the events were done in conjunction with NFL or MLB players—and take in the applause justly. I knew I still had not healed completely, but I was on the right path and that was good enough for the time.

A few years ago I was invited by a friend to attend a summit in Vail, Colorado, called "Vail Living Well." For three days I took in panels, lectures, and presentations delivered by prominent academics from Michigan, Harvard, Stanford, and MIT. During breakfasts, lunches, and dinners I sat next to these brilliant minds and asked questions about the objective aspects of improving one's health. All the usual suspects emerged: good health was about a proper diet, exercise, consistent sleep schedule, and negative stress reduction, they said. One of these academics was a monk who taught ethics at MIT. He taught us the most valuable lesson I have ever learned: life is suffering. It is only by accepting that fact that we can lessen it. I had been saying something close to that in speeches for years, but he helped concretize it for me.

I left Vail with a much more thorough sense of what it took to get my body and mind performing at their peak. I applied that new understanding and saw great results right away. Still, I had another problem that I had yet to fully confront.

You'll remember that earlier I wrote about the VA's inadequate distinction between Traumatic Brain Injury and the illness PTSD. In an act that always felt like the VA medical community just had thrown up their hands in defeat, my medical file simply had a slash between the two acronyms: PTSD/TBI. I assumed this was to signify that I had both issues, but there was no clear way to discern between the two. I was branded with an indecipherable problem that was so complicated it would be best to just leave it be, it seemed.

But, I was done laying my problems at the feet of others. I got online and searched for any information I could find on brain injuries—I found that I had demonstrable signs of TBI. I remembered that the VA sent me a letter listing all the most common symptoms of both brain injury and Post Traumatic Stress Disorder:

Common Symptoms of PTSD

1) Re-experience the event over and over again

You can't put it out of your mind no matter how hard you try

You have repeated nightmares about the event

You have vivid memories, almost like it was happening all over again

You have a strong reaction when you encounter reminders, such as a car backfiring

2) Avoid people, places, or feelings that remind you of the event

You work hard at putting it out of your mind

You feel numb and detached so that you don't have to feel anything

You avoid people or places that remind you of the event
3) Feel "keyed up" or on-edge all the time
You may startle easy
You may be irritable or angry all the time for no apparent reason
You are always looking around, hyper-vigilant of your surroundings
You may have trouble relaxing or getting to sleep

I certainly dealt with some of these symptoms—I had experienced them all at one point or another—but it begged the question: What specific event? Most of us have many more than one traumatic experience in war. Were *all* of them to blame? The most common answer to that question is, "Yes. All these events, or even just one could cause the disorder." That idea just didn't hold water with me.

The paper goes on to say:

"People who have PTSD have experiences from all three of these categories that stay with them most of the time and interfere with their ability to live their life or do their job."

Okay, I guess I may have experiences from all three of those categories often, but I had already decided they weren't going to rule *any* portion of my life any longer. How should I go about making sure I am in control of my own fate even with the effects of PTSD manifesting themselves from time to time, I wondered. Further, it was clear to me that there were problems affecting my life that didn't seem to be PTSD-related, problems that had emerged only after my injury.

I struggled to defy my impulsivity. Executive function was a huge problem for me. I am highly forgetful. In not so small ways, too. For example, I often forget where I am going. Once while on a run near my friend's house, I forgot which road was his. I just ran past it—I had been to this place dozens of times.

The paper goes on to talk about symptoms of TBI:

Common Signs of Brain Injury:
Difficulty organizing daily tasks
Blurred vision or eyes tire easily
Headaches or ringing in ears
Feeling sad, anxious or listless

Easily irritated or angered
Feeling tired all the time
Feeling light-headed or dizzy
Trouble with memory, attention, or concentration
More sensitive to sounds, lights or distractions
Impaired decision making or problem solving
Difficulty inhibiting behavior—impulsive
Slowed thinking, moving, speaking, or reading
Easily confused, feeling easily overwhelmed
Change in sexual interest or behavior

The last 150 pages of this book, and the decade it took to live it, look in retrospect like an aggregate of those symptoms played out in one person's experience. I had long understood that the VA wasn't taking my brain injury very seriously, but after reading that paper it became immediately apparent that *I* had not taken the brain injury I incurred seriously enough.

As Dr. Jordan B. Peterson and the Buddhists—and as I had been saying in my private conversations and speeches for years—rightly point out, life *is* suffering. Suffering is universal. Tragedy is a part of the human condition. Of course, it is true that some lives suffer more than others, but all people confront pain, misery, and death. We ourselves and everyone we know and love is going to die—and before they die they are going to suffer things that before they happen seem unimaginable. *Being* itself is unfair. We can either accept that *fact,* or we can spend our lives avoiding it. Avoidance will not change the reality. Pain and suffering are byproducts of living.

What was I to do with the fact that my brain—the organ we use to process reality—was permanently damaged?[83] I didn't want to blame my own personal failures, and they were many, on something that was out of my control. I knew that was too simple an answer. The temptation to use this new information as a scapegoat was strong, but deep down in

83 Modern neuroscience has opened the question as to whether brain damage is truly irreversible.

my core I knew that taking that path would only lead me toward more suffering. I wasn't going to do that again. I decided that the best I could do was accept that I had incurred an injury that had made—and would continue to make—my life harder than it was before. It was time to move forward with that fact fully internalized. Scapegoating would be another copout, more cowardice. I was done with that road.

A good friend of mine, and a Green Beret we call "Preacher," stopped over around the time I discovered this problem.[84] While we were visiting I shared with him my new world view about the importance of humility and acceptance, and how I felt the Mountain could teach a man both things.

"There is a forbidden mountain hike on the Big Island of Hawaii that you have got to do. You have to start your ascent at around midnight, so that you can reach the peak before the sunrise. The view is incredible."

I was a little puzzled by his description of the "Forbidden Mountain" in Hawaii. Weren't all mountains in America publicly accessible?" I wondered. I later found that the mountain itself was not forbidden in modern times, but it had once been seen as a place only the warrior kings could travel. He preferred the old way of conceptualizing it, and so do I. It adds an element of reverence to the hike that those who set off under a different pretext miss. Luckily for me, it turned out that I already booked a trip to visit a friend from the Iraq War on the Big Island. I was to be leaving in a couple of months.

When I researched and put together a plan for the adventures I was going to take in the Aloha State I decided that, given the steep grade and long treks I would encounter on Mauna Kea and Mauna Loa, I needed to greatly improve my cardiovascular health before I set off. *If I am going to complete these climbs I am going to have to live a truly Spartan life for the next 40-50 days,* I thought to myself.

I put together a workout plan and decided to scrap booze altogether. Alcohol is little more than a hindrance to a man with an endurance-based goal.

---

84 He got the nickname Preacher when he became a certified minister so that he could marry my wife and me.

I maintained my early rise time and added ruck marches to my schedule. One day I ran a couple miles, the next I loaded a rucksack with 50 pounds a walked five miles. This schedule was improving my strength, but I knew I wasn't getting in enough mileage; so I implemented a new strategy: instead of setting out with a fixed distance to run, I just ran as far as I could. Then, when I was convinced I could not run so much as another foot—I sprinted 100 more yards.

Same with the ruck sack. I walked as far as I thought I could go and then I put down the ruck and sprinted another hundred yards. After a week or two of this I changed it up and did the sprints before the ruck or run, and I upped the sets to three sets of 100 yards, then five sets of 100 yards the next week.

When my friends came over to the house to drink I hung out with them, but only drank coffee or water. Mentally I had never felt better, but physically I was in a lot of pain. It was an interesting reversal of the order of my problems.[85]

I was beginning to have serious doubts as to whether my skeleton was going to hold up through the training, let alone the hikes. But, after the 40 or 50 days or grueling workouts and what I hoped would be sustainable progress, I found myself sitting at Salt Lake International Airport waiting to board an eight-hour flight to paradise.

Sitting on that airport bench I pondered what it was going to be like to watch that sun come up, to accomplish another goal, this one truly grand. Training for the climb had given me a reason to be that was specific and concrete, an objective sense of purpose. I had overcome physical hurdles before, many of which are detailed in this book, but I had yet to do anything that was above the capability of an average person. This hike was something beyond average. I was excited to feel like I was achieving something grander than mediocrity. I could hardly wait to sit up there in the clouds, triumphant once again. What I couldn't see in the moment was that the Mountain would teach me another unexpected

---

85 I think this change in perceived hierarchy of problems was due to the amount of pain I was in. Just like in Walter Reed when my physical pain was great, I thought little of my mental health. I think this probably has evolutionary roots. What importance does psychological health have to the animal who is focused on survival?

lesson. Maybe you could say it would concretize and deepen one I had already learned, but was not taking seriously enough.

I pulled out my cell phone and browsed through the apps, nothing much was happening on my social media pages, so I opened a dating app and flipped through the pictures. I came across the profile of a beautiful brunette girl who obviously had rural Utah roots. On her page were a few pictures of her at weddings, one hanging out with her dog, and another of her shooting her bow. In truth, she didn't seem anything like the other girls on the site. Her mere presence there was a mystery to me. I swiped right, assuming not much would come from it.

When I landed in Kona and powered up my phone. The first notification that popped up was an icon indicating that she and I had "matched." This girl, RanDee was her name, became the focus of conversation as soon as my friend picked me up from the airport. My buddy Dusty, as was typical for him, was not at all interested in talking about some girl I found on a dating site. Our flight landed in the dark, so he changed the subject and explained to me why the street lights of Kona were soft orange in color, rather than bright yellow like most others:

"There's a telescope on the top of Mauna Kea, the mountain you keep calling, 'the Forbidden Mountain.' It's like one of the most powerful telescopes on the planet, so they have a deal worked out with the island to help limit light pollution," Dusty said.

"That's cool. I have seen that telescope in some documentaries before. It's called the Keck Observatory, right?"

"Yeah, brah. It is supposed to be an amazing scope."

As much as I am fascinated by the solar system and space in general, my mind was elsewhere; specifically on this girl, RanDee.

When we got to his apartment he introduced me to his roommate and a few of his friends. His roommate was a polite Jewish girl from New York, named Rebecca. He had another friend there called Stephanie.

"This is the girl I have been telling you about, brah. She's the one with the hands," he said.

He had been teaching her to box for some time. Now and again he would call me with some question about boxing and her name would always come up. I was happy to finally meet her. She called him "Coach," even when we were hanging out informally. That took some getting used to, but she and I hit it off right away. After about a half an hour I brought up RanDee again. I figured these ladies would have some good advice.

"So, while I was in the airport I matched with this pretty country girl."

"Have you talked to her?" Rebecca asked.

"Not yet. I don't want to send her the same tired old pickup lines that I send to every other girl I match with. This girl is too classy for that. And besides, another fling is totally disinteresting to me. I am almost 30 years old, I have a kid and I am probably as close to healthy as I am ever going to get. I want to have a real relationship and grandbabies. Want to be seriously committed with an equally serious person."

"So just send her a normal message. Ask if she wants to meet up for drinks," Stephanie mused.

Frankness. Now, there is a concept that has become novel in the modern world.

I pulled my cellphone out of my pocket and sent her the most basic message I had ever dispatched on a dating site:

"Hey RanDee, I am vacationing in Hawaii for a week, but let's meet up for drinks after I get back."

The next morning when I woke up there was another notification on my dating application. She responded:

"Okay. I am also on vacation. Checking out Bali with my roommate. I will message you when I get back home. We can meet up then."

The most pressing loose end was tied up. It was time to go experience the Big Island and prepare for my hike on the Forbidden Mountain.

In contemporary times Mauna Kea is open to us all, but I still liked the idea of visualizing it as a forbidden hike. It was as if that made it call for a sort of respect within the climber. He must demonstrate reverence for the *Ali'i* who once ruled the island if he wished for safe passage. I was going to the volcano to learn, not to trespass. To experience, not to take. Additionally, I made a lot of sacrifices to cleanse myself in the buildup to the climb. I hoped that offering might satisfy the spirit of Kamehameha the Great, who I liked to envision guarding its slopes.

Around the middle of my trip, after we spent a day hunting for sheep on Mauna Loa and another deep-sea fishing, it was finally time to head for the Forbidden Mountain. Around midnight, I tossed my rucksack in my buddy's car and headed out. It took roughly two hours to get from the south side of Kona to the visitor's center at the mountain. The drive was only about 65 miles long, but to a mainlander the speed limits are impossibly slow in Hawai'i. The locals don't appreciate the way those of us from the continental states speed, either. They see our rush to get from point A to point B as a sin against their higher value of "Island Time." There's a wisdom in that way of framing the world. For me though, Island Time was cutting into my hiking time.

When I arrived at the Visitor's Center it was 2:00 A.M. and sunrise was supposed to be at 6:00 A.M. That left me only four hours to get to the top. Barely enough time for an able-bodied and experienced hiker—I was only one of those things.

I started out up the main road which zig zags its way up the western face of the dormant volcano. Just as I had hoped for, there was no one else around. A couple miles into the trek I hit a trail that cut up the side of the mountain. I struggled to stay on the footpath in the pitch dark of the night. Halfway through the climb I noticed that vans carrying tourists to the summit were beginning to scale the road below me. *I must not be doing very well on time,* I thought. I checked my watch: 4:00 A.M.

Most of the terrain at the higher elevations of the mountain is comprised of a type of lava rock that the locals call *a'a*. The surface of these flows chips off into little chunks called "clinkers." In the light of my headlamp these clinkers looked like the kind of lava rock that people use to decorate their flower beds. When the rocks pile up in thick layers it causes sloppy footing. Like walking up a sand dune; except that instead of sand, these are loose, jagged, rocks with sharp edges.

I struggled through the *a'a* for an hour or so. The rocks were killing my joints. Every time my foot slipped during an ascending step my ankle rolled and twisted my knee. That was the last thing I needed, another joint injury. The idea to stop and take a break crept into my consciousness. *Can't stop. I'll never beat the sun.*

The area above my right knee joint, where the CT Scans once

releveled a nonunion, burned every time my muscles tightened.[86] I could feel my legs swelling through my pants. I slowed the pace for a few hundred yards, but my watch constantly reminded me of the need for urgency. I knew I would never beat the sun if I didn't hurry. I was dead tired. Slowly, but steadily—like I had done a hundred times before—I lifted one leg and dropped it in front of the other. I slogged on, doing my best to ignore the pain.

Another hour passed by while I trudged along in a trance. The mountain was getting *steep.* Steep like the country I used to try to avoid on elk hunts. I knew I must be getting near the summit, but it was still too dark to see.

Four hours went by, twilight emerged. I could make out the various peaks. I glanced at my watch. Only about half an hour till official sunrise. *I need to pick a peak and climb it,* I thought. I kept my eyes fixed on the tallest one I could make out. My legs were trembling. I was used to that. Any time I push myself beyond the limit my legs feel like leather bags filled with flaming Jell-O. *Would be a shame to give up now. Almost there.*

Once on the side of the peak the rock was so loose that I fell down on every other step. It was like trying to climb a pile of gravel several hundred yards high. I scratched and clawed my way up the last few hundred feet. The sun was peeking over the ocean.

I didn't make it.

My hands and knees were covered in specks of blood from fine cuts gouged out by the *a'a.*

Why not just get out my camera now? I didn't make it anyway. That would be cheating.

True, but cheating who?

When I finally reached the top of the peak the sun was already showing—I had failed.

Across the sky for as far as I could see was a cascade of color. The horizon was washed with pink and orange, green and yellow bands of

---

86 Since writing this book I have learned that the burning sensation is caused by a few large bone spurs which have grown out from the old fractures.

misty light. Below me, over the city of Hilo, rested a blanket of clouds which gave the sunrise a foreground of bright white and subtle hues of gray. I was born in the Rocky Mountains. I had long insisted that there was no sunrise on earth as powerful as those we were graced with in Utah. In fact, when I was in high school my friends from nearby towns and I used to argue over whose hometown had the best sunrises and sunsets. None of that mattered in that moment. This was more beautiful than them all.

The Forbidden Mountain is the gateway to the grandest sunrise on earth.

I reflected on my life from atop that volcano. All twenty-nine years of it. I hadn't quite accomplished my goal of beating the sunrise, but I had been blessed enough to see it anyway. Wasn't that the real goal? Why let an arbitrary thing like a watch ruin that?

I thought about everything I had overcome along the way, my physical injuries, my ego, my mental health problems and brain injuries.[87] I felt accomplished, but I wondered, what was next? What goal could I set my mind to after I climbed the Forbidden Mountain? That's when it hit me: I was Sisyphus, perpetually rolling a big rock uphill. Living in eternal struggle—of my own choosing!

Setting goals and completing them makes one feel empowered and accomplished. It's as desirable a feeling as I have ever encountered. It is addictive, but it doesn't make one *whole.*

Overcoming a serious obstacle is an important developmental step, and one that we should experience from time to time as a reminder of the power of human will, but it's a juvenile step nonetheless.

I sat atop that mountain and all around me were eight more peaks to climb. What should I do with them? Should I climb them all and chase that feeling all over again? No. That can't be what life is about. It can't be about who can endure the most hardship, that is only slightly better than nihilism. I thought back to the bitter windy slopes of the Wasatch mountains:

---

87 To some degree. Clearly, I have not bested them completely and it is an open question as to whether I can fully overcome the brain injury. I think probably not.

The mountain is a microcosm of everyday life. We matter only to the extent that we make a difference for others, our experience is only significant when we strive to make being itself more tolerable. Regardless of how wronged or tormented we may have been in our own lives.[88]

I was then, and am now, convinced that we can only truly strive to live an honorable life after we have learned to overcome great struggle. But, we must beware—struggle itself can become a lighthouse.

***

When I got back from Hawaii I messaged RanDee again. We met up for drinks the next night. She says she knew we would marry the first time she met me. That's a little too fairytale-like for me, but I will tell you when I knew.

On our second date, we met up at my house to have dinner and put new fletchings on some of her arrows. During the first date she claimed that she wanted to learn how to fix her own arrows when they were damaged. About fifteen minutes into the project she changed her mind:

"I don't think I like fletching arrows. Maybe I will just have my brother do them from now on."

Or I just take care of them for you, I thought.

We decided we would go for a walk instead.

She told me about all the issues she had during previous relationships and all the ways other men had failed to live up to the standard her father set for her. I walked alongside her staring at the joints between the concrete slabs beneath our feet. *I am walking next to this girl without so much as a noticeable hitch in my step, I have come so far, but have I truly grown into manhood properly? Is my moral compass recalibrated enough to deserve such company?* I wondered.

In hindsight I think the answer to my internal question is coded in the

---

88 This idea has surely been influenced very heavily by Dr. Jordan B Peterson. I would hate to plagiarize him, but I don't know exactly what he has said on the subject verbatim. I only know that my thinking has been heavily influenced by him since I first wrote this book. Many of my thoughts were turbid before I found him and they are now echoes of his. I thank him for the clarity he has given me.

way I responded to a few questions she posed to me:

"So, are you fully recovered from your injuries, then?"

"No, I am not yet." It would have been so easy to lie to her. To justify a small black lie would be all too easy, especially to a question as loaded as this one—and on a second date even. But, I didn't.

"Like, what sorts of problems do you deal with?"

The concrete scratched the bottom of my boots as we walked along. I watched the joints pass by rhythmically, my mind was whisked back to Balad and Walter Reed. *How can I answer that one without turning this into a conversation about myself,* I wondered.

I remembered on the first day of one of my college classes a professor asked the students, "Introduce yourselves and tell us your story in five minutes or less. Everyone has a story," she said.

Yes, but not everyone wants to share their story so trivially, I thought then. I felt the same way with RanDee. Not that she would trivialize my life's history, just that it was not the time to tell it. I wanted to hear more of hers, not share mine.

"My legs and hand will never be one-hundred percent healed, my back probably won't either, but I have learned to cope with those things—"

"You don't have PTSD anymore?" She interrupted.

"Yes, I do. But that is a problem that I am actively trying to solve, and I feel like I will get to the bottom of it one day. My brain injury is a different thing. That I don't think I can fix. I am afraid it will be like this forever."

This on our second date. My God!

"So, what does that mean? Your brain seems to work fine."

"My problems are less noticeable to the casual onlooker. I am impulsive and terribly forgetful. Concentration is a major issue for me and I can't tolerate certain types of light for very long.

"My impulsivity is not an issue of character, though. I am not going to cheat on you. My problem is I will impulsively decide I want to try something new, or buy something new, or make a serious decision without thinking through the risks enough. That sort of thing." I got a little uncomfortable when I noticed that she was just staring at me and not responding. I went on, "I also have a difficult time with executive function and focus. I will forget about appointments, bills, birthdays, that kind of stuff. And, I can't manage my own schedule at all. I mean, I have been doing it for years, but it isn't really working out. Sometimes I am on top of things, other times I feel like I am failing miserably at things a 15-year-old should be able to do."

"That's okay, I am good at all that stuff. I manage a dental clinic for a job now, managing our lives would be easy."

I told her every single thing that I thought made me unfit to be a good partner in a relationship—upfront and honestly—the full truth—and she just smiled at me. That's when I knew.

RanDee and I were married about two years later in a beautiful barn that we rented in northern Utah. We later moved back to my home county and started a small family together with my daughter, our newborn son, two dogs and some livestock. In the end, like the iconic buffalo of the American West, tenacity and strength were not enough to save me. I did my best to steel myself against the onslaught of injury, but I failed. I was not—and am not—strong enough to live at my best alone. It was not until I showed my true weaknesses to a person who loved me that the deepest wounds began to heal. "So they are no longer two, but one flesh. Therefore what God has joined together let no man separate." (Matthew 19:6.) Her strengths filled the void in my being, and mine filled hers. This was no cliché, either. My problems were real and I was not strong enough to overcome them alone. I wasn't so lost as to have been suicidal or anything of the sort, but I was saved by her love. She turned the chip away from the wall and filled it with her own heart. She's more than just a partner, she truly is the better part of me.

I often look back at my time on the Forbidden Mountain and smile. I didn't "make it" so to speak, but I got what I had gone there for. Perhaps this is pure superstition, though I think it too premature to tell for certain, but it could be that the ghost of those dead *Ali'i* did welcome me on those volcanic slopes. I learned a lot from their sacred mountain, and one thing is for sure—I left Hawai'i ameliorated. A different man. A better man. Freed from my life of perpetual endurance and on to one of balance, truth, ownership, selflessness, and love.

Finally, now that I have a partner to help me through the world, I hope to live a life of Honor. One that those heroes of mine laid to rest in their sacred shrine at Arlington can find comfort in.

Rest easy, Warriors. I'll see you on the other side.

AFTERWORD

A Retrospective

What can we learn from this story? Authors are often told that they need an answer to this question before they even touch a pen. I didn't have one clearly articulated enough to aim toward at the outset. All that I knew for certain was that telling the truth as best as I know how—letting one's heart bleed on paper—might help another who is in chaos.

Not everyone who reads this book will have been wounded in combat, I knew that much, but I think this story is universal in some sense. We all suffer.

Some friends told me when I set out to write that the proper way to do it would be to focus on the inspirational part of my journey. People like that kind of thing, but the physical success is too flimsy. It's like when a motivational speaker tells you that the secret to life is "to be happy." It's thin and weakly thought out. That idea can't even get you to quit smoking for God's sake. If the secret to life is the endless pursuit of happiness then why give up cigarettes? Smoking is quite pleasurable for a smoker. Now, you might object that idea by saying that smoking leads to cancer and that's not going to make your future-self very happy. That is true, but "happiness" as a mode of being can't even get you far enough into the future to *worry* about cancer. I tried that philosophy—it's *not* sustainable. Try telling a parent that life is about being happy after they have just lost a child. It's a mindless statement and will always produce the opposite result given enough time.

My descent into nihilism was accelerated by the pursuit of happiness. In fact, many of my closest friends thought that I was a joy to be around because I was so ostensibly positive—and I was. I am naturally an optimistic guy. The problem is when you aim at pleasure and happiness that optimism becomes a misdirected sail. *I want to get high, but I know I can't quit if I go back to drugs. Sure you can—you've done it before!*

Life is not about happiness, that much I know. The people who preach this sort of thing are peddling a false gospel—they're false prophets:

"Watch out for false prophets. They come to you in sheep's clothing, but inwardly they are ferocious wolves. By their fruit you will recognize them. Do people pick grapes from thornbushes, or figs from thistles? Likewise, every good tree bears good fruit, but a bad tree bears bad fruit. A good tree cannot bear bad fruit, and a bad tree cannot bear good fruit. Every tree that does not bear good fruit is cut down and thrown into the fire. Thus, by their fruit you will recognize them."

I am not writing about theological doctrine here, what I am getting at is an existential truth. I think The Bible says some things about the human experience that are *true,* this is one of them. I followed the Way of those false prophets for awhile and the bitterness of their fruits lead me to Hell. It is not the right way to *be* in any serious sense. Another thing these false prophets often preach is that unconditional love of self is what will keep a person properly oriented in the world, but this is also false. There's no room in this philosophy for the role of guilt. Real guilt. The kind that burns inside each person's heart when he or she knows they've done wrong—the kind of guilt that *transforms.* If we try to love ourselves unconditionally then we will perish in our hubris. Selflessness and responsibility heal; unwarranted love of self destroys. We should not love ourselves when we fail, we should be ashamed and we should let that shame point us toward the good. Denying our own consciences is just another lie. Its deception will lead us to Hell. Just look around, which person who espouses the 'Just Be Happy' theory do you want your kids to follow? If this is the proper Way then why do we venerate the heroes of our past?

Balance is important—we must not be too hard on ourselves—but *truth* is life's blood. Each time we do wrong we cut at ourselves and spill its curative powers for naught.

We know we must take care of our mental, physical and spiritual (or emotional if you prefer) health. We learn this in grade school, but the people teaching haven't seen the darkness. People who wish to instruct others have too often lived naïve, sheltered lives. Their opinions are weightless. There's no power in them. They serve no purpose to a soul who has been crushed by the horrors of life outside the womb of ignorance.

I am not one of those and thus I am careful to say I know very little about the world. I have seen the darkness and have walked through Hell. I don't have all the answers—I wouldn't dare be so presumptuous—but I have learned a few things in the last ten years. This three-tiered approach to overall health isn't perfect, but it is the best we have right now.

Taking care of your physical health is the simplest. You have to eat a healthy diet. No junk food, take it easy on the sugar. Don't over indulge on spirits, wine or beer. You have to get up early. Force yourself into a regimen and don't break it. You have to do something physical every day. The fastest way to relieve depression and laziness is to enforce strict discipline. We all know this stuff—intuitively I think. This is the simplest step to growing into a fully developed and strong person, but it isn't easy. It is very hard. It's all hard.

The physical fitness is the easiest problem to solve, but it is not the most important. As we begin to take our earthly vessels more seriously we must also work on our mental health. This is where the complexities and dangers start to mount. Studying makes one's mind stronger, but what should a person who is seeking answers to life's biggest questions study? Where should they look for purpose? Can we even begin to find purpose if we don't know who *we are?*

Aleksandr Solzhenitsyn wrote, "A man is the product of his whole experience—that is how we come to be what we are." I think this is an undeniable fact, but it is important (as he points out in his books) to understand our capacity for malevolence and cowardice if we are to find ourselves in our histories. Our experiences can shape us in two ways: better or worse. We make that decision for ourselves. When troubles come—and they will come—it is up to us how we quarrel with them, but we can't do it properly if we don't see ourselves clearly. We must know who we really are at our core: divine and reprehensible.

It would be easy to read my descent into nihilism as a chain of unfortunate causal events. I was wounded, this depressed me. I was heavily medicated, this increased my depression and lead to addiction. Addiction lead to despair, that anguish lead into nihilism, that nihilism lead to suicidal tendency. This chronological line may be accurate in some sense, but even if it were an accurate depiction of the events in my life—how would accepting that frame work help me in the future? How could I learn from my mistakes—I couldn't! That would mean that my suffering was in vain, none of it mattered—nothing matters. Nihilism.

When I followed that logic I became so lost in the darkness that I nearly never got back out. I at one point, like Tolstoy, I stopped taking guns out shooting because I didn't want to tempt myself. At nights when I was home alone I would take my pistols apart putting the slide in one drawer, the barrel in another, and the guide spring in another. Then I locked the frame in a safe. "At least this way I will have taken time to think it through before I touch the barrel to my temple," I said to myself. How can a world view that produces such contempt for life be *true* in any useful sense? It can't, and it isn't.

Once I walked through Arlington awe struck by the honor and sacrifice those hundreds of thousands of heroes had demonstrated. On wobbly, throbbing legs, I stood above the grave of my brother-in-arms and wept at the vanity I had shown. The ungratefulness. Complaining about my pain and suffering in the presence of such mountainous character was abhorrent to me. I swore an oath to them, I was going to live for those who could no longer live for themselves.

Foolishly I tried to fulfill this oath by "living life to its fullest." By partying, and drinking, and pleasure seeking—I didn't know the Way.

Neither do those who cite useless phrases endlessly to justify their depravity and vanity. I was wrong, and I almost lost my life running from the Truth. From truth I knew at a young age and have since rediscovered: Integrity, ownership, responsibility, discipline, courage, honor, selflessness—those virtues are *true*! I can think of no better way to honor the sacrifices of those great men than to endlessly pursue the "good," the truth.

The question then is *how* do we live for the greatest possible good? We have already discussed the need to respect our bodies—to show gratitude for the gift of life—but, we must also balance our mind and spirit.

Dr. Jordan B. Peterson says there is only three reasons why we suffer: 1) We are fragile and human. Our lives are finite and the Universe we frame them in is infinite. 2) We are treated harshly by the rest of the world and our societies. That is true for us all. 3) The rest of it can be laid right at our own feet!

Peterson teaches that, "The proper way of getting through [suffering] is to adopt the mode of authentic being. That is something like refusing to participate in the lie, in deceit. To orient your speech as much as you can toward the truth. And to take responsibility for your own life and perhaps the lives of other people."

I spent almost a decade suffering things that in my youth I never could have imagined. Some caused by life, some were caused by associating with the wrong people, other bouts by society, but *most* can be laid directly at my own feet.

When I was wounded I made a clear choice, one of the few choices I have ever made that I am deeply proud of. I decided that I would rather put my flesh in harm's way than have a friend of mine put at risk for reasons that I did not think worthy. When I was lying on the ground bleeding to death I was in a great deal of pain—torment that you cannot imagine if you've not endured it—but I wasn't *suffering*. I was serving my country, my family, and my brothers.

I didn't truly suffer until I started lying to myself and to others about my problems with nightmares, stress and sleep. Those lies built into other lies, and those lies built into more, until one day I was a suicidal-nihilistic-addict.

I created my own Hell and it nearly destroyed my soul.

A very special woman lives in my town. She was assaulted by some peers while in high school. The girls who attacked her were so evil that they beat her to the brink of death. She suffered irreversible brain damage. It is noticeable when you talk to her—but that isn't all one sees in her. There is a kindness and a love for life in her eyes that too many mentally able people scoff at. Her soul is especially clean, that purity radiates from her. You can't help but feel small around such a person (which is why the weakest among us scoff at them). My wife just had her first baby, a son. During labor her liver failed and the doctors had to perform an emergency C-Section on her. My son had a few problems of his own, he recovered rather quickly, but my wife did not. During the week we spent in the hospital trying to get my wife's liver functioning again this wonderful woman came over to my house and fed our animals, watered our garden and our flowers, and put our chickens to bed. No one ever asked her to do it, she just heard that we were in need and acted in the way her sweet spirit thought natural—to sacrifice her time for strangers! Charity and compassion.

If a woman who has endured all that she has can be so selfless—so *good*—what excuse do the rest of us have?

Peterson says that the dragon of mythology is mankind's best attempt to describe the unknown. Fear and chaos. Since discovering his lectures I have adopted this way of framing the problems of life.

You can't hide from a dragon or he will burn down your entire village and all that you love and care about with it. You must face him. When I ran from the dragons my life crumbled, split apart and burned. It was like my soul itself was fractured.

Then one day I decided I would face my problems one at a time. I wanted to own them. When I did, or at least started to, I improved almost instantaneously. Then more popped up. More dragons. I think this is why we feel overwhelmed when we try to take on our problems—there are always dozens more than we thought there were and it is not until we emerge from our cowardly little hiding places that we can see them all clearly. This overwhelming feeling can crush us if we have not stiffened our spine for combat. That is why I think it is important that we crush our most pressing physical obstacles before we try to take on the mental ones. If we can stop eating terrible diets that we know are killing us; if we can run when others say we can't walk, if we can put down the bottle that is drowning our soul, then we *know* we can do anything. The lessons we learn on the physical journey will steel our resolve for the longer—much harder—fight for our mental and spiritual health.

Sometimes when we first emerge and feel completely overwhelmed we run back to our hiding places. We see so many little dragons that we are afraid the aggregate of issues will demolish us. Maybe that isn't the worst thing. Sometimes armies must retreat in order to regroup and acquire some help before they fight again another day. We can use this philosophy as well—but we can't make it a habit. We must go back into the fray again the moment we are ready. And again.

Then we become practiced. We have dulled our swords on so many small dragons that we understand their weaknesses as well as we do our own. This gives us the ability to take them out more easily—to see them for the miniscule issues that they often are. Fear makes the wolf bigger than he is. The best antidote for fear is experience.

The first step then is to get the physical body in order, no matter what that takes—no matter how steep the climb may be. The next is to stand up for truth in your own life—all the time. I swore an oath to my brothers in Arlington, I failed to keep it many times and will probably fail again, but I am on the right course now. Those failures will happen less and less often as I gain more and more experience. You may not have a national shrine to cling to as a guiding light, but maybe you're a mother or father. You have your children and their futures, certainly my kids are the center piece of my life now. What better thing could you do for them than to get yourself together. To lead them by example. To face your mistakes, fears, and the chaos of life with a steeled spirit and a selfless heart? Nothing.

Teach them to manifest courage, integrity, honor and selflessness in their own lives by living those virtues so fully that they cannot help but to see them displayed.

We know there are three levels of health, and that total health requires all three be balanced: physical, mental and the spiritual. Perhaps, there is something transcendent that comes after we achieve that harmony. Nirvana. I don't know yet because I am still working on developing my mental and spiritual health, but I hope we all find out.

Slay your dragons—or, they will consume you.

Made in the USA
Monee, IL
20 January 2021